Moral Cultivation and Confucian Character

SUNY series in Chinese Philosophy and Culture

Roger T. Ames, editor

Moral Cultivation and Confucian Character

Engaging Joel J. Kupperman

Edited by

Chenyang Li and Peimin Ni

SUNY PRESS

Cover art woodcarving portrait of Joel Kupperman courtesy of Michael Kupperman

Cover art: background image © Leshabu / Dreamstime.com and Confucius image © Liang Zhang / Dreamstime.com

Published by State University of New York Press, Albany

Printed in the United States of America

For information, contact State University of New York Press, Albany, NY
www.sunypress.edu

Production by Diane Ganeles
Marketing by Kate McDonnell

Library of Congress Cataloging-in-Publication Data

Moral cultivation and Confucian character : engaging Joel J. Kupperman / edited by Chenyang Li and Peimin Ni.
pages cm. — (SUNY series in Chinese philosophy and culture)
Includes bibliographical references and index.
ISBN 978-1-4384-5323-1 (hardcover : alk. paper)
ISBN 978-1-4384-5322-4 (pbk.: alk. paper)
1. Ethics. 2. Character. 3. Confucianism. 4. Kupperman, Joel J. I. Li, Chenyang, 1956–, editor of compilation.

BJ1521.M765 2014
170—dc23 2013045657

10 9 8 7 6 5 4 3 2 1

To Joel,

A mentor and a *junzi*

Contents

Part II. Moral Cultivation and Material Well-Being

Part III. Responses and Comments

Acknowledgments

We would like to thank the following individuals for their contribution to the making of this volume: Paul Bloomfield, who organized the "Character: East and West" conference in honor of Joel Kupperman at the University of Connecticut in Storrs, on May 20 and 21, 2011, which provided a valuable venue to us to discuss Joel's work and to contemplate this project; Roger Ames, for his able assistance with the mini-conference that we organized in honor of Joel Kupperman, held in conjunction with the Tenth East-West Philosophers Conference in Honolulu, on May 23 and 24, 2011; Karen Kupperman for her persistent help along the way; Michael Kupperman for his professional drawing of Joel's portrait that appears on the cover of this book; Li Jifen and Sun Qingjuan for their technical assistance with the preparation of the manuscript; Jonathan Sim for assisting with proofreading and for preparing the index; and at SUNY Press, Nancy Ellegate, our acquisitions editor, for her guidance along the way; Jessica Kirschner, for her timely assistance. Diane Ganeles and Kate McDonnell, for their efficiency and professionalism in handling respectively the production and marketing of this book. This project was supported by a generous grant from the Centre for Liberal Arts and Social Sciences of Nanyang Technological University (NTU) and NTU research grant M4080394. Finally, we thank our respective family members, Ying and Sophie (for Peimin), Hong, Fay and Hansen (for Chenyang), for their continuous understanding, support, and love. The long-lasting friendship between these two families is traceable all the way back to our student years under the guidance of Joel Kupperman.

C. L., P. N.

Foreword

Fred Dallmayr

The political thinker Hannah Arendt once remarked that the task of responsible human agency is "to think what we are doing." What this comment endorses or recommends is neither the descent into mindless activism nor the escape into abstract metaphysics, but rather a continuous learning process where thought is seasoned through practical experience. The recommendation, one can readily see, had a critical edge: it opposed the prevailing dichotomy (in the West) between rationality and arbitrary whim—a dichotomy undergirding the equally glaring hiatus between the academy and public life. Fortunately, in our time, Arendt's position is no longer an isolated exception: her plea to reconnect thinking and doing finds resonance in several contemporary philosophical perspectives—including above all the perspective of "virtue ethics" which by now has a global or cross-cultural reach. By contrast to the focus on invariant principles or private emotions, virtue ethics—from both an Aristotelian and an Asian/Confucian vantage point—emphasizes the reflective cultivation of practical life, that is, the ethical shaping of human conduct in its relation to fellow-beings and the world.

The present volume pays tribute to Joel Kupperman as a scholar, teacher, and practitioner of virtuous life. As reflected in his writings, teachings, and personal interactions, Kupperman is one of those all-too-rare people: an individual who "practices what he preaches," whose everyday conduct exemplifies in a concrete manner the meaning of the legacies he investigates and transmits. I was not fortunate enough to be closely acquainted with Kupperman; but even my limited contacts (at conferences and on other occasions) convinced me that I was in the presence of a knower/doer, of an erudite expert on ethical philosophy who allowed his learning to infiltrate and pervade his "persona" or character. Together with many colleagues and probably with all of his students, I benefited from this exposure to a life well lived, to this concrete exemplification of virtue in our time.

As the assembled contributions to this volume show, the precise meaning of virtue ethics, in both the Aristotelian and the Confucian traditions, is a matter of debate and allows for different readings. In this debate, Kupperman himself placed an accent on the formation of "character" in ethical conduct, an accent which departs to some extent from "role" conceptions (as well as other conceptions) of virtue. As it seems to me, however, these different accents do not cancel a deeper commonality: the recognition that role performance depends on the cultivation of personal dispositions which, in turn, are shaped by interpersonal contexts. Perhaps, such a linkage of form and content, of outside and inside, best captures Kupperman's harmonious approach. No matter which accent one prefers, however, the fact remains that his work has given new impulses to a great variety of interpretations and thus provided a boost to the reinvigoration of virtue ethics in a global setting. For this service, we all—Western and Asian comparativists—are deeply indebted and grateful to him.

Introduction

Chenyang Li and Peimin Ni

This volume grew out of two events in celebration of the fiftieth anniversary of Joel J. Kupperman's teaching career in philosophy. The first was "Character: East and West—a Conference in Honor of Joel Kupperman," organized by the Philosophy Department of the University of Connecticut, in Storrs, on May 20 and 21, 2011. Joel Kupperman, David Wong, and the editors of this volume were among the attendees. The second event was a mini-conference in honor of Joel Kupperman, held in conjunction with the Tenth East-West Philosophers Conference in Honolulu, on May 23 and 24, 2011. The mini-conference was organized by these editors, attended by Roger Ames, Henry Rosemont, Jr., Karyn Lai, Kwong-loi Shun, Sor-hoon Tan, whose papers are included here, and Joel Kupperman. Other invitees to the mini-conference, Philip J. Ivanhoe, Robert C. Neville, and Bryan Van Norden, although unable to attend, have graciously made their contributions to this volume in honor of Kupperman.

As former students with the good fortune of having studied with Kupperman, we can speak the world of our mentor. Kupperman is not only a learned scholar and a thought-provoking philosopher, but also a most caring teacher, who has the ability to convey deep insights with a good sense of humor. Though his research and publications encompass a broad range of ethics, aesthetics, moral psychology, metaphysics, applied philosophy, and the philosophy of mind, his major intellectual focus has been on ethics. Much of his early work in this regard was a reaction to a widespread assumption by philosophers that judgments of values or of rightness were to some degree subjective. In the 1960s, there was much talk about "pro-attitudes," or inclinations. In two books, *Ethical Knowledge* (1970) and *The Foundations of Morality* (1983), Kupperman argued that there are cases in which some judgments of rightness or of value could reasonably be considered objectively right, or to be wrong. Most distinctive about him as an ethicist, however, is his engagement in Asian and comparative philosophy. Kupperman's interest in Asian philosophy began early when he was an undergraduate student in Herrlee G. Creel's seminar on Chinese philosophy at the University of Chicago. He began to publish on Asian and comparative philosophy in 1960s. In a time when Asian philosophy was virtually excluded from philosophy departments in universities across North America, Kupperman was one of the few mainstream Western philosophers who had the vision, knowledge, and yes, the courage, to bring Asian philosophy into philosophical discourse. His signature work, *Character* (1991), synthesized Western, Chinese, and Indian philosophies in developing a character-based ethics. Along with his other very influential publication *Learning from Asian Philosophy* (1999), and many articles, Kupperman's work in comparative philosophy has set a model for fruitfully navigating wisdoms of both East and West to address philosophical questions of our times.

Kupperman never does Asian philosophy for its own sake. He is not a "scholar" of Asian philosophy in that sense. Kupperman is an ethicist and a philosopher. His goal, as stated in *Learning from Asian Philosophy*, is "to gain contributions to philosophical enterprises that are, in the end, primarily Western rather than Chinese or Indian" (1999, 3). In doing so, Kupperman never for a minute fails to be a serious mainstream Western philosopher. He studies and borrows from Asian philosophers in ways most philosophers in Britain and America study and use Descartes and Locke: as reminders of problems or lines of thought that we might have forgotten about or ignored, and as suggestive philosophical activity that we can continue, revise, or debate in our own philosophical work (Ibid.).

As a Western ethicist, Kupperman maintains that ethical philosophy in our age "needs to be comparative," because without some knowledge about differences among traditions of ethical thought, it is all too easy to conclude that "reason" requires what amounts to a structural feature of most Western ethical thought. Given everyone's own tradition, if he or she is "compelled" to think in a certain way, then it may seem obvious that this is the path of reason. Furthermore, if the reference points are mainly Western systematic ethics of the last two and a half centuries, it is easy to conclude that the primary task of normative ethical philosophy is to arrive at principles that yield decision procedures. It would follow that any project of transforming oneself into a certain sort of person is secondary to that of arriving at reliable moral decisions (Kupperman 2010). Comparative approaches to ethical study, or for that matter to philosophy in general, encompass using ideas and concepts from one philosophical tradition to interpret, understand, and develop ideas in another tradition.[1] As such, comparative philosophy has added advantages compared to a philosophy that is confined to a single tradition. It allows us not only to think "outside the box" but also to acquire additional tools in solving problems within one's own tradition. Philosophizing in response to contemporary problems in a global age, we need to draw on intellectual resources from both West and East. In this regard, Kupperman has provided a good model for us.

As David Wong puts it, "Too many contemporary philosophers have nothing to say on a subject if they cannot hope to identify the singular truth. Alternatively, most of what they have to say is that there is no final word or singular truth, as if that were all that was left to say. . . . The tone of much of Kupperman's work is that of a gentle and wise interlocutor who refrains from lecturing to us on what the good life is, but rather assists us in our individual and collective endeavors to live a good life by articulating much good advice and well-taken cautions" (see p. 97 in this volume). Kupperman's *Learning from Asian Philosophy* illustrates that we can make judgments or estimates of activities or forms of activity and speak of the knowledge of values without being able to supply conclusive grounds. Countering the widespread tendency to center philosophical judgments on logic, in particular, he articulated in a recent essay on "Half Truths" in the English journal *Ratio* (2012) that judgments of value cannot be examined straightforwardly in terms of logic or logical influences. None of this, in his view, precludes awareness that some activities or forms of activity can have considerable positive or negative value. But this does indicate that judgments or estimates of this sort are highly unlikely to be very widely shared, or to be demonstrable.

Things not demonstrable may nevertheless be illustrated. A good example is how Kupperman absorbs ideas and insights from Confucius and other Asian thinkers as well as Aristotle and Hume in developing a character-based ethics. He finds that Kantian and utilitarian ethical theories have largely ignored the ways in which decisions are integrated and shaped over time in a person's life. Through comparison with Confucius's and other Asian philosophers' emphasis on ritual and cultivation of one's demeanor or style of conduct, Kupperman reveals that Western ethicists in the last two hundred years have focused mainly on the "big moments" in which people make critical ethical decisions, and largely ignored "the moment-to-moment texture of the large part of our lives" as a "free-play zone" (see Kupperman 1999, 167–169). His study of Chinese Philosophy led him to believe that a good deal of personal interaction that did not quite involve moral issues nevertheless could be (to a significant degree) deplorable or praiseworthy, and could affect the value in a life. Nuances and styles could matter. The preoccupation with decision making makes being ethical a bitter business, as if being ethical is a joyless obligation rather than a constituent of an excellent life. Furthermore, he points out that by laying down minimal demands of ethics for everyone, modern Western ethicists largely failed to see that there can be sliding scales of ethical requirements. He reveals that, contrary to our intuition, being ethical actually has more to do with cultivating one's character so that one's live options are narrowed down when immoral things become unthinkable, rather than making right choices when facing with alternative options. "At the extreme, a Confucian sage, say, would have no choice to make, in that a wide variety of unworthy actions would have ceased to be live options" (Ibid., 136). Yet on the other hand, this insight is fully consistent with our intuition that the value of a life is very much related to the kind of person one manages to become. He also notices Confucius's observation that a person's faults often go along with his virtues (*Analects* 4.7). If this is true, Kupperman infers, developing virtues has its natural limitations. Character-based ethics is not just about individual virtues; it is about building a character as a way of life, which is less likely to lend itself to compartmentalization. In his view, Western virtue ethics have largely overlooked the interrelationships between virtues and failings within a character.

Drawing insights from his comparative study, Kupperman sheds light on many things that people who work exclusively in one tradition tend to miss. In his book, *Value and What Follows* (1999), he focuses on how judgments of values connect with estimates of what is worth seeking or avoiding in life, and points out that there often are misconceptions about this, especially if people emphasize pleasure or immediate satisfaction. His other book, *Six Myths About the Good Life* (2006), examines the values that are important in our lives, and explains how easy it is to miss these. For the purpose of broadening people's vision across different traditions, Kupperman has also recently published a book entitled *Theories of Human Nature* (2010), surveying various views of what human nature is, and edited a book entitled *Human Nature: A Reader* (2012), which brings together ways in which human nature has been treated in different traditions.

The value of Kupperman's works is not limited to the specific philosophical insights they provide, but also reflected in the way he does philosophy. He inspires people to make a deeper reflection on the function of philosophy itself (e.g., how it is related to Asian philosophy which is sometimes dismissed as "wisdom literature"), and how philosophy communicates and what counts as really effective communication.

With regard to philosophical communication, we want to mention another salient feature of Kupperman's scholarship: his amazing ability to unpack complicated issues in simple terms and to spell out things in a concise fashion. He pays attention to the style of writing as much as to the content of what he is writing about, or to put it more accurately, his writings exemplify his moral character as well as explain what moral character is, although in no way does he suggest that his is the only right kind of character.

It is with all these that Kupperman has triggered widespread resonances—not necessarily agreements but varieties of responses that truly vitalized the field. As a snapshot of these resonances, this volume opens with a foreword by Fred Dallmayr, who himself is an exemplar in comparative philosophy, and followed by ten essays by eleven authors. All these chapters deal with issues of contemporary significance on ethics, and do so from a Confucian perspective or comparative perspective, or both. They share Kupperman's hallmark of philosophizing on pertinent issues across ethical traditions, yet, in diverse ways, they respond, expand, and engage in critical dialogues with Kupperman's views. This is, in our view, the best way to celebrate Kupperman's achievements. Instead of just explaining and elaborating on Kupperman's contributions, the essays in this volume all have distinctive merits of their own, making the volume a lively platform of contemporary scholarship on ethics in its own right. As Dallmayr aptly reminds us in his foreword, the varied views on reading Confucian ethics as presented in this volume do not cancel a deeper commonality: the recognition that role performance depends on the cultivation of personal dispositions which, in turn, are shaped by interpersonal contexts.

We begin with the article by Roger Ames and Henry Rosemont, Jr., who in the last decade or so have been developing a "role ethics" from Confucian philosophy. Ames and Rosemont acknowledge that, in seeking to replace virtue ethics with character ethics, Kupperman challenges the "snapshot" view of ethical decision making in virtue ethics and equally the "big moment" ethics we associate with Kant and Bentham and Mill, and that his character ethics points us in the right direction for appreciating the role that family has in developing moral competence. They argue, however, that Confucian role ethics in taking family relations as the entry point for developing moral competence has more to offer contemporary conversations in moral philosophy than other approaches. Kupperman's character ethics, according to Ames and Rosemont, has several limitations. First, character is individual-based and presupposes a reified conception of a unified and discrete self. There is for Kupperman a definite individuality to the self that serves as the ground and locus of one's character development. Role ethics makes no appeal to superordinate, substantive categories such as "self" or "character," but instead locates "person" gerundively as the embodied, social activity of thinking and feeling within the manifold of relations that constitutes family, community, and the natural environment. Person thus understood is a complex event rather than a discrete "thing," a process of "becoming" rather than an essential "being," an on-going "doing" rather than an autonomous "is," a configuration of concrete, dynamic, and constitutive relations rather than an individuated substance defined by some subsisting agency. Second, Confucian role ethics would resist the uncritical substance ontology underlying Kupperman's conception of agency that requires a separation between the agent of conduct and the conduct itself. The Confucian concept of *ren* is a gerundive notion—a verbal noun—that is descriptive of consummate "person-ing." Third, Kupperman's character ethics has little to say about the body as the root through which human conduct, being nourished and grown, becomes refulgent. Hence he fails to appreciate the dramatic role that the body has as integral to achieving personal identity and consummate conduct. Fourth, Kupperman fails to appreciate the vital role that the process of moral imagination plays in the moral life. Fifth, in reading Kupperman's *Character*, the expectation is that we learn from it a conceptual vocabulary that enables us to think about personal moral development in a more cogent and nuanced way, rather than that we become inspired by the exhortations and the models of the cultural heroes to become better people. Finally, even though Kupperman values the role of family in the moral life, he did not accord family the vital importance that it deserves. In comparison, role ethics is fully family-centered.

Unlike Kupperman or Ames and Rosemont, Philip J. Ivanhoe reads Confucius (Kongzi) as a virtue ethicist. Taking a comparative approach in explicating Confucius, Ivanhoe argues that, if we consider Confucius's teachings as a whole and seek to interpret them comprehensively and systematically, we will come to understand his ethical philosophy as an expression of virtue ethics and more particularly as a form of virtue ethics that shares important similarities with the kind of view one finds in Aristotle. Such an approach enables us to account for and understand centrally important features of Confucius's thought that might otherwise go unnoticed. For example, even though Confucius did not develop a specific theory about human nature, it is clear that his philosophy relies upon a general and distinctive concept of human nature and its flourishing. One critical feature of Confucius's view of human nature is that at birth, one's nature is underdeveloped and incomplete; we can and must cultivate our original nature by developing a set of virtuous dispositions in order to attain an ideal form of life. In all three respects—being founded on notions about human nature, focusing on the cultivation of a set of virtues, and aiming at an ideal form of life—Confucius's philosophy distinguishes itself as an expression of virtue ethics. Similar to Aristotle in explicating his virtue ethics, Confucius insists that the good life can only be found in the right kind of community and that such a community is constituted by special relationships between and among properly cultivated human beings. For Ivanhoe, Confucius is neither a character ethicist, nor a role ethicist, but a virtue ethicist and must be read as such.[2]

Going beyond the question about virtue or character, Bryan Van Norden tackles a more fundamental question about the nature of value. Following Kupperman's contrast between Platonic realism, which takes values as "spectral furniture of the universe," and what Van Norden calls "anthropocentric realism," he endorses Kupperman's recommendation to reject the first approach, and elaborates the latter in his own way. Van Norden argues that, just like the notion of "poison" is meaningful only in the context of living organisms and yet it is objective whether something is poisonous to an organism, "value" for humans is anthropocentric, i.e., meaningful only in relation to humans, and objective in the sense that either what is valuable is a means toward what is intrinsically good for humans, or is itself intrinsically good for humans. Citing early Confucian Xunzi as an example of anthropocentric realism, and rejecting the widespread argument from disagreements for ethical non-realism, Van Norden, again, in agreement with Kupperman, defends the version of anthropocentric realism that admits varieties of distinct but equally adequate forms of human conduct, such as marriage ceremonies, funeral rituals, etc. Van Norden's own position is more inspired by Aristotle than by Xunzi, who Van Norden thinks "fails to do justice to pluralism." He phrases Aristotelian rationality as "the simple recognition that 'Why are you doing that?' is always a legitimate question to ask of a human being," and argues that Hume's famous view about the nonrational nature of value is question-begging (as it depends on his stipulative definition of rationality). He moves on to reject four "inadequate answers" and defend six "adequate answers" to the "Why question," the question about what is or is not objectively valuable for humans. Van Norden concludes his essay with a definite but open position: As philosophy is dialogical, so if one disagrees with his view, he is willing to ask "Why?" and will begin a dialogue with the person.

Comparing to the previous chapters, David Wong's appears to be less ambitious, as it focuses on just one specific emotion—love and its place in a good life. His essay belongs to the kind of project that Kupperman has done so much to renew in a contemporary setting but has not been explored in depth by Kupperman himself. However, readers will soon realize how rich and broadly significant Wong's essay is. Through his discussion of a wide array of accounts of love, including well-known philosophical accounts such as those given by Harry Frankfurt and J. David Velleman, filial love in Confucian texts, and psychological and neuroscientific studies of love and attachment, Wong lays out three forms or faces of love—the kind that answers to no reasons, the kind that answers to reasons grounded in personal qualities of the beloved, and the kind that answers to reasons grounded in relationship. He shows any account that makes one of these the only or primary mode of love to be inadequate. The tensions and apparent conflicts between these forms answer to the complexity and changing nature of the human needs to which love answers. Wong's fair-minded, pluralistic approach and his style of clear articulation and tight reasoning, which have gained him the reputation of being one of the most prominent scholars in comparative philosophy today, are well exemplified in this essay.

Making ancient ideas appealing to contemporary readers is a challenge for today's students of Asian philosophy, even from a comparative perspective. Following Kupperman's lead but extending beyond Kupperman's own discussion, Kwong-loi Shun espouses a Confucian account of equanimity. By "equanimity," Shun denotes a cluster of qualities such as calmness of the mind, maintaining one's balance in the face of trying circumstances, and being unperturbed in seemingly alarming situations. He begins with a puzzling observation: Confucian thinkers often attribute the good person such qualities as ease of mind and being free from anxiety, qualities that are usually unassociated with the ideal person in contemporary ethical theories. Shun draws on both early and later Confucian thought to extract a more elaborate account of these qualities and of how they are grounded in a complete orientation to the ethical in the Confucian tradition. On the account developed by Shun, the state of mind described as equanimity is not a matter of one's immediate responses to one's environment, and is not something that comes and goes as the way one relates to environment changes. While there is a sense of calm, of being at rest and at peace, of not moving around or being agitated, and of being in control of oneself and not being a captive of one's environment, the state of mind under consideration here also involves a certain reflective stance, namely, one's awareness and affirmation of the fact that one is flowing along with the ethical. It is a more enduring state that is grounded in this reflective stance, and it involves a certain outlook, posture, or orientation in life, having to do not just with one's feeling a certain way, but also with the way one views and relates to the world. Reflective equanimity is a posture toward adverse conditions of life that is grounded in the awareness that these other conditions of life pale in significance compared to the importance of following the ethical path. Such a state of mind is an integral part of Confucian moral cultivation and the moral life, and perhaps an important quality possessed by persons of a good character.

Robert Neville has been a representative of "Boston Confucianism," a contemporary Confucian school that brings Confucianism into lively dialogue with mainstream Western philosophy. Deeply rooted in the Xunzian philosophy of ritual propriety, his work complements Kupperman's, which has more to do with Confucius and Mencius. Neville argues that the Western "subject-object" dichotomy has turned other people into the actual or potential experience of them. From the perspective of the Confucian ritual, a person's relationship with others is not seen as a subject-object contrast but as constituted by a natural standpoint within which individuals interact, most often in ritualized, meaningful, roles. An individual understands herself or himself to be one among many individuals in the dance of a ritual. The other individuals are also players in that ritual pattern. The fundamental reality of the ritual, or nexus of rituals, makes players of us all. In the process, each player needs to individuate the playing: I see my individuating to be part and parcel of the ritual reality, just like the individuations being cultivated by the others. In Neville's view, ritual is a fundamental dimension of the human reality. In it, both "I" and "Others" are individuated as persons. Neville's Xunzian approach to individuation provides an important philosophical dimension to Kupperman's character ethics.

The next group of essays by Chenyang Li, Sor-hoon Tan, Peimin Ni, and Karyn Lai are all concerned with the idea that a good life must extend beyond, though does not exclude, material well-being. Though this thesis seems like common sense, the prevailing materialistic culture in the world, the difficulties and the urgency in overcoming the materialistic tendency, and the theoretical complexities involved and revealed by these essays all warrant serious treatment.

Inspired by Kupperman's work on material good and the good life, Chenyang Li's chapter examines the relationship between material well-being and moral cultivation in early Confucianism. Confucians advocate both material well-being and moral cultivation. While people seldom question the value of these two pursuits, their relationship is by no means intuitive. Various passages in the classic texts suggest varied possibilities. Li analyzes four possible solutions to this relationship. First, material well-being is not a precondition for moral cultivation, but it improves human life in a separate dimension and, therefore, it is good on its own. Second, material well-being is a precondition for moral cultivation and must be achieved before cultivating character. Third, Confucius and Mencius have different virtues in mind when they say that one needs material well-being in order to cultivate (one set of) virtues *and* that one does not need material well-being to cultivate (another set of) virtues. The fourth view, which Li supports, is that, whereas a small portion of people may be able to become morally cultivated without a decent level of material well-being, the large majority need material well-being as a foundation for moral cultivation. Introducing a concept of "statistical necessity," Li argues for a Confucian view that, while in principle each individual person possesses the capacity for self-cultivation even without adequate material provisions, statistically a population cannot be well-cultivated without adequate material provisions. Therefore, Confucians maintain both that an individual should strive for moral refinement regardless of his or her material circumstances, and that material well-being in a society is essential toward achieving a good society.

In her essay, Sor-hoon Tan explores the relationship between materialistic desires, pursuit of profit, and wealth on the one hand and ethical life on the other, and reveals interesting complexities in Confucian attitudes to the tension between them in the *Analects* and the *Mencius*. Her study shows that there is no doubt that the highest ideal for both

Masters is that of a person who loves the ethical so much that she is willing to sacrifice all materialistic goods and even her life. They are however realistic enough to recognize that materialistic desires are common and dominate the motivations of the average human being, and the idea that ethical life precludes these desires is more likely to turn people away rather than lead them toward the Confucian way. Nor is it necessarily the case that what is profitable and what is ethical are always opposed. In the Confucian view, it is possible to satisfy materialistic desires, gain wealth and honor while living ethically.

Peimin Ni's chapter points out an elephant in the room: while we expect individual persons to be morally decent and care for more than material possession and consumption, social entities in today's world increasingly revolve around economic standards and submit to the whim of the market. Extending Kupperman's study of character and his insights about the value of Confucianism to the ethics of social entities, the chapter breaks the taboo of avoiding the topic for fearing stereotypes against groups of people. Ni argues that in most cases we can meaningfully apply the word "self" to social entities, which is not only irreducible to mere collections of individual persons, but often a source of individual selves, and hence the ethics of social entities is not reducible to but rather should be placed within its dynamic interrelation with the ethics of individual persons. Viewing this point in the context of this book, we implicitly see a path where Ames-Rosemont's and Kupperman's views about self might be reconciled. Ni takes the character of social entities roughly as their culture, which is reflected in and shaped by but not reducible to their primary functions, structures, and operational regulations. It is their continuity of commitment, which is difficult to break up in the short run, as illustrated by what Ni calls "the Red Lantern Effect," but not impossible to alter in the long run. Having summarized the limitations of the "lowest-common-denominator" approach, Ni proposes a Confucian way to shape the character of a social entity—model emulation, and suggests that, to avoid conceiving creativity as merely acting "out of character," we should more accurately understand character cultivation as a process of acquiring artistic abilities, or using his favorite term, "*gongfu*."

The chapter by Karyn Lai extends Kupperman's character ethics to social entities and aims to rectify the tendency in recent scholarship on Confucian business ethics that, in her view, overly and wrongly puts building harmonious relationships as fundamental and central to Confucian business ethics. She argues that, although relationships are a key aspect of Confucianism, what is fundamental in Confucian ethics is the cultivation of character, from which good relationships manifest. If relationships were to be taken as central, it would lead to difficulties such as making compromises for the sake of maintaining good relations, or nepotism. However, this shift of center from relations to the cultivation of self does not entail an acceptance of the notion of self as an autonomous choice-maker who makes single, disconnected decisions and actions, but rather a longitudinal understanding of a person as the development and manifestation of character over time. Lai concludes her essay with three features of the Confucian cultivation of character to be pertinent for business: that a business should not be limited to gaining its own profit; that a business should not just occasionally do a charitable thing, but to have a long-term commitment of making it part of its core business to contribute to the society; and that a business should constantly reevaluate its objectives in light of their situatedness within particular social, political, legal and ethical contexts.

This volume concludes with Kupperman's "Responses and Comments." Kupperman acknowledges the differences between the views expressed by contributors and his own. However, he sees these different views as revealing various aspects of the issues under consideration. Each of us has some kind of blind spot and collectively we "see" a fuller picture. If there is one substantial difference of views, it is the one on self between Kupperman, on the one hand, and Ames and Rosemont on the other. Ames and Rosemont charge that Kupperman holds on to a notion of "reified self" and retains a clear distinction between the self and the character. They do not think there can be such a clear distinction. Kupperman acknowledges the influence of Indian philosophy on him, but does not give up such a notion of self entirely. In his view, although the image of an individual agent functioning in an autonomous way is overworked in recent Western philosophy, it does not mean that it can be abandoned. For Kupperman, it is the idea of the individual agent functioning in an autonomous way that takes on personal meaning. In Dallmayr's view, these differences are more of a matter of different "accents" than fundamental disagreements. Kupperman does not deny that persons exist in relationships; Ames and Rosemont do not entirely rule out the relative independence of the self. As Dallmayr says, no matter which accent one prefers, the fact remains that Kupperman's work has given new impulses to a great variety of interpretations and thus provides a boost to the reinvigoration of virtue ethics in a global setting. For this service, we—Western and Asian comparativists—are all deeply indebted and grateful to Kupperman.

Notes

1. See Stephen Angle 2010. It is conceivable, of course, that one could philosophize on common problems shared by more than one tradition, draw on more than one tradition, and advance a thesis in between and across traditions. That would also fall into the category of comparative philosophy broadly construed.

2. Besides virtue ethics, character ethics, and role ethics, for a debate on whether Confucian ethics can be properly read as a form of care ethics, see Star 2002 and Li 2002.

References

Angle, Stephen (2010). "The Minimal Definition and Methodology of Comparative Philosophy: A Report from a Conference," *Comparative Philosophy*, 1.1: 106–110.

Kupperman, Joel J. (2012). "Half Truths." *Ratio*, 25.2: 148–163.

———. (2010). "Why Ethical Philosophy Needs to Be Comparative." *Philosophy*, 85: 185–200.

———. (1999). *Learning from Asian Philosophy*. New York: Oxford University Press.

———. (1991). *Character*. New York: Oxford University Press.

Li, Chenyang (2002). "Revisiting Confucian Jen Ethics and Feminist Care Ethics: A Reply to Daniel Star and Lijun Yuan." *Hypatia: A Journal of Feminist Philosophy*, 17.1: 130–140.

Star, Daniel (2002). "Do Confucians Really Care? A Defense of the Distinctiveness of Care Ethics: A Reply to Chenyang Li." *Hypatia*, 17.1: 77–106.

PART I

Moral Cultivation and Confucian Virtues

Engagements and Developments

1

From Kupperman's Character Ethics to Confucian Role Ethics

Putting Humpty Together Again

Roger T. Ames
Henry Rosemont, Jr.

Reinstating Family in Moral Philosophy

With a few oblique exceptions (such as Aristotle, Rousseau, and Hegel), the family, and the relations among and between family members, have not received much detailed attention from Western philosophers and theologians. And much of what notice family has received has been in a more negative than positive light with respect to the capacities of this social institution to enable full human development. Plato, for example, strictly forbade all forms of family life for the guardians of his Republic as corrupting of their abilities to govern and protect the citizens.[1] A few Christian savants have made tolerable remarks about the institution of marriage and the family, but to most of them married life, being profane, is decidedly inferior to the loftier existence of the monk or nun, who, because of their abstinence from worldly desires and pursuits, are—or should be—closer to God.[2]

But humans are social beings, and the socialization process begins and develops in the family. Thus, if morality is the form and content of our social relations, then thinking about morality must include thinking about the family, and to the extent that the family is neglected in thinking about morality, to just that extent will morality be broken, like Humpty Dumpty. Herein we would like to try to piece him together again.

Two contemporary exceptions to our generalization about the neglect of family and familial relations in Western moral philosophy are the late Susan Moller Okin and Joel Kupperman, both of whom have given long and careful attention to the role of this institution in their detailed treatments of justice and character, respectively. The focus of our interest in these two philosophers has to do with their understanding of the relationship between person and family in achieving justice and in developing personal character, respectively. We find that Okin provides us with a clear statement of the problem that the current inequitable institution of family poses for achieving a just society, and that Kupperman's character ethics points us in the right direction for appreciating the role that family has in developing moral competence. In this article we will assay these two positions as we have come to understand them, and then turn to a consideration of the importance of family in our real experience to make the argument that Confucian role ethics in taking family relations as the entry point for developing moral competence has much to offer contemporary conversations in moral philosophy. Finally, returning to Confucian role ethics, we will invoke the *Great Learning* (*daxue* 大學) as the first of the *Four Books* that lays out the Confucian project of personal cultivation within family, community, and tradition.

Okin and the Importance of Family in Formulating a Theory of Justice

Okin, while somewhat critical of John Rawls, is still building on his influential theory of justice. She makes the argument that developing a sense of justice in our adult political life cannot take place unless justice is first learned and practiced in the family. Indeed, in her influential work, *Justice, Gender, and the Family*, Okin reserves a key place for the family, and is sharply critical of those moral theorists who think that they can ignore it.

We offer our critique of Okin here to make clear how the Confucian formulation of justice would begin from family life itself rather than from the abstractions of either principles or discrete and autonomous individuals. Rather than starting from a reflection on justice in the life of the family itself, and then extending a familial conception of actualized justice into the public sphere, Okin instead chooses to draw upon an abstract, public definition of justice—that is, an equality of opportunity for all—to restructure the institution of family. Her assessment of family inequities is persuasive. But her thin Rawlsian solution of constructing ideal institutions and policies that can then be applied to achieve a quantifiable justice defined largely in terms of equal distribution of work and compensation among generic individuals is much less satisfying.

Okin offers a compelling argument that the institution of family as it is presently constituted by a hierarchical structure of roles saturated by a pervasive gender bias is fundamentally unjust. And given the crucial importance of family as the veritable "school of justice" in the moral development and education of children, the assumption that we can construct a just society on such a tenuous foundation is, as she properly claims, untenable. This being the case, it is both undeniably true and at the same time deplorable that most scholars who would offer us a theory of justice have chosen to do so while ignoring the family altogether (for example, Bruce Ackerman, Ronald Dworkin, and Robert Nozick).[3] The alternative to those thinkers who would neglect the institution of family is another group of theorists who, in using a false gender neutrality, are able to skip over the issue of gender discrimination within the family and community by pretending it does not exist (for example, Alasdair MacIntyre and Derek Phillips).[4] And then there are those few scholars late and soon who actually take the family into account, but who would exempt it from the demands of justice by claiming that the norms governing their idealized conception of family such as love, fidelity, and trust are of a higher order than simply respect for what is just and fair (for example, Jean-Jacque Rousseau, David Hume, Michael Sandel, and Roberto Unger).[5]

Okin frames the problem well, but her solution is disappointing. While she does seek to rectify the family as a patently unjust institution upon which so much of social justice is built, and on which justice ultimately depends, she offers a Rawlsian-inspired attempt to apply the principle of justice to a family of autonomous individuals in order to establish equal opportunity among them. Okin's ostensive solution is in fact an integral part of the problem itself, requiring as it does the retention of a foundational individualism as central to the definition of what it is to be a human being while relying exclusively upon a principled understanding of justice as the instrument for effecting a just world. Her underlying assumption is that an abstract principle of justice can be mechanically applied to abstract individuals who are conjoined by extrinsic, causal relations. As such, she ignores the intimacy, mutuality, and particularity that is invariably defining of relations in real families, and the always particular context from which putative principles ultimately derive and to which they are to be applied. This reductionism with respect to the subject of justice is targeted quite sharply (although almost surely unintentionally) by feminist philosophers Martha Minow and Mary Lyndon Shanley in the introduction to a special issue of *Hypatia* they edited on the family when they note as "a paradoxical characteristic of family life" the fact that "the individual must be seen simultaneously as a distinct individual and as a person fundamentally involved in relationships of dependence, care, and responsibility."[6] They are correct on this point: If we presuppose that human beings should be seen as fundamentally discrete, autonomous individuals then family life does indeed become paradoxical.

With respect to the inequities that are pervasive in the institution of family, the greatest source of injustice for Okin is gender discrimination and its implications for work and pay. And she would solve these ubiquitous inequalities that attend gender by terminating the distinction of gender altogether. But how do we do this, and would erasing gender solve the problem even if we were able to do so? Whatever attempt we might make to reconceive the human experience in a non-gendered way, we must begin from the fact of gender as a sexual and a historical difference, and then ask: Is it desirable to construct a society free of gender discrimination in which the seemingly distinctive practices of "mothering" and "fathering," "sistering" and "brothering," are made obsolete terms? Said another way, it might be thin justice for women that is premised upon them becoming ungendered persons rather than remaining women, and thin justice for family members as well by reducing them to generic individuals rather than allowing them to be the unique persons they are within their thick familial bonds.

Does not the appreciation of real differences—those of gender, generation, and most importantly, personal differences—give the lie to the idea that justice is to be achieved by treating all people the same? Like Okin, we are keenly aware of the profound influence that family has on moral development, and we certainly agree with her that family should serve as the "school of justice" for our children, but not in a way that eliminates any interesting notion of family by making it into a committee of fungible equals. Should we not instead strive for a society in which gender differences like all other real differences are an integral part of a much more robust conception of justice?

A Confucian Critique of Okin's Theory of Justice

Viewed from a Confucian point of view, if Okin's book were to reflect the process we *ought* to follow in formulating a practicable conception of justice, it would have to be retitled *The Family, Gender, and Justice*. That is, a Confucian critique of Okin would begin by arguing that consideration for the wholeness of experience would require that we start with life in the lived family within which not only sex and gender but also ubiquitous patterns of hierarchy have been familiar distinctions, and try to reconstruct a vision of all relations, gender included, that would best serve the interests of the many diverse and constantly shifting roles lived by each member of the family. The goal would not be to enforce a simple equality among the family's distinctive members, but rather to achieve a parity that saves productive differences as much as possible, while precluding coercion in all of the relational transactions that are defining of family life, keeping in mind at all times that family relations are always changing to a certain extent as the family members all grow older.

Since we basically agree with Okin that gender is largely a social product rather than a distinction determined by human biology, we can and must strive to redefine gender difference in a way that replaces an oppressive inequality with a complementary and productive parity. Ironically, a heavy-handed conception of distributive justice that, in imposing a quantifiable standard of equity on family, fails to respect the processual, phasal, and resolutely hierarchical nature of family life, is itself reductive and violent, becoming a procedural strategy for enforcing conformity at the unacceptable expense of excising real differences and their creative possibilities. In failing to accommodate family roles lived through richly textured and constantly changing patterns of both natural and socially constructed differences, such a theory is an anathema to the optimizing of the family experience for all of its members. After all, it must be this aspiration to optimize the family experience that is surely the ultimate goal of any conception of real, actualized justice. To our minds, Okin does not "do justice" to the particularities of persons in families or to the correlative nature of relations, and as a consequence fails to do justice to the notion of justice itself.

Kupperman and the Role of Family in Early Character Development

Against this background, we now turn to Joel Kupperman's contribution to this discussion of the relationship between persons and family. In the field of ethics over the past generation we have witnessed a sustained dissatisfaction with narrow rule-based approaches to ethics, and have seen developments in different quarters that are seeking to reinstate different dimensions of the human experience that have been excluded from consideration. The revival of virtue ethics, the rise of sentimentalism, of particularism, and of care ethics, and a sustained professional reflection on the role of emotions and somaticity in the moral life are all attempts to understand ethics in a more holistic way.

Kupperman's work is an important contribution to this sea change in ethics. His main argument is that ethical philosophy should be structured around the development of character as it begins in family relations and is further developed within the context of community and tradition. In his earlier work—especially in his seminal monograph *Character*—Kupperman has formulated a doctrine of "character ethics" that he posits as a robust alternative to familiar versions of virtue ethics. And he sees in the Confucian emphasis on personal cultivation a close analogue to his long-term concern with character development. With his formulation of this doctrine of character ethics, he is glad to break ranks with those who would advocate virtue ethics, and is further prepared to argue that Confucius himself should be included as a fellow character-ethicist.[7]

In seeking to replace virtue ethics with character ethics, Kupperman is doing his best to put the humpty-dumpty of ethical philosophy back together again. That is, he challenges what he calls the "snapshot" view of ethical decision making in virtue ethics, and equally the "big moment" ethics we associate with Kant and Bentham and Mill.[8] This fragmenting approach to our understanding of ethics has introduced a plethora of fractures and fault lines into what he takes to be the relatively seamless process of developing the qualities of character that enable us to express a moral competence in our daily conduct. Such compartmentalizing, while acknowledging relevant issues in ethics, seems at the same time to isolate and decontextualize them. While virtues, for example, are generally classified and treated separately and simply, Kupperman's appeal to character development requires that we appreciate the interpenetration among personal qualities and accommodate their true complexity, and further that we take the aggregate of both positive and negative qualities into consideration at the same time. For Kupperman, "selves are constructed during a life rather than being present at birth."[9] That is, he attempts to restore process and duration to the notion of human development, to respect the interpenetration of virtues in time, and to abandon any severe distinction between what one does and what is done to one.

> Anyone's character is likely to be affected, at any point in life, by social norms, a person's social class and family relations, how that person spends most of her or his time, and so on; as these factors change, a change in character will be the natural (although not inevitable) result.[10]

Kupperman is adamant that character development is importantly dependent upon the contexts of community and tradition:

> To the extent that a person can be viewed as creating a character, this self-creation does not take place in a void: It occurs against the background of types of people in a community and in relation to social roles and options that are available. It is impossible not to be, in some sense, a person of one's time, however many prevailing opinions and attitudes one rejects . . . Tradition and a network of more or less common understandings thus underlie the development of individual character.[11]

Kupperman's robust conception of character is more personal and particular than virtue traits, and has an active, continuous, and particularizing role that both unifies and stabilizes lives through time. Consistent with the continuities and context recovered with this processual understanding of the development of character, Kupperman challenges any atomistic view of choice that would reduce it to serial discrete, impersonal decisions, by seeing choice itself as a process in which a continuing current of commitment and responsibility serves to unify ostensive judgments:

> The decision-procedure is oriented toward single decisions, viewed as disconnected from other decisions, in a way which ignores or slights the moral importance of continuity of commitment. . . . Many of the most crucial "choices" in our lives turn out to be clusters of an indeterminate number of choices, most or all of which point in the same direction, which are

> such that many are not reflective or explicit. Any model of choice in human life must take account of this.[12]

In the various dimensions of character development, Kupperman wants to understand moral conduct in a vital and more holistic sense by reinstating in significant degree the processive nature, the always specific context, the particularity, and the growth that are all characteristic of moral conduct. But even though Kupperman has taken us in the right direction by restoring some of the continuities in human conduct that have been underrepresented in virtue ethics, we would contend that he does not go far enough. We are able to identify several remaining disjunctions and dichotomies in his own theory of character ethics that prevent him, like all of the king's men, from reinstating the wholeness and the capaciousness of our actual moral experience.

First, Kupperman insists on retaining the default concept of a discrete, separate, and reified "self" as the emergent product of character development:

> Normally, a human organism will regard herself or himself as having a single self, with the life of the organism as its outer boundaries, and this will coincide with the view of outside observers. . . . A normal human being begins life with a protoself, and a self begins to appear in the course of early childhood. It is constructed within the protoself, typically not by conscious decisions but rather by the formation of habits and attitudes and the emergence of characteristic ways of thinking and behaving.[13]

For Kupperman, "character approximates the nature of self" where "character is to the major matters of life as the nature of self is to all of life."[14] That is, there is for Kupperman a definite individuality to the self that serves as the ground and locus of one's character development that becomes manifest in its more important undertakings.[15]

And when we ask the question: What then is the relationship between this self, its character, and its conduct? Kupperman would retain a clear distinction between the self and the character it has accrued that "flows" from this self into its actions:

> Character certainly has a causal role in behavior: In many cases, part of the explanation of why someone behaved in

> such and such a manner must be that he or she is such and such a person. But another part of a causal explanation of behavior will be features of the situation.[16]

In Kupperman's more recent work, and specifically, in the two versions of his "Tradition and Community in the Formation of Character and Self,"[17] he presents a view of the role of the family in personal development that is certainly more robust than Okin's, but that still retains this reified conception of a unified and discrete self. In this essay, Kupperman does insist upon the importance of family, community, and tradition in the formative process of creating the foundation for a moral self in the following terms:

> Tradition is, in Confucius' presentation of the development of a good self, not only a source of inspiration and advice but also (more importantly) a source of modeling. The right kind of parent-child relation, in his view, has this character. One develops a self that of course is separate but is not entirely separate: there will be elements reminiscent of parents, who in turn had developed selves that included elements reminiscent of their parents, and so on.[18]

Kupperman's notion of the self as a "self-as-collage" includes "elements derived from outside sources" that have both a causal and a constitutive status and "layers that represent the absorption (or sometimes, rejection) of various influences at various stages of life, going back to early childhood."[19] Although he often references and seems to appreciate the relational nature of the Confucian person, he is still consistent in maintaining that an individual can be accurately described, analyzed, and evaluated independently of other human beings. With this assumption of an individual and discrete self, he interprets persons in families in an importantly different way than we do from a role ethics perspective.

We maintain that the familiar dualisms such as subject/object, agent/action, mind/body, nature/nurture, and so on, that arise from substance ontology have little relevance for the notion of relationally constituted persons integral to Confucian role ethics. Indeed, this Confucian conception of person makes no appeal to superordinate, substantive categories such as "soul," "self," "will," "faculties," "nature," "mind," "character," and so on, but instead locates "person" gerundively as the embodied, social activity of thinking and feeling within the manifold of relations that constitutes family, community, and the natural environment. Person thus understood is a complex event rather than a discrete "thing," a process of "becoming" rather than an essential "being," an ongoing "doing" rather than an autonomous "is," a configuration of concrete, dynamic, and constitutive relations rather than an individuated substance defined by some subsisting agency.

Herbert Fingarette made this point elegantly some time ago, when he said: "For Confucius, unless there are at least two human beings, there are no human beings."[20] In any moral (or political) sense, role ethics is the claim that we can neither be well described, analyzed, or evaluated as persons apart from the other persons with whom we interact, and that persons are best described, analyzed and evaluated morally (and politically) in terms of the specific roles that guide their actions with specific others.

A Confucian Critique of Kupperman's Character Ethics

We would argue that Confucian role ethics in several important ways offers a basis for a more capacious vision of justice than Okin does, and a more holistic vision of the moral life than Kupperman's character ethics does. First, consistent with the spirit of Kupperman's attempt to restore wholeness to experience, Confucian role ethics would insist on the primacy of relationships, and would preclude any notion of final individuality. Personal discreteness is a conceptual abstraction and strict autonomy a misleading fiction; association is a fact. And the roles we live are simply the way in which this fact of association is further stipulated and specified.

We hasten to make the point that giving up the notion of a superordinate "self" far from surrendering one's personal uniqueness, in fact, enhances it. That is, the "natural kinds" talk that usually stands behind claims about a shared human nature and a concomitant essential self mitigates the degree of difference we find in a Confucian notion of person where person is constituted by a dynamic manifold of always specific relations.

Second, Confucian role ethics would resist the uncritical substance ontology underlying Kupperman's conception of agency that requires a separation between the agent of conduct and the conduct itself. The notion of *ren* 仁 that is central to Confucian role ethics entails no such agency/action dichotomy. *Ren* requires a narrative rather than an analytic understanding of person. And *ren* is cultivated by correlating one's own conduct with those models close at hand rather than by acting in concert with some abstract moral principles.[21] It is for this reason that it is often unclear whether *ren* denotes a consummate person or the conduct of such a person, or like its cognate *ren* 人, whether the referent is singular or plural. *Ren* is an open-ended generalization made off of particular historical accomplishments of consummate conduct rather than referencing some innate and essential element that is characteristic of all members of the set called human "beings." Indeed, *ren* is a gerundive notion—a verbal noun—that is descriptive of consummate "person-ing."

Third, Confucian role ethicists would fault Kupperman for failing to appreciate the dramatic role that body has as integral to achieving personal identity and consummate conduct. He appeals to the familiar language of "a psychological field which is present in a newborn infant and which continues throughout that infant's life,"[22] but has little to say about the body as the root through which human conduct, being nourished and grown, becomes refulgent. It is no coincidence that the simplified graph for body 體 is 体—that is, quite literally, the graphic denotation of the root of a person. The body—always a collaboration between person and world, between organism and environment—is at once carnal and vital, seen and lived, receptive and responsive. Not only does the world shape the body, but through our bodily sensorium we structure, conceptualize, and theorize our world of experience.[23] Indeed, it is because the body is the medium through which our ancestors and their culture live on in us that keeping one's body intact has been the first among the several precepts of family reverence (*xiao* 孝).[24]

Fourth, while Kupperman appeals to a language of process to express character formation and the choices that are made to effect this transformation, he again has little to say about the vital role that the process of moral imagination plays in consummate thinking and living. In Confucian role ethics, it is our educated imagination that, drawing upon all of our human resources, defers action until we can conjure forth the full range of possibilities that allows for optimal growth in our relationships. And said plainly, it is this growth in relationships that is the very core of morality.

Fifth, Confucian role ethics does not compete with virtue ethics or any other ethical *theory* but is rather a vision of the moral life that resists the theoretical/practical divide. When we read Kupperman's monograph, *Character*, the expectation is that we learn from it a conceptual vocabulary that enables us to think about personal moral development in a more cogent and nuanced way. When we read the Confucian canons, however, the aspiration is higher. The expectation is that while we certainly can appropriate a cluster of terms that enable a critical reflection on our conduct, we ought, more fundamentally, to be inspired by the exhortations and the models of the cultural heroes to become better people.

And finally, despite the incisive, sensitive, and nuanced reading Kupperman always gives the *Analects*, and in spite of what he has to say about the importance of family in that text, we believe that Confucian role ethics requires that much more be said about this institution. And it is to this task that we now turn.

A Meditation on the Importance of Family in Ordinary Experience

Kupperman surely believes, as do we, that it is of great importance worldwide to bring the family center stage in thinking about how to address the Herculean economic, social, political, and environmental tasks we face today. Surely a great many families can be characterized as sexist, oppressive, or just generally dysfunctional. But many more of them are not, and families are not going to disappear as an institution no matter what some people might wish. Moreover, admitting that "family values" has regularly been employed conceptually in the service of arch-conservative social and political orientations, reinforcing patriarchy, sexism, homophobia, and worse, family values can nevertheless quite straightforwardly be modified along much more progressive social, political, and economic lines; or so we want to claim in advancing an ethic of roles that is grounded in family.

But if our efforts are to receive serious consideration, the concept of individualism as it has been advocated in liberal thinking must be challenged at its core. We believe that an ethics of roles inspired by our own reading of the classical Confucian texts offers a real alternative to a foundational individualism that can constitute one such line of engagement. The challenge of role ethics, however, will not be worth much unless accounts of human interactions can be given in nonindividualistic moral terms that do not fly in the face of our experiences in and of family life, and our intuitions about them. Thus we want to take the opportunity of this celebration of the Kupperman oeuvre to invite him to comment on how well, or how poorly, the following sketch of some distinctive elements of family life from a role perspective meshes with his sympathetic, but still seemingly individualistic interpretation of persons, especially as he believes his account better captures more basic intuitions about human interactions by employing the concept of individual character and creativity as they apply to human beings.

Apart from Okin, Kupperman, and a few other feminist philosophers, the neglect of the family in modern Western philosophy has continued through the twentieth century. The reason for the neglect is easy enough to discern on (at least) two counts. First, family matters have long been considered to be *private* matters, whereas morality is concerned with one's *public* persona.[25] In part this distinction has come about as an implication of increasing sympathy for the idea of the separation of church and state, with the church left to dictate duties and obligations that are mandatory only so long as the person involved accepts the creed of a specific church. That is to say, such obligations are in the *personal* or private sphere, and would cease being binding if one forswore the creed. In the *public* sphere, however, moral duties and obligations are seen to be mandatory in the society in which one lives, full stop; the only alternative is exile.

An even more important reason, we believe, for not examining potential moral concerns pertaining to the family is that the dominant Western moral theories are largely grounded in the concept of human beings as fundamentally rational, free, and autonomous individuals (who are also usually self-interested). Whether this idea (presupposition, actually) is taken descriptively or prescriptively is not important in their advocacy that we must treat all other human beings as free, rational, and autonomous individuals.

But we do not see or treat our parents, grandparents, and children in this way. Family relations, especially the most basic of them—namely, those between parents and children—cannot be described, analyzed, or evaluated on the basis of free and rational autonomous individuals interacting with one another, for parents are implicated in the lives of their children, and children in the lives of their parents. That is to say, a significant element in how both parents and children define who they are, is in terms of the other.[26] Herein lies a part of the paradoxical nature of family life when viewed from an individualistic perspective, as noted earlier.

In other work we chose to translate *xiao* as "family reverence" rather than the more common "filial piety."[27] There are several reasons why we abandoned the standard translation, beginning with the Christian flavor that "piety" tends to evoke that is altogether out of place in the

Confucian context. An even more important reason is that it is the family that is the locus of one's spiritual development in Confucianism. A person is engaged in a fully secular family, but it is at the same time engaging in what we see as an authentic religious discipline that one undergoes in fulfilling familial roles, sacralizing them and then extending them outward to non-kin. This being so, it would perhaps be appropriate to begin thinking a bit more *reverently* about families—our own first, and others too, as the Confucians seem to have done.[28]

Roles in Marriage, Family, and Parenting

To quickly sketch this different perspective from which to see persons, think of how different we become, in a very real sense, when we marry. We remain part of the family whence we came, but our roles within them are altered as we are now forming another family of our own, and we also enter into the family of the spouse we have chosen. All of these relationships change us in significant ways, as every married person knows well.

We are changed even more when our first child is born, followed by that child's siblings, all of whom contribute much to the definition of who we have been, who we are now, and who we will be, just as we too have contributed significantly to who they have become. Hence, when it is "my daughter" or "my son" that must be used in the description of a supposedly moral situation involving a mother or father, the adequacy of formulating and acting upon some abstract principle vanishes. If we as parents do not have the requisite cognitive and affective resources within us to ascertain the most appropriate means of dealing with our own children in any given situation, Kant can no more assist us than can Bentham or Mill, or any other universalist moral philosopher, for that matter. We do not look for a rule that will apply to all abstract individuals all of the time, but rather are genuinely concerned about what it is most appropriate to do with *this* son or daughter, *right now*.

Role ethics has a bottom-up rather than top-down orientation, in that it is based on and develops out of immediate human experience, grounded in family life, not on the rational development of universal principles to be employed by abstract unencumbered individuals whose obligations are always altogether general. Of course parents do not live solely in the immediate present when living their roles with their children; they must remember their past interactions, and contemplate future ones as well. But these, too, are ongoing elements of our daily experience, as every parent, we believe, will attest.

We must take time into account when discussing the responsibilities of parents to and for their children, and the children's responsibilities toward their parents. Consider for a moment a situation that is deeply moral in role ethics, but might well be invisible from other, universal moral perspectives. The situation is from the standpoint of a son. Should I place my aged mother in a nursing home, or keep her in mine? Well, that might well depend on how old I am when I ask the question. If I'm 35, I might well believe I will maximize utility for my wife, children, and co-workers by moving her to a nursing home. And I can formulate a universalizable maxim for doing so, believing strongly that I would not want to be a burden to my children, and following the same maxim, would want them to institutionalize me. At 60, however, I might answer the question differently. Understanding how even the best of such institutions diminishes human flourishing, and given my ever-declining vigor, I might well not be able to formulate a maxim about institutionalizing my parents that I would want my own children to follow, nor can I intelligently calculate benefits for all concerned.

Returning to the parental role, time enters equally into all deliberations we make in the discharge of our responsibilities to and for our children, deliberations not totally circumscribed by the ages of any of us, for each of us must think, and act in accordance with details of the past, the present, and the future in ascertaining how to fulfill our role as father or mother.[29] We must, in the first instance, think about the *present* when attending to that dimension of our paternal role as responsible *caretakers*, seeing, that is, to the needs of our children for food, shelter, clothing, books, security, love, and more. In addition to *caring* for them, however—meeting their physical, mental and emotional needs—we are also aware of our responsibility for *raising them* to become adults, and now we must attend no less carefully to the *future* than to the present. This is to say that as parents, we must not only attend to our children as they are right now but also as we believe it would be best for them to become in the future. There are certain ways we should like our children to be when they grow up, and certain ways we do not want them to be, the details of which will be largely dependent on our children's mental, physical, and psychological makeup. The details will, however, be equally dependent on our own family history, our ethnicity, citizenship, and other social factors that have largely determined the hopes, fears, dreams, and goals we have not only for ourselves, but altogether naturally have for our children as well. Without such factors we would not be who we are, nor would we be a family in any meaningful sense of the word.

In raising children our stated concern is not solely, or perhaps even mainly, to seek to maximize the possibility of their later becoming fully autonomous and free individuals, rationally choosing their own futures, as moralities grounded in individualism would demand. (*Teachers* might conceivably hold this or a similar goal for *students*, but the case with *parents* and their *children* is radically different). But that demand is in our view not only impossible to meet, it is an undesirable one; to a brief consideration of which we now turn, again with a focus on temporality.[30]

Family and the Ordering of Values

We attempt to live in accordance with an order and pattern of values that influences importantly who we are and what we do. We have these values because we believe them to be good ones, and we endeavor to exemplify them in our conduct with our offspring no less than with others. Needless to say we will endeavor to instill our value ordering in our children, for a major part of our parental responsibility is to have them become value-oriented, and if we do not orient them toward our own ordering, which others might we use? How could we conceivably choose among them?[31] This is not to say we do not reorder our values at times, for many people do. Some who place patriotism above an aversion to killing may volunteer for military service, and then combat, but later become pacificists. Others leave, or join a church. Still others come to have more, or less sympathy for the plight of the poor. Our opposition to capital punishment may wither if one of our own children is brutally murdered, and so on.

Presumably, however, we alter our values in a reasoned way. We can explain why we no longer accept violence as a means of settling disputes, or come to see the evasiveness of "blame the victim" arguments with respect to poverty, and we can explain these changes in discussions with our children (and with parents as well). But at any given moment, we believe our value orderings are pretty good ones, we attempt to reflect them in our actions, we look forward to discussions with our children about them, and we want our children to embrace them and model them. *Caretakers* may not have to do these things with respect to the young, but *parents* must, and it would be decidedly unfilial for the children not to take them seriously.

A Non-Exemplary Son: Immoral as Well?

Consider a person whose chosen career has been that of a union organizer. He has enjoyed his work overall, and been extremely proud and happy when another labor unit, through his efforts, votes in a union to represent their interests in negotiations with the corporate hierarchy. His career has not made him rich, but has provided the wherewithal to send his son to college, and to law school thereafter, a goal the boy has embraced since his high school sophomore year. Now, after passing the bar exam the son announces that the best job offer he has had came from the largest union-busting firm in the state, and he has accepted it.

It seems to us that any pride and joy the father might take at this turn of events—the son has a good job, and clearly chosen it independently—would almost immediately be replaced by depression, perhaps severe. And this would not simply be because of the choice the son has made, but because of the way the father now had to view his own role as a father in a very different, much more negative manner, namely as largely a failure. It is not merely that the father secretly might have wished for the son to choose to become a labor lawyer; had the son chosen real estate law, criminal law, or become an assistant district attorney, the father might or might not have been a bit disappointed, yet no more than that. But for the son to embark on a career that was the antithesis of the values of solidarity and social justice his father has lived for and attempted to embody, would be proof positive to him that his fathering had been radically deficient in some vital respects.

It might be tempting to think here that the father is just being self-centered in some way or another, either by wanting to live vicariously through his son's work, or by being a dogmatist, or simply not thinking of how the son might take pride in the knowledge of his independence and ability to make up his own mind. But if we shift attention directly to the son himself as he begins a career devoted to undoing his father's life work and dreams, what would we think of him? Notice that so long as we merely see him as an individual who has made a rational choice, we will probably just shrug our shoulders and say "So what?" Our strong sense, however, is that if we focus on him as a *son* of *this* father we would not think much of him, very probably seeing him as unfeeling, or worse. We would certainly characterize him as *self-centered* for being so unmindful of the significance of this decision for his father, who, because of his son's decision, has become a much-altered person, and not merely because of his sadness. We would hold the son in low regard because of his lack of gratitude, and also because of his *irreverence* toward his family, with untoward consequences for the others with whom his life has been intertwined.[32]

Parents must, of course, balance their guiding conduct toward their children with an appreciation of the uniqueness of each one of them. The desired goal would be to have them take on these values not merely because they are the values of their parents, but because the children believe such values are *good* values, and want to commit themselves to them for this reason. And it seems that this goal can only be achieved on the basis of the *love* of the parents for their children, and not because of an abstract moral *rule* or *principle*. Returning to the union-organizing father, how could he possibly assign a higher place in his values to the categorical imperative or the utility principle than to the priorities that have given his life meaning, purpose, and satisfaction?

The Dysfunctional Family Objection

It might be objected here that all of this is well and good, but what do we do with fathers who don't love their children very much, and are rigid dogmatists to boot? How can we be reverent toward such a family? Don't we need some more general moral principles applicable to these situations? If love can bring the parental behavior into accord with the requisite moral principles without invoking the principles upon reflection, fine, this objection might continue; but how do we handle the unloving or uncaring parents—of which, obviously and unfortunately, there are a great many today—without more general moral principles?

Such an objection is very probably the most common to be made about the particularistic nature of Confucianism.[33] In reply, first, it may be irreverent, but not irrelevant to turn the question around. In cases of wretched fathers, why would we have any reason to believe they will see the light and become good Kantians or Utilitarians? Surely almost all such fathers will not have read any of the works of these philosophers, and how will we make them do so? At any level even remotely resembling the practical, how can this kind of objection be seen to have more force against Confucius than Kant, Bentham, or Mill?

More importantly, the question underlying the objection cannot be answered as stated, because it is requesting a rule or a principle to follow, and, we are arguing that there are no such rules or principles to be gleaned from the texts of early Confucianism; it is particularistic to the core. But this does not mean there is no answer to the question, for there always is one, only framed differently.

If I see that my father is unduly indoctrinating my younger siblings, and seems to show indifference to them, I must first ask why he is this way, and attempt to correct the cause of the problem if possible. If the first question cannot be answered, my next question is whether or not I have the capacity to change his behavior in order for my siblings to flourish. If the answer is "Yes," I do so. If my answer is "No," I must then ask whether I can help my mother change him. Or ask my uncles and aunts (his brothers and sisters), or his parents (my grandparents) to get him to change his ways. And if all else fails, I can then simply do my best to shelter my siblings from my father as best I can whenever he is being overbearing or abusive. In an extreme case, I may have to ask for outside assistance from a public agency, or in a desperate situation, from the police. In sum, what I do is dependent on who *I* am, who *my* father is, and the specific personalities and capacities of other members of *my* family. But there is always an answer to the question that we obtain upon reflection at times, but without invoking universal rules or principles.

The Primacy of Family in Confucian Role Ethics

The moral of the story thus far should be clear: When dealing with relationships between parents and children we cannot see any of the participants as free, autonomous individuals, for they are too intimately bound up with one another not only in their interactions, but in their sense of who they are, have been and will become as well; in all cases, bonded by love. What it means, in large part, to be a father or a mother is to be sensitive to the personalities, abilities, and feelings of their children at all times, taking these into account both when caring for them *now*, and raising them with an eye to the *future*. And what it means to be a son or daughter, is to be sensitive to the beliefs and feelings of one's parents before electing and following any significant goal in their lives, a sensitivity that must be maintained throughout their parents' lives, as a matter of loyalty. This loyalty does not preclude remonstrating with parents (or others in authority), of course, as all the texts of classical Confucianism make clear.

How much of each behavior and attendant attitude parents should seek to instill in their children depends in part on their own value ordering, but depends even more on the specific personalities of the children. For Confucians, challenging authority is not to be taken lightly; but neither is loyalty or obedience if these qualities are not exhibited outwardly without a proper inward orientation. For them, these qualities were reciprocal, and every parent and teacher had to be aware of when and how best to inculcate the appropriate feelings to accompany appropriate behavior. In the first book of the *Analects*, for example, we find "It is a rare thing for someone who has a sense of familial and fraternal responsibility (孝弟) to have a taste for defying authority" (1.2). But at the same time, "As for young people contributing their energies when there is work to be done, and deferring to their elders when there is wine and food to be had—how can merely doing these things be considered as being familially reverent?" (2.8). Somehow true family reverence would provide insight into when authority might be defied, for Confucius equally noted that "To see what it is appropriate to do, and not do it, is cowardice" (2.24).

The textual evidence suggests that the early Confucians did not think too long or hard about the institution of the family *qua* family either, but for very different reasons than their Western counterparts: The family is seen as so basic for human flourishing as to be self-evident, and hence not in need of detailed analysis or justification. For the Confucians, the question is not *whether* the family is necessary for human beings to develop and flourish, for it is obvious that it is, and without it, it is assumed that one does not have the means to become human.[34] The question is rather *which* behavior models are most appropriate in a family in order for its members to develop and flourish.[35]

The early Confucian texts are certainly not simply child-rearing manuals, but they *are* child-rearing manuals in part, and read with care and sensitivity still have much to teach parents (and teachers) today about how to nurture the young in the present, and raise them with an eye to the future. Conversely, what it means to be a son or daughter is in part to be sensitive to the beliefs and feelings of one's parents before electing and following any significant goal in their own lives, a sensitivity that must be maintained throughout their parents' lives, as a matter of loyalty. And perhaps after their deaths as well.

A Thought Experiment: On Reviving Family Reverence

There is a third factor of time that parents must take into account in meeting their responsibilities both to care for and raise their children. In addition to the present and the future, parents must attend to the past. Here, it seems to us, the early Confucians have much to say to everyone today, with their detailed concern for rituals, especially those involving ancestor veneration. Perhaps it is with respect to our dead forebearers that the concept of *xiao* as family reverence can be seen most vividly, most religiously, and most importantly, as a strategy for strengthening the roles of those still alive.

Much of who and what we are may be traced fairly directly to our ancestors, from our appearance to our native tongue, from our ethnicity to the specifics of the socialization processes we have undergone. Most of our tastes in food, music, dress, avocations, and more can usually be traced directly to our parents and grandparents, and their grandparents in turn. (In a number of cases we can also trace our antipathy to certain of these tastes, or others, directly to them, too.) The odds are that each of us bears a strong physical resemblance to one or more of our grandparents or great grandparents. Like it or not, we belong to a family, and moreover, a family with a history (and perhaps more than one). It follows from this that the more we know of our familial past, and the more we stay in touch with it, the better we can know who we are now, and envisage possibilities of who we might, or should become.

This point is obvious to the families of the rich and the powerful. Probably each member of the Rockefeller, Kennedy, Bush, and Vanderbilt families has a strong sense of who they are, and a sense of belonging to a special group, with a special history. All of them can very probably name not only their four grandparents, but most of their eight great-grandparents as well. Most ordinary Americans cannot do this, but the point still applies equally to all families. Each of us almost surely has a hero or heroine or two in the family tree, and very probably an occasional villain as well. Each of us has eight great-grandparents. Their fame or infamy may have been great or local, but the histories of all families should be seen as special to the members thereof. Yet in order to obtain that sense of *belonging* to a family with a history (which every family has), you must know about that history, especially the lives of the ancestors who made that history. It behooves all of us, then, to learn of our family's history, to listen carefully to the stories told to us by our grandparents and their siblings, to look at old photographs, and/or do a bit of genealogical detective work. Knowing where we have come from provides major clues as to who we are, and might become, as we continue developing the history of our family—and contributing to it.

Learning our family's history is not merely in pursuit of justifying a coat of arms on the silverware; genealogy and heraldry are very distinct enterprises. And we should not engage in studying where we came from just in order to brag about some past hero to whom we are related. Great granduncle Tom may have been a fine sheriff in a Western frontier town; but on the other hand he might have been a horse thief properly hanged by a fine sheriff in a Western frontier town.

To our mind there is no better way to obtain this sense of belonging, of feeling the continuity of a family line, than by a ritual honoring of the ancestors on occasion, especially for parents and grandparents. It should thus be a significant dimension of our role as parents to instill in our children this sense of coming from, and belonging to a family with a history. And we must demonstrate our responsibilities to our own parents and their parents in turn, teaching them that these responsibilities do not cease at their deaths. It is our responsibility to our forebearers to see that their memory is not entirely erased by time; for we are truly dead only when no one knows who we were.

Hence, in order to be appropriate models for our children we should periodically engage in a ritual that honors our ancestors, a ritual that might be widespread throughout our culture, or more locally, or it might be a ritual unique to our own family's heritage, or we may well have to initiate a ritual on our own to pass on to our children. We each enrich the lives of our children by continuing to discharge our responsibilities toward our parents and grandparents after they have died by remembering them via a ritual of remembrance.

It may sound strange to say that we can owe a debt to the dead, but it is not. Even atheists can understand the obligatory nature of keeping a deathbed promise.[36] And does not every son and daughter raised in a loving home "promise," even if only implicitly, not to forget their parents, nor to let our own children forget them? Rituals, especially family rituals, have tended to occupy the thoughts of most Western philosophers no more than the family has, but rituals can form a basic bond for families, and significantly affect our self-identification, as well as our sense of worth.[37]

To see this point another way, consider the fact that a great many people invariably "talk" to the tombstone when they visit a cemetery to pay respects to a deceased relative, teacher, or friend. There is nothing surprising about this, as it is altogether human. We *know* the deceased cannot hear us, but we speak anyway "as if they were present."[38]

As members of families then, and especially as we become parents, our roles take on religious no less than moral, social, and political significance. In meeting our manifold responsibilities to our children, and our parents, we are obliged to attend carefully to the present, to the future, and to the past, and thereby we become enabled to see, and feel ourselves linked closely to what has gone before, what is now, and what will come tomorrow; a small, but not inconsequential brush with immortality—here, now, in *this* world.[39]

For this insight, if for no other, all of us owe a continuing debt to the early Confucians. In the past, ritual practices honoring ancestors undoubtedly stemmed from the almost universal belief in ghosts and spirits, benign and malevolent, in keeping with the theologies of the world's religions. This occurred in China too, of course, and here is where the peculiar genius of the early Confucians is of such great relevance today, over and above the social, political, and economic insights they can provide us as we undertake the task of seriously re-thinking the family. The Confucians also show us how these rituals and customs can continue to be moving, satisfying, and sustaining even for the increasing number of us the world over who give no credence to the idea of ghosts and spirits. Even in the absence of such entities, or deities, we may indeed be reverent—especially toward our families.

In conclusion, it seems that our lives have been, and always will be lived through roles that have encumbered us since earliest childhood, interacting with others to contribute to their flourishing as they contribute to ours, making it all but impossible to ascertain what I might be as an individual self in any meaningful sense. Rather, do we seem to be the sum of the roles we live, roles that we first learned how to live and practice in family, and roles that we continue to live and practice in family today.

All of these perspectives—personal, social, moral, and spiritual—on the lived family are visible from the vantage point of a role ethics centered on persons as constituted by the others with whom they interact; they are much more difficult to see, or appreciate, from the standpoint of any other ethical system built on the fiction of human beings as free, autonomous, and isolable individuals like the person in A. E. Housman's poem: "I, a stranger and afraid // In a world I never made."[40]

Confucian Role Ethics in the Confucian Project

Descending from our meditation on the importance of family in ordinary life, we return to the *Great Learning* 大學, that sets out to define the Confucian project, taking family feeling as the entry point for developing moral competence. The central message of this terse yet comprehensive document is that while personal, familial, social, political, and indeed cosmic cultivation is ultimately coterminous and mutually entailing, it must always begin from a commitment to personal cultivation within the roles and relations of family and community. Said another way, personal cultivation for the relationally constituted person is irreducibly social, with its locus of cultivation being the roles and relations that begin radially with family itself. In the language of the *Great Learning*:

> There is the important and the incidental in things and a beginning and an end in what we do. It is in realizing what should have priority that one approaches the proper way (*dao*). . . . Once they saw how things fit together most productively, their wisdom reached its heights; once their wisdom reached its heights, their thoughts were sincere; once their thoughts were sincere, their heartminds knew what is proper; once their heartminds knew what is proper, their persons were cultivated; once their persons were cultivated, their families were set right; once their families were set right, their state was properly ordered; and once their states were properly ordered, there was peace in the world.[41]

Each person stands as a unique perspective on family, community, polity, and cosmos, and through a dedication to deliberate growth and articulation, everyone has the possibility of bringing the resolution of the relationships that locate and constitute them within family and community into clearer and more meaningful focus. The "learning" (*xue* 學) of the *Great Learning* is the cultivation of productive, transpersonal habits of conduct that radiate out through family, community, and polity to ultimately transform the cosmos. The meaning of the family is implicated in and dependent upon the productive cultivation of each of its members, and by extension, the meaning of the entire cosmos is implicated in and dependent upon the productive cultivation of each person within family and community. Personal worth is the source of human culture, and human culture in turn is the aggregating resource that provides a context and a resource for each person's cultivation.

While certainly having important theoretical implications, the enduring power of this Confucian project as it is given shape in the *Great Learning* is that it proceeds from a relatively straightforward account of the actual human experience. Confucianism is a pragmatic naturalism in the sense that, rather than relying upon metaphysical presuppositions or supernatural speculations, it focuses instead on the possibilities for enhancing personal worth available to us here and now through enchanting the ordinary affairs of the day. A grandmother's love for her grandchild is at once the most ordinary of things, and the most extraordinary of things.

Confucius, by developing his insights around the most basic and enduring aspects of the ordinary human experience—family reverence, deference to others, friendship, a cultivated sense of shame, the centrality of education, the politics of community and country, intergenerational responsibility and respect, and so on—has guaranteed the continuing relevance of Confucian role ethics, and not for the Chinese alone.

Notes

1. *Republic* 5.465 c–e. See also the beginning of Book 8: "We are agreed, then, Glaucon, that the state which is to achieve the height of good government must have community of wives and children and all education . . ." Plato 1961. Aristotle criticizes Plato's "community of wives and children" in Book II of the *Politics*, 1260b–1266a, but nowhere comments on the equality of women that flows from the Platonic ideal. His own view of the nature of the family, however—as described in Books VIII and IX of the *Nicomachean Ethics*—while nearer to our modern view, is nevertheless justified, in the end, by religion, and conducted on the basis of reason, with misogyny, chauvinism and slavery somehow becoming "reasonable," to him if not to us. Aristotle 1984.

2. Beginning with Paul, who says in 1 Corinthians 7:38, "[H]e who marries his betrothed does well, and he who refrains from marriage will do better."

3. Ackerman 1980, Dworkin 1977, Nozick 1974.

4. MacIntyre 1981 and 1984, Phillips 1986.

5. Rousseau 1959–1969, Hume 1975, Sandel 1982, Unger 1975.

6. Minow and Shanley 1996.

7. Kupperman 1991, 108–109.

8. "Big moment" is Kupperman's own term. See Kupperman 1971.

9. Kupperman 1991, 37.

10. Kupperman 1991, 56.

11. Kupperman 1991, 111.

12. Kupperman 1991, 70, 74.

13. Kupperman 1991, 38, 43–44.

14. Kupperman 1991, 47

15. Kupperman 1991, 19.

16. Kupperman 1991, 59.

17. There are two versions of this essay, with the later one included in Kupperman 2004, and the earlier one in Kupperman 1999.

18. Kupperman 2004, 115.

19. Kupperman 2004, 117.

20. See Fingarette 1983.

21. *Analects* 6.30.

22. Kupperman 1991, 43.

23. See Ames 2011, especially 102–114.

24. See Rosemont and Ames 2008, 105.

25. This private/public distinction was not drawn by the early Confucians with respect to males, although an "inner-outer" (*neiwai* 內外) variation on it was at the basis of Confucian gender discrimination. The Confucians did draw a distinction between the family and the government, but in many respects the latter was simply a radial extension as the family writ large. There were a number of dimensions of the Confucian family that we would consider "public" today, notable among them being the performance of many rituals.

26. We will claim that *all* interpersonal relations and interactions can be fruitfully described, analyzed, and evaluated on the model of parents and children, benefactor and beneficiary—even the interrelations between friends, neighbors, colleagues, and others. Nothing of ethical significance, we are arguing, will be lost by abandoning a foundational individualism.

27. Rosemont and Ames 2008.

28. It might well be objected that the overall view of the family portrayed herein is so wildly idealistic as to not be worth taking seriously. Two quick replies: (1) The picture suggested here might be more realistic than a number of accounts of the family—East and West—have been. Individualism is supposed to have been a characteristic only of the family in the West. Until the nineteenth century children were seen largely in economic terms. The nuclearization of the family in the West contributed greatly to the rise of capitalism, and many more stereotypes of the history of the family, whether compiled by sociologists (Western families), anthropologists (non-Western families), or by historians, comparative or otherwise. In *The East in the West* Jack Goody (1996) challenges these stereotypes, as well as the disciplinary methodologies that have generated them. His analyses, and his citations should be read by everyone interested in the structure(s) of families—East and West. (2) Perhaps we are indeed idealistic, but "there is nothing wrong with building castles in the sky," said Thoreau; "That is where they belong. Now put the foundations under them."

29. In proffering this analysis of the several dimensions of parental roles we have profited much from a paper by William Ruddick 1988. Although his concerns were bioethical in nature—conflicts between doctors and parents vis-à-vis the treatment of children—his insights, especially his distinction between caring for and raising children, are no less appropriate for the issues we deal with herein.

30. Even here a caveat should perhaps be entered: If one of our former ethics students were to defend the autogenocide of the Khmer Rouge in Cambodia, for example, we would surely believe we had failed, at least to some extent, as teachers.

31. We emphasize the prioritization of values to make it clear that we do not believe it is possible to "take on a new set of values" as most people would be inclined to say. One cannot logically take on a whole new set of values, but only reorder the values they (and everyone else except sociopaths) already have. How, for example, could one ever get you to change your mind about the worth of a particular value except by appealing to a more basic value you both share? Everyone values security, everyone values freedom; but different people order those values differently. And if members of one camp convince some members of another to change their minds, these latter have not "taken on a whole new set of values," but have simply reordered the values they have long held, sometimes, but not always, permanently. In situation X, freedom trumps security, but in Y the opposite ordering might obtain.

32. Aristotle would not agree with us at all, for he held that despite the fact that his seemingly "unfriendly doctrine" on this score was "opposed to the opinions men hold," he nevertheless claimed that ". . . [T]he fortunes of descendants and of all a man's friends should not affect his happiness . . ." Aristotle 1984, Book I, 1101a–b.

33. Usually couched as a conflict arising from the fact that good Confucians are supposed to serve in government when called upon, on the one hand, and the fact that the ruler you are now serving is a thoroughgoing rotter; what to do? What rule or principle will Confucius follow? If we are correct in our interpretation, however, there are no such rules or principles to be found in the early texts. But we may nevertheless resolve the conflict easily. Rather than searching for an abstract principle, we must ask, as one who is serving in government, whether *this* ruler, here now; is he reformable? If the answer is affirmative, we must ask a second highly specific question: Do we have the qualities and skills to reform him? If the answer to this question is also affirmative, King Wen becomes our model exemplar, and we continue to serve, remonstrating all the while. If the answer to the first question is "yes," but is "no" to the second, Confucius himself becomes our model, as we return to family and community, and "serve government" from there, as *Lunyu* (the *Analects*) 2.21 makes clear, and 7.16 and 8.13 reinforce. And if we answer the first question "No, we don't believe he is reformable," then we must raise the flag of rebellion, with King Wu as our hero and precedent-setter. In sum, no conflicts; there is always a decision procedure. It is always highly particularistic—but none the worse for that, it would seem.

34. David Hall and Roger Ames have argued for the family being the most foundational of all metaphors in Chinese thought. See their *Anticipating China*, SUNY Press, 1995, esp. pp. 271–77; see also their references there to the sociological work of Ambrose King.

35. This would explain why "family reverence" (*xiao* 孝) appears relatively infrequently in the *Analects* in comparison to the other terms of ethical import for Confucius. Only later is *xiao* treated at length in its own right in the *Xiaojing*. See our translation of this text, Rosemont and Ames 2009. Our Introduction to the text takes up some of the themes elaborated upon herein.

36. See Nagel 1979, 6.

37. Aristotle would be in opposition again for he focused only on the ontological status of the dead. He did not believe we should think or act on behalf of them, or when considering or justifying our actions, "For it seems . . . that even if anything whether good or evil penetrates to [the dead], it must be something weak and negligible, either in itself or for them, or if not, at least it must be such in degree and kind as not to make happy those who are not happy nor to take away their blessedness from those who are" Aristotle 1984, Book I, 1101b.

38. *Analects* 3.12, and see also 11.12. For further discussion of the psychological dimensions of engaging in mourning rituals, see Rosemont 2007.

39. For more on the spiritual sense of time and nonphysical immortality, see Rosemont 2001.

40. Housman 1922.

41. Zhu Xi 1969: *Daxue* 1a–2a: 物有本末，事有終始，知所先後，則近道矣。。。 物格而後知至，知至而後意誠，意誠而後心正，心正而後身修，身修而後家齊，家齊而後國治，國治而後天下平。

References

Ackerman, Bruce (1980). *Social Justice in the Liberal State*. New Haven: Yale University Press.

Ames, Roger T. (2011). *Confucian Role Ethics: A Vocabulary*. Hong Kong and Honolulu: The Chinese University of Hong Kong Press and University of Hawai'i Press.

Aristotle (1984). *The Complete Works of Aristotle*. Edited by Jonathan Barnes. Princeton: Princeton University Press.

Dworkin, Ronald (1977). *Taking Rights Seriously*. Cambridge: Harvard University Press.

Fingarette, Herbert (1983). "The Music of Humanity in the Conversations of Confucius." *Journal of Chinese Philosophy*, Volume 10.

Goody, Jack (1996). *The East in the West*. Cambridge: Cambridge University Press.

Housman, A. E. (1922). *Last Poems*, Poem XII. New York: Henry Holt & Co.

Hume, David (1975). *Enquiry Concerning the Principles of Morals*. Oxford: Oxford University Press.

Kupperman, Joel J. (2004). "Tradition and Community in the Formation of Character and Self." *Confucian Ethics: A Comparative Study of Self,*

Autonomy, and Community. Edited by Kwong-loi Shun and David B. Wong. Cambridge: Cambridge University Press.
———. (1999). *Learning from Asian Philosophy*. New York: Oxford University Press.
———. (1991). *Character*. New York and Oxford: Oxford University Press.
———. (1971). "Confucius and the Nature of Religious Ethics," in *Philosophy East & West*, Volume 21.
MacIntyre, Alasdair (1981). *After Virtue*. Notre Dame: University of Notre Dame Press.
———. (1984) *Whose Justice? Which Rationality?* Notre Dame: University of Notre Dame Press.
Minow, Martha, and Mary Lyndon Shanley (1996). "Introduction to a Special Issue on the Family and Feminist Theory." *Hypatia*, 11.1.
Nagel. Thomas (1979). "Death." *Mortal Questions*. Cambridge: Cambridge University Press.
Nozick, Robert (1974). *Anarchy, State, and Utopia*. New York: Basic Books.
Phillips, Derek L. (1986). *Toward a Just Social Order*. Princeton: Princeton University Press.
Plato (1961). *The Collected Dialogues of Plato*. Edited by Edith Hamilton and Huntington Cairns. New York: Pantheon Books.
Rosemont, Henry Jr. (2007). "On the Non-Finality of Physical Death in Classical Confucianism." *Acta Orientalia Vilnensia*, 8.2.
———. (2001). *Rationality and Religious Experience: The Continuing Relevance of the World's Spiritual Traditions*. Chicago: Open Court.
Rosemont, Henry Jr., and Roger T. Ames (2008), *The Chinese Classic of Family Reverence: A Philosophical Translation of the* Xiaojing. Honolulu: University of Hawai'i Press.
Rousseau, Jean-Jacque (1959–1969). *Discourse on Political Economy* in *Oeuvres Completes*. Paris: Pleiade, Volume 3.
Ruddick, William (1988). "Parenthood: Three Concepts and a Principle." *Family Values*. Edited by Laurence Houlgate. Florence, KY: Wadsworth Publishing Co.
Sandel, Michael (1982). *Liberalism and the Limits of Justice*. Cambridge: Cambridge University Press.
Unger, Roberto (1975). *Knowedge and Politics*. New York: The Free Press.
Zhu Xi 朱熹 (1969). *Sishu jizhu* 四書集註 (Collected Commentaries on the *Four Books*). Taibei: Yiwen yinshuguan.

2

Kongzi and Aristotle as Virtue Ethicists

PHILIP J. IVANHOE

Introduction

In recent years a number of philosophers who study Chinese ethics have produced major works comparing the ethical philosophy of Kongzi ("Confucius") and Aristotle.[1] In some of my own writings, I have described early Confucians as sharing the general approach of virtue ethics, and of course Aristotle offers one of the most famous examples of virtue ethics in the Western philosophical tradition.[2] Joel J. Kupperman has argued that character offers a more person-specific account of ethical evaluation and requires less precise categories and performance regularity than traditional forms of virtue ethics.[3] I see his point and it is a good one, especially for contemporary times, but I do not think this is how classical Confucian thinkers tended to see things. While they did take a more comprehensive view of ethical evaluation and in this regard "character" can in some respects be more helpful than lists of specific "virtues" for understanding their position, they were inclined to believe that with enough cultivation of the right sort people could become remarkably regular in their behavior and that sages are more or less flawless examples of a fairly specific moral ideal. Even Xunzi, who explicitly argued that human nature is bad, holds this remarkably optimistic and quite precise picture of human potential. In these respects, their view seems more like traditional Western accounts of virtue ethics.

In this essay, I would like to talk more specifically about some of the ways in which the comparison between Kongzi and Aristotle holds, some of the ways in which it does not hold, and some of the ways in which it requires qualification. In my conclusion, I will use this particular comparison to sketch an argument for the value of comparative studies in general. My primary points will be that comparing and contrasting the thought of philosophers such as Kongzi and Aristotle can facilitate achieving a clearer and more penetrating understanding of both, can help us to avoid at least one clear ethical failing, and can enhance the quality of human life. Like all philosophy, comparative philosophy helps us sort out and understand more clearly the phenomena under consideration. One of the great strengths of certain examples of comparative philosophy is that they have the practical effect of bringing out important features not only of *other* traditions but of our home traditions as well. It is not that it is conceptually impossible for us to grasp such features without the comparative project, but the process of comparison often greatly facilitates such understanding by allowing us to take up in imagination an alternative yet related perspective on a shared set of human concerns.

Why Virtue Ethics?

Understanding Kongzi's philosophy as an example of virtue ethics enables us to account for and understand centrally important features of his thought that might otherwise go unnoticed. For example, despite Kongzi's lack of a specific theory about the character of human nature, it is clear that his philosophy relies upon a general and distinctive concept of human nature and its flourishing. Early Confucians such as Mengzi ("Mencius") and Xunzi proposed explicit *theories* about human nature. Kongzi's writings express a consistent *concept* of human nature by making a cluster of specific claims about human needs, capacities, tendencies, and the like. This concept of human nature in turn informs and shapes his more general ethical views.[4] One critical feature of Kongzi's view of human nature is that at birth it is underdeveloped and incomplete; we can and must cultivate our original nature by developing a set of virtuous dispositions in order to attain an ideal form of life. In all three respects—being founded on notions about human nature, focusing on the cultivation of a set of virtues, and aiming at an ideal form of life—Kongzi's philosophy distinguishes itself as an expression of virtue ethics. Kongzi's philosophy shares each of these general features with Aristotle's approach to ethics, and there are further similarities between their views. For example, both Kongzi and Aristotle insist that the good life can only be found in the right kind of community and that such a community is constituted by special relationships between and among properly cultivated human beings.[5]

If we consider Kongzi's teachings as a whole and seek to interpret them comprehensively and systematically, we will come to understand his ethical philosophy as an expression of virtue ethics and more particularly as a form of virtue ethics that shares important similarities with the kind of view one finds in Aristotle. Among other things, the last part of this claim is intended to highlight the fact that Kongzi, like Aristotle, advocates a particular form of life as the natural flourishing of human nature. This distinguishes their type of virtue ethical theory from traditional sensibility-type virtue ethicists such as Hume or contemporary advocates of such a view, such as Nel Noddings, Virginia Held, or Michael Slote.[6] Nevertheless, this in no way entails that Aristotle's and Kongzi's ethical philosophies are essentially the same or that Aristotle is somehow the standard against which we should measure the success of Kongzi's ethics. Even the simple sketch of their views that I have provided above should make clear that a great deal depends on *what* their specific conceptions of human nature are like, *how* they think we best can develop ourselves to become good, *what* the good person is like, and *what* kinds of relationships constitute the ideal community. On these issues, we find significant differences between the philosophies of Kongzi and Aristotle, and these have profound implications for other aspects of their respective ethical views. I would like now to describe some of these differences and how they contribute to further distinctions between the thought of Kongzi and Aristotle.

Kongzi's and Aristotle's Ethical Philosophies

As noted earlier, we do not find an explicit theory about human nature in the *Analects*, but in the course of this work, Kongzi says many things that point to a fairly clear concept of human nature and its role in his ethical philosophy. Among such claims are that human beings possess the capacity and at least some inclination to care for other human beings and to develop a sense of themselves as morally responsible agents participating in a greater ethical community. He further believes that human beings can only flourish and find fulfillment in the right kind of community. He spent much of his own life looking for and working to develop just such a community. One of the most distinctive claims Kongzi makes about human nature is that our moral sensibilities find their source and paradigm in natural feelings among family members. These are the earliest and most characteristic features of human nature and the beginning of a moral life.

This last point is an extremely important feature of Kongzi's philosophy, for it establishes certain fundamental emotional responses as the source of ethics and the family as the paradigm for ethical relationships and political order. These claims also point to the greater importance of care or benevolence over virtues such as justice, and here we find interesting differences between our two thinkers. In these respects, Kongzi's ethical system is more like certain aspects of another Western virtue ethicist, David Hume, than Aristotle. Hume, too, pointed to the feelings of benevolence and generosity within the family and small kin groups as both an important source of moral feelings and the first kind of ethical community in human history. Moreover, he made clear that within such communities, as within modern families, benevolence and generosity take precedence over justice.[7] In general, in Confucian political theory, certain emotion-based kinship virtues play more primary and robust explanatory roles than civic virtues. The order of explanation for Confucians begins with the family and moves out to justify a particular structure for social relations. In the case of Aristotle, the order of explanation runs very much in the opposite direction. One can see this general trend in modern political theorists such as Rawls as well; in the case of Plato, this difference is dramatically represented by his advocacy of the dissolution of nuclear families for the good of the state.

Aristotle offers a detailed and sophisticated description of human nature. He begins by asking: What is the *ergon* "characteristic activity" of human beings? He concludes that it is rational activity; whenever we act intentionally, we use our reason to set and negotiate both our ends and means, and we do this to an extent that distinguishes us among all the creatures on earth. While our feelings are important for determining what is good for us and in our deliberations about how to realize the best kind of life, reason plays, or at any rate should play, the commanding role in these pursuits. Reason is what enables us to balance and coordinate our various needs, desires, and capacities with those of others in ways that serve both self and society. We need reason to ensure that every member of society gets what he or she deserves and this pursuit—justice—is a cardinal virtue in Aristotle's ethical scheme. Moreover, rational activity itself is an important good for us and is our most "godlike" capacity. The best kind of life for Aristotle is one that enables a person to engage in pure rational activity or contemplation—a search for truth—as much as possible.[8]

While Kongzi and Aristotle concur that at the core of the good life for human beings are certain states of character, we find important differences in their conceptions of the virtues. Both agree that virtues are excellent dispositions to perceive, feel, intend, and act in fairly specific ways and that the virtues are critical both for one's own flourishing and the success of one's community. And yet, because of their different conceptions of human nature, both tacit and explicit, they emphasize different sets of virtues. Kongzi places great importance on what he regards as the natural virtues of filial piety and brotherly respect and sees these affectionate and deferential dispositions as the sources and paradigms for more general virtues such as humanity and conscientiousness. Given his family-based ethic, which is structured by a set of rituals and related norms, he has no pressing need for and expresses no virtue that corresponds to Aristotelian *dikaiosune* "justice." Some have translated 義 (*yi*) as "justice" and see Kongzi as centrally concerned with this virtue. While there are reasons to see similarity here, there is no good case for equating these terms. For early Confucians, *yi* as a virtue concerns a sense of falling short of the proper norm or ideal. In this general respect, it resembles Aristotle's sense of justice, but, unlike the Aristotelian virtue, *yi* was not thought of as a disposition to accord with the law and fairness and was not primarily concerned with issues concerning distribution or retribution.[9] Aside from justice, Kongzi's very different conception of human nature and its flourishing leaves no room at all for Aristotelian virtues such as *megalopsuchia* "greatness of soul." In this respect, his ethical views are closer to Christianity, which dropped *megalopsuchia* and added humility to its list of core virtues. The reasons for this similarity, though, are quite different and revealing. For Christians, the great-souled man, who is primarily concerned with honor and feels that he deserves much, misconstrues his nature as a finite and fundamentally flawed creature of God. For early Confucians, to claim much or focus one's attention on what one deserves is to direct one's attention and energy toward the wrong ends.[10]

Another distinctive feature of Kongzi's conception of virtue is that he sees the character of the good person in terms of its effect upon others. The Chinese character 德 (*de*), which is commonly translated as "virtue," most often is not used in the sense of the Greek *arête*. Rather than a particular excellence, as in "strength, beauty, or temperance is a virtue," *de* more often means something like "moral charisma." It is a kind of psychological power associated with excellence that has the ability to attract, sway, and inspire those around the person who possesses Virtue.[11] One finds no clear equivalent notion in Aristotle's ethical philosophy.[12]

We find other important similarities and differences when we turn to compare Kongzi's and Aristotle's views about how best to *develop* one's character. Kongzi places great emphasis and offers considerable detail about the role of ritual training and tradition in the cultivation of virtue. He appears as a consummate teacher throughout the *Analects*, and one of his most important legacies is not only his model of teaching but also the reflective inquiry about teaching that his example generated. Kongzi's early follower and defender, Xunzi, discussed the process of learning in considerable detail and insisted upon the critical importance of teachers for the task of self-cultivation. One characteristic feature of the Confucian tradition is its attention to the nature and practice of teachers and good teaching.[13] Aristotle does not explicitly discuss teachers or teaching, though he does insist on the need to be brought up well in the sense of being properly habituated to virtue.[14] In general, the themes of teachers and teaching are not prominently represented in his work or in the Western philosophical tradition in general. It is not an exaggeration to say that these themes are not a substantial concern in most contemporary research universities either. As a partial defense of this claim, note first that teaching plays at best a minor role in hiring, tenure, and promotion in such institutions. Second, there is not a single endowed chair dedicated to good teaching at any major research university. Third, the interest in teachers and teaching is quite seasonal. It waxes full during orientation and graduation, when more parents and alumni are present, and tends to fade into relative obscurity throughout the rest of the year. The relative neglect of teachers and teaching in the Western tradition may reflect a greater characteristic faith in the power of individual reason to find its own way to the truth. Descartes's famous meditations offer one dramatic expression of this sensibility; this feature of his philosophy, even more than his views about mind and body, serves to distinguish his thought from both Aristotle's and Kongzi's.

As noted above, Aristotle believed that one needed to be brought up properly in the sense of being habituated to virtue.[15] He did not provide much in the way of detail concerning how this is to occur, but the idea roughly is that guided experience is the only way to acquire a *sense* of the value of certain activities, principles, traits, and states of affairs.

Without this grounding in what is worthwhile, one has no foundation upon which to build a reflective and sophisticated theory of value, which in turn disciplines, refines, and strengthens one's commitment to virtue.[16] While there is little direct evidence to support the claim that Aristotle thought ritual should play a role in at least early education, it seems that we must infer that like Kongzi he relied to a considerable degree upon traditional culture—though in his case of course it was Athenian culture—as the source of much of the learning that constituted "being brought up properly." Aristotle's emphasis on the need for proper *activity* highlights the importance of proper practice, and this implies at least something like ritual, in the sense of standard practices. Nevertheless, we do not find any analysis or developed discussion of the nature or role of such practices.

Both Kongzi and Aristotle rely upon what some have called the "good person criterion" to help describe what it is to live a proper life. While neither simply defines the good in terms of what the good person would do, both insist that acting well requires a special kind of perception and judgment, and so it is natural to find both appealing to a kind of moral connoisseur in the course of presenting their ideals of a proper life.[17] Despite these broad similarities though, their respective descriptions of the good person are quite distinct.

Kongzi's "gentleman" has cultivated himself to be a good son, loving father, loyal brother, and humane civil servant. He has done this by dedicating himself to a protracted and intensive course of learning aimed at internalizing the ideals and lessons of traditional culture. Seeing himself as a member of this cultural legacy, both in terms of being a recipient of its special goods and responsible for its integrity and continuing flourishing, is an important part of his own self-conception. Fulfilling this ideal requires him to engage in prolonged and extensive reflection, but this reflection is focused primarily on interpreting, understanding, and applying an inherited body of wisdom.[18] The gentleman's reflections include both practical and theoretical forms of reasoning, but the ideal life for Kongzi has no clear place for theoretical contemplation *per se*. The unencumbered search for truth simply is not an ideal to which early Confucians aspired.

While pure contemplation is not an ideal, Kongzi's gentleman is to develop and maintain a remarkable level of *self-awareness* concerning not only his actions and speech but his internal thoughts and musings as well. This awareness and attentiveness amounts to a kind of meditative practice, though one lacking in any formal regimen such as one finds in most forms of Buddhism. There is a parallel here with "prayer," which was a common form of religious practice in Kongzi's day. While Kongzi showed no inclination to engage in formal prayers of supplication, passages such as *Analects* 7.35 make clear that he thought his daily practice of the Way meant he lived a life of continual prayer. The remarkable emphasis on awareness and attentiveness in early Confucianism helps explain why many later neo-Confucians found Buddhist meditation quite appealing and in fact incorporated more formal regimens of "quiet-sitting" into their own practice.[19] This general perspective on the ethical life generates a kind of tension, but one that proved to be remarkably productive for Confucian philosophy. According to Kongzi, an ethical person must, on the one hand, be regularly if not constantly concerned with his or her own moral improvement.[20] Nevertheless, on the other hand, those most successful at moral cultivation will not entertain thoughts of their own ethical achievements or worth. Thinking about *making* oneself morally worthy was a constant concern, but thinking of how good one is or what that warranted in terms of recognition and reward did not contribute to one's moral achievement and manifested an excessive and unproductive concern with oneself.[21] In this respect, Kongzi's "gentleman" offers a strikingly different ideal than Aristotle's great-souled man, whose primary concern is honor and who claims and feels that he deserves much.[22]

Aristotle's complement to Kongzi's *junzi* "gentleman" is the *phronimos* "man of practical wisdom." As the very name suggests, this is someone whose life is guided by reason. The *phronimos* organizes his life so that it offers him the best chance of realizing *eudaimonia*—often translated as "happiness" or "flourishing" and in many contexts synonymous with *makarios*, which means "blessed" or "fortunate."[23] As students of Western philosophy know, Aristotle believed that our souls are divided into rational and irrational parts. The irrational is further divided into a nutritive or vegetative part and our appetites and desires. The nutritive part is amoral but our appetites and desires can be good or bad depending on whether or not they follow reason. The rational part of the soul displays various intellectual virtues—when it reasons well—and the second element of the irrational soul displays the moral virtues when it complies with reason.

Given that the characteristic activity of human beings is the exercise of reason, our souls are most satisfied and fulfilled when we engage in rational activity. Were we more like gods, we would in fact spend all of our time in contemplation and would live perfectly happy lives, impervious to the vicissitudes of human existence. Since we are creatures, though, that live our lives in between the extremes of gods and beasts, we must do the best we can to organize our lives according to reason. This leaves Aristotle with a different kind of tension than we found in Kongzi's ethical ideal. For Aristotle, the best kind of life is that of the gods. While he makes clear that this is not possible for us, he nevertheless argues that we should lead as godlike an existence as possible. This means we should organize our lives so that they afford us the greatest opportunities to pursue pure contemplation. And yet, since we are not gods, it is not wholly evident why we should try to focus our reason on theory more than the practical affairs of life. Given the kind of creature that we in fact are, should we not find our greatest satisfaction and fulfillment in the creation and enjoyment of culture—as Kongzi's gentlemen did—rather than in theoretical contemplation? Shouldn't we use our reason to strive to live the most prosperous, rich, and humane lives possible, rather than *the most* godlike?[24]

The final set of issues I would like to explore concerns Kongzi's and Aristotle's views about human relationships and how these contribute to their respective conceptions about the ideal human community. As noted earlier, familial relationships play a preeminent role within Kongzi's ethical philosophy. They are understood as both the source of and model for ethical life. This explains not only why they occupy such a central role in Kongzi's discussion of virtue but also why we see him invoke various familial relationships as paradigms for political organization as well. Kongzi's moving and inspirational ideal community is not a *polis* led by elite politician-warriors, nor a Kingdom of Ends, but roughly the family writ large, a society in which, as it says in *Analects* 12.5 "all within the four seas are brothers."[25] This idea remains an important feature of contemporary Chinese culture within which people call and refer to one another using familial terms such as *jiejie* 姐姐 ("sister"), *didi* 弟弟 ("brother"), *ayi* 阿姨 ("aunt"), and *shushu* 叔叔 ("uncle"). Here we see another similarity with certain Christian communities, which seek to engender a sense of common purpose and mutual love among their members and embody their belief in all being children of God, through the practice of referring to one another as if they were members of a natural family: i.e., "sister," "brother," "father," and "mother."

Given the role that familial relationships play in Kongzi's ethical theory, it is no surprise that the virtue of filial piety is so prominent in his teachings.[26] This leaves a much less important role for conceptions of friendship in general, which offers a dramatic contrast with Aristotle's philosophy. While friendship does play a role in Kongzi's ethics and in early Confucianism in general, it is a much less central feature of his thought and the early tradition that followed him. Friendships become important as one begins to develop and extend one's basic moral sensibilities out beyond the family. The *Analects* opens with a passage that clearly expresses the importance of friendship as a cherished good within Kongzi's ideal life. Among other things, friendship with the good—and for the early Confucian Mengzi, this included friendships with the ancients as well as those living in one's own age—could help one to develop one's self and serve one's society.[27] Nevertheless, for early Confucians, the role such friends played was always posterior and supplemental to that played by family members. Later Confucians, under the influence of Daoist and Buddhist thought, practice, and institutions, developed more robust roles for friendship. For example, Li Zhi of the Ming dynasty argued that friendship should replace kin relationships as the primary focus of Confucian self-cultivation. He also argued that an equal friendship between wife and husband should serve as the model for married life.[28]

While Aristotle discussed the importance of the family in many of his works, family relationships did not play a central role in his ethical philosophy. In contrast to Kongzi, the natural affection between family members, and especially between parents and children, was neither the source of nor paradigm for ethics. As we already have noted, Aristotle grounds his ethical philosophy on a particular conception of rational activity. For him, the most pressing and revealing example of rational activity governing human relationships is not the family but the *philia* "friendships" that exist between privileged male citizens who shared a humanly fashioned, public, political life.[29] It should not escape our attention that one important feature of this shared political life was fighting together in defense of the *polis*. Aristotle began his reflections on ethics from the perspective of a male citizen, and his thinking was informed by the question of what kind of man would make the best companion and comrade for other men engaged in business of life, politics, and warfare.[30] This was the beginning of morality for Aristotle, and it helps us to understand why a discussion of friendship is such an important theme in his *Nicomachean Ethics*, occupying fully one-fifth of that work. The contrast with Kongzi is dramatic; the reasons for the contrast are revealing, and their implications far-reaching.

Conclusion

I have endeavored to offer further evidence and argument for my claim—defended at greater length in other work—that Kongzi is best thought of as a virtue ethicist of the type that is exemplified by Aristotle in the Western philosophical tradition. I have made a special effort to show that this claim should only be understood as describing the general approach and structure of their respective ethical philosophies. When we explore the contents of their views, we discover deep and far-reaching differences. For example, I have argued that both Kongzi and Aristotle base their ethical philosophies on conceptions of human nature and its cultivated flourishing, even though Kongzi's views on human nature must be largely inferred if we look exclusively at the *Analects*, while Aristotle offers an explicit, sophisticated account of human nature. Both Kongzi and Aristotle defend the view that the most satisfying and fulfilling life for creatures like us can only be found in the right kind of community, and that such a community must be constituted by people who have developed particular virtues or excellences of character. While their ethical philosophies share these important general approaches and structures, we find profound differences in their respective conceptions of human nature, self-cultivation, and human flourishing. As a consequence, their ideal communities are distinctively different as are their lists and conceptions of the virtues.

By way of conclusion, I would like to address briefly the question of what we have learned in the course of this comparison and specifically what, if any, purpose has been served in *comparing* the philosophies of Kongzi and Aristotle. Comparative philosophy often is treated as a transparent and uniform discipline or approach, but in fact people pursue it in very different ways, with very different motives, and aiming at very different goals. Some practice it without having any clear sense of what distinguishes it from other types of philosophy or *why* it is worth pursuing. Others seem to believe that the primary aim of comparative philosophy is to show the superiority of one tradition over another; one version of this is the "death of analytic philosophy" approach, which contends that contemporary analytic philosophy has somehow led us into a dead end and only Chinese or some other non-Western tradition can point the way out. Others write comparative philosophy from the perspective of establishing a kind of cultural parity: if the West has a certain view, the Chinese and other traditions have it too! Still others seem to think that by studying other traditions, Westerners can see things in their home tradition that they *could not possibly see* without engaging in such comparison. I do not endorse or practice comparative philosophy from any of these angles, though I have learned things by reading examples of each of these approaches.

Among other ends, comparative studies can help us to understand and appreciate aspects of the thought of different thinkers that we may not have understood or seen as easily or clearly apart from such exercises. As noted earlier, I do not believe that such comparison is *necessary* in order to reach such understanding, but I do believe that often it is of great practical benefit for facilitating such insight and appreciation. Comparative philosophy can also make the strange more familiar or make the familiar quite strange.[31] That is to say, on the one hand, it can help us to understand thinkers from other traditions by showing how they are grappling with problems and employing approaches that at least to some degree are familiar to us from our acquaintance with thinkers in our home tradition. On the other hand, comparative philosophy can lead us to see aspects of philosophies from our home traditions in a new and revealing light by making these features more salient or bringing out their distinctive nature through comparison and contrast.[32]

We can more easily grasp the general shape of Kongzi's ethical philosophy when we see it as an expression of a certain kind of virtue ethics. And yet this should not in any way obscure or diminish the distinctiveness of Kongzi's particular form of this type of ethical theory. The central importance of social roles and rituals in Kongzi's philosophy and his intriguing discussion of moral charisma should lead us to wonder about the adequacy of Aristotle's account of the development and nature of virtue. On the other hand, Aristotle's theory of human nature and his analysis of the types, values, and roles of reason should lead reflective Confucians to look at Kongzi's philosophy more critically and has the potential to inspire and empower constructive reinterpretations and defenses of Confucian thought. The contrast between Kongzi's use of familial paradigms and Aristotle's focus on types of friendship raises questions for both traditions and should do the same for any reflective person interested in the nature and value of human life.

In addition to facilitating greater mutual understanding of individual thinkers and traditions, comparative philosophy offers rich opportunities to understand and appreciate different ethical values and the lives of which they are a part. Such greater understanding and appreciation can help us to avoid the common error of thinking that our own values and form of life are the only proper way for human beings to live. Avoiding such a moral deformation is necessary if one is truly to respect other human beings and lead a fully satisfying life. We must not merely tolerate differences but work to understand and appreciate alternative values. This requires a considerable, though not unreasonable, amount of effort. One cannot simply note or describe differences; one must work one's way into alternative forms of life through a process of sympathetic understanding. Aside from helping us to avoid thinking we already know all there is within heaven and earth, such greater understanding and appreciation of other ethical lives offers the opportunity to experience new realms of value; sharing such goods with others and incorporating them into one's own life and the lives of those one cares about present additional reasons for engaging in the task of comparative philosophy.[33]

I have only attempted to sketch some similarities and differences between the ethical views of Kongzi and Aristotle and have made uncharacteristically general claims about how some of these features describe tendencies within the Confucian and Western traditions, respectively. My remarks are not intended as offering a vigorous or definitive defense of these broader claims; rather I offer them as suggestions for further study of both Kongzi and Aristotle. I do hope they present enough food for thought of sufficient flavor and interest that others will return to these themes and ideas as well as the larger implications of and need for comparative work in their teaching and research.

Acknowledgments

Thanks to Erin M. Cline, Eric L. Hutton, Jack Kline, Chenyang Li, Jan Szaif, and Justin Tiwald for corrections and suggestions on earlier drafts of this essay. I dedicate this essay to Joel J. Kupperman whose work and personal example have inspired and guided me in my own efforts at philosophy, comparative and otherwise.

Notes

1. For example, Sim 2007, Yu 2007, and Van Norden 2007. These authors take the contents of the *Analects* as in general representative of the ethical philosophy of Kongzi and the accepted corpus of works attributed to Aristotle as representative of his ethical philosophy.

2. For example, I argue that a virtue ethics approach is the most plausible and revealing way to understand early Confucianism, and I compare its advantages to several of the most influential accounts that one finds among contemporary Western philosophers in chapter one of Ivanhoe 2002b. Note though footnote #36 in that chapter for the kind of qualifying remark that I discuss below.

3. For the most thorough presentation of his view, see Kupperman 1991.

4. Confucian thinkers throughout its 2,500-year tradition have expressed near unanimity in holding that Kongzi had a distinctive conception of human nature. One reason for such a belief is that many texts outside the *Analects* attribute to Kongzi explicit and sophisticated views about human nature. For example, the Qing dynasty Confucian Dai Zhen cited the views attributed to Kongzi in the *Great Appendix to the Book of Changes* as his definitive theory of human nature and the key to understanding his philosophy. For a discussion of this issue, see Ivanhoe 2002a.

5. Kongzi emphasizes the value of the right kind of community. For example, see *Analects* 4.1. He also talks about how this requires one to develop oneself into a *junzi* "gentleman." Aristotle goes to considerable lengths describing the need for and character of the ideal *polis* and how this requires one to cultivate oneself into a *phronimos* "man of practical wisdom."

6. Some have argued that Kongzi and Mengzi are best thought of as sensibility-type virtue ethicists and specifically what Slote calls "agent-based" as opposed to "agent-centered" virtue ethics. For example, see Lou Shirong 2010 and the discussion of Van Norden's book by Angle 2009 and Slote 2009. For my views on why different thinkers in the Confucian tradition are best understood as virtue ethicists on the model of Aristotle, see Ivanhoe 2012.

7. For these ideas, see David Hume, *An Enquiry Concerning the Principles of Morals*, Section III, part 1. The contrast that I am drawing here between Aristotle and Kongzi is important but not absolute. For example, Aristotle notes that the state originates in the family (*Pol.* I.2, 1252a24–1252b16) and criticizes Plato for wanting to disband the family (*Pol.* II.1, 1260b27–1261a8). In the *Nicomachean Ethics* (VIII.1, 1155a20–30), he claims that for people who have "unanimity" (*homonoia*) and friendship, justice is not necessary. But he also argues that the family and the village exist "to satisfy everyday needs" and only find completion in a proper *polis*, which exists "for the sake of living well" (*Pol.* I.2, 1252b12–29). The translation is by Reeve 1998. Thanks to Justin Tiwald and Eric L. Hutton for discussions on this set of issues.

8. For this idea, see *NE* X.7, 1177b. Aristotle's ideal life would seem to be what many contemporary philosophy professors might choose. Compare Kongzi's approval of Zeng Xi's description of his ideal day in *Analects* 11.25.

9. None of what I have said should be taken as implying that Kongzi lacked anything like a *sense* of justice. For a comprehensive and penetrating exploration of this issue, see Cline 2006.

10. Eric L. Hutton 2002b offers a revealing discussion of why *megalopsuchia* finds no place in the Confucian picture of virtue.

11. I follow David Nivison's policy of capitalizing Virtue when it is a translation of *de*. For a description of distinctive Daoist and Confucian forms of moral charisma, see my essay, Ivanhoe 1999.

12. Plato though does talk about the attractive power of the Good, which is similar in spirit to early Chinese views about Virtue. Iris Murdoch has described and defended this notion with great clarity and insight. See Murdoch 1970.

13. A number of eminent Confucians wrote essays on the topic of teaching and sophisticated reflection on the character of good teachers and good teaching figures prominently in works such as the *Liji* "Book of Rites."

14. See *NE* II.1, 1103b. Aristotle goes into somewhat greater detail concerning moral education at the end of the *Politics*. For a collection of passages from Aristotle's writings that concern education, see Burnet 1967.

15. For an insightful analysis of Aristotle's views on moral education, see Burnyeat 1980.

16. This process may of course lead one to emend or wholly reject certain traditional views.

17. For more on the idea of being a moral connoisseur, see Wallace 1991 and Hutton 2002a.

18. For this sense of "reflection," see Ivanhoe 1990.

19. Thanks to Eric Hutton for helping me to see the importance of this connection.

20. For an excellent anthology focused on this general aspect of ethical life, see Wilburn 2007.

21. For example, see *Analects* 4.14. I have discussed this issue in considerable detail in regard to the Daoist tradition, with some mention of the parallel concern among Confucians, in Ivanhoe 2010.

22. See *NE* IV.3, 1123b–1125a.

23. For revealing discussions of the close relationship between *eudaimonia* and *makarios* ("blessed" or "fortunate") see Nussbaum 1986 and McMahon 2006, 3–4, 68, etc.

24. In "Aristotle on *Eudaimonia*," Thomas Nagel explores what he sees as the tension in Aristotle's work between more "comprehensive" and "intellectualist" accounts of "flourishing." He argues that these reflect a deeper ambiguity in Aristotle's conception of human nature. See Nagel 1980. One could see Nagel's account of this aspect of Aristotle's philosophy as reflecting his own concern with what he takes to be the irreducible tension between more objective and subjective points of view.

25. The ideal for early Confucians is thus like that expressed in Friedrich Schiller's immortal lines in *To Joy*: "Alle Menschen werden Brüder, wo dein snafter Flügel weilt."

26. I have offered an in-depth analysis of this aspect of early Confucian philosophy as well as a defense of filial piety as a modern virtue in Ivanhoe 2007.

27. For this idea, see *Mengzi* 5B.8.

28. For Li Zhi's views, see Lee 2011.

29. For a good introduction to the theme of friendship in the Western philosophical tradition, including important essays on Aristotle's contribution, see Pakaluk 1991 and Badhwar 1993.

30. One of the few places in modern Western society where the issue of friendship still has the gravity of Aristotle's discussion is within the military. This is because having the right comrades remains an issue of extreme importance within this context. This also helps us to understand how those who have served together, who have lived, suffered, and fought together as a *band of brothers*, often remain friends for life, even when they go on to lead remarkably different lives.

31. This idea finds its earliest expression in the work of the medieval poet and philosopher Georg Philipp Friedrich Freiherr von Hardenberg (1772–1801), better known by his pseudonym, Novalis, who defined romantic poetry as "the art of appearing strange in an attractive way, the art of making a subject remote and yet familiar and pleasant."

32. The works of Joel J. Kupperman offer some of the most insightful, inspiring, and elegant examples of the advantages I outline here. For example, see Kupperman 1999, Kupperman 2006, and Kupperman 2010.

33. I describe and argue for the kind of view that one can gain through proper comparative philosophy in Ivanhoe 2009.

References

Angle, Stephen C. (2009). "Defining 'Virtue Ethics' and Exploring Virtues in a Comparative Context" in *Dao: A Journal of Comparative Philosophy*, 8.3: 297–304.

Badhwar, Neera Kapur. Edited. (1993). *Friendship: A Philosophical Reader*. Ithaca, NY: Cornell University Press.

Burnet, John, Trans. (1967). *Aristotle on Education; Being Extracts from the Ethics and Politics*. Cambridge: Cambridge University Press.

Burnyeat, Myles F. (1980). "Aristotle on Learning to Be Good." *Essays On Aristotle's Ethics*, 69–92. Edited by Amelie O. Rorty. Berkeley, CA: University of California Press.

Cline, Erin M. (2006). *Confucius, Rawls, and Justice Without "Justice" in the Analects*. PhD Dissertation. Baylor University.

Hutton, Eric L. (2002a). "Moral Connoisseurship in Mengzi." *Essays on the Moral Philosophy of Mengzi*, 163–86. Edited by Liu Xiusheng and Philip J. Ivanhoe. Indianapolis, IN: Hackett Publishing Company.

———. (2002b). "Moral Reasoning in Aristotle and Xunzi" in *Journal of Chinese Philosophy*, 29.3: 355–84.

Ivanhoe, Philip J. (1990). "Thinking and Learning in Early Confucianism" in *The Journal of Chinese Philosophy*, 17.4: 473–93.

———. (1999). "The Concept of *De* ('Virtue') in the Laozi." *Religious and Philosophical Aspects of the Laozi*, 239–257. Edited by Mark Csikszentmihalyi and Philip J. Ivanhoe. Albany, NY: SUNY Press.

———. (2002a). "Whose Confucius? Which Analects? Diversity in the Confucian Commentarial Tradition." *Essays on the Analects of Confucius*, 119–33. Edited by Bryan W. Van Norden. New York: Oxford University Press.

———. (2002b). *Ethics in the Confucian Tradition: The Thought of Mengzi and Wang Yangming*. Revised Second Edition. Indianapolis, IN: Hackett Publishing Company.

———. (2007). "Filial Piety as a Virtue." *Working Virtue: Virtue Ethics and Contemporary Moral Problems*, 297–312. Edited by Rebecca Walker and Philip J. Ivanhoe. Oxford University Press.

———. (2009). "Pluralism, Toleration, and Ethical Promiscuity" in *The Journal of Religious Ethics*, 37.2: 311–29.

———. (2010). "The Theme of Unselfconsciousness in the *Liezi*." *Riding the Wind with Liezi: New Essays on the Daoist Classic*, 129–152. Edited by Ronnie Littlejohn and Jeffrey Dippmann. Albany, NY: SUNY Press.

———. (2012). "Virtue Ethics and the Confucian Tradition." *Cambridge Companion to Virtue Ethics*. Edited by Daniel Russell. Cambridge: Cambridge University Press.

Kupperman, Joel J. (1991). *Character*. New York: Oxford University Press.

———. (1999). *Learning from Asian Philosophies*. Oxford: Oxford University Press

———. (2006). *Six Myths about the Good Life: Thinking about what has Value*. Indianapolis, IN: Hackett.

———. (2010). *Theories of Human Nature*. Indianapolis, IN: Hackett.

Lee, Pauline Chen (2011). *Li Zhi 李贄 (1527–1602), Confucianism, and The Virtue of Desire*. Albany, NY: SUNY Press.

Lou, Shirong (2010). "A Defense of Ren-based Interpretation of Early Confucian Ethics." *Taking Confucian Ethics Seriously: Contemporary Theories and Applications*, 123–43. Edited by Yu Kam-por, Julia Tao, and Philip J. Ivanhoe. Albany, NY: SUNY Press.

McMahon, Darrin M. (2006). *Happiness: A History*. New York: Atlantic Monthly Press.

Murdoch, Iris (1970). *The Sovereignty of Good*. London: Routledge and Keegan.

Nagel, Thomas (1980). "Aristotle on *Eudaimonia*." *Essays on Aristotle's Ethics*, 7–33. Edited by Amelie O. Rorty. Berkeley CA: University of California Press.

Nussbaum, Martha C. (1986). *The Fragility of Goodness: Luck and Ethics in Greek Tragedy and Philosophy*, 329–33. Cambridge: Cambridge University Press.

Pakaluk, Michael, Ed. (1991). *Other Selves: Philosophers on Friendship*. Indianapolis, IN: Hackett Publishing Company.

Reeve, C. D. C. (1998). *Politics*. Indianapolis, IN: Hackett Publishing Company.

Sim, May (2007). *Remastering Morals with Aristotle and Confucius*. Cambridge, NY: Cambridge University Press.

Slote, Michael (2009). "Comments on Bryan Van Norden's *Virtue Ethics and Consequentialism in Early Chinese Philosophy*." in *Dao: A Journal of Comparative Philosophy*, 8.3: 289–295.

Van Norden, Bryan W. (2007). *Virtue Ethics and Consequentialism in Early Chinese Philosophy*. Cambridge, NY: Cambridge University Press.

Wallace, R. Jay (1991). "Virtue, Reason, and Principle" in *Canadian Journal of Philosophy*, 21.4: 469–95.

Wilburn, Brad, Ed. (2007). *Moral Cultivation*. Lanham, MD: Rowan and Littlefield.

Yu, Jiyuan (2007). *The Ethics of Confucius and Aristotle: Mirrors of Virtue*. New York: Routledge.

3

Anthropocentric Realism about Values

Bryan W. Van Norden

> For if the Good predicated in common is some single thing, or something separated, itself in itself, clearly it is not the sort of good a human being can pursue in action or possess; but the latter is just the sort we are looking for in our present inquiry.
>
> —Aristotle, *Nicomachean Ethics* I.6

> The rules are the beginning of order, but the gentleman is the origin of the rules.
>
> —Xunzi, "The Way of a Ruler"

It is a commonplace to observe that, in contemporary academia, there is no connection between being a person who studies ethics and being an ethical person. However, my sense is that Joel Kupperman is both. Indeed, I think if Kongzi were alive today, he would recognize Kupperman as the sort of "gentleman" (*junzi*) that he hoped to produce via his process of ethical cultivation. But a gentleman like Kupperman does not seek acclaim, and I will honor his preferences by praising his character no more.

Some Typologies

While I fall far short of Kupperman in the more important level of practice, I am pleased that I share many of his views at the level of theory:

realism, particularism, pluralism, and fallibilism. (1) *Realism*: Values are, in some sense, objective. This does not entail that they are objective in the way that properties like mass or entities like zebras are. However, neither are they purely subjective (in the way that my preference for chicken over fish is subjective) or a result of mere intersubjective consensus (in the way that "Three strikes and you're out" is).[1] (2) *Particularism* (or contextualism): Values are highly context-sensitive. If we ask, "Is it permissible to lie?" the right response is to ask back, "About what? To whom? In what circumstances?" and many other questions. Although there is a strong presumption in favor of honesty, it is defeasible in many situations, ranging from the trivial example of fibbing to a friend about a surprise birthday party to the weighty example of Miep Gies hiding Anne Frank and her family from the Nazis.[2] (3) *Pluralism*: There are a variety of incommensurable kinds of value. As a result, there are a plurality of worthwhile ways of life. It might be better for Bloggs to become an FBI agent and for me to become a college professor (because of our respective aptitudes, interests, and traits of character); but my life of theoretical inquiry and teaching is not intrinsically better than Bloggs's life of practical action and intervention. The two of us can achieve different but equally valuable varieties of human flourishing and manifest distinct but equally worthwhile forms of virtues such as benevolence and integrity.[3] (4) *Fallibilism*: Because there are evaluative facts that we can be wrong about, and because value is so context-sensitive, and because we cannot fully appreciate values in other ways of life that we have not experienced[4]—for all these reasons, we must be continually mindful of the possibility of error in our valuations.[5]

In this essay, I am going to focus on the first thesis: realism. Realism can take different forms.[6] (i) The default target of anti-realists often seems to be Platonic realism. The Platonist holds that ethical values are part of the fabric of the universe, and would be there whether any human beings had existed or not. For the Platonist, values are not reducible to natural or physical properties, but they are similar to them in that their existence does not depend upon human cognition or motivation. (ii) Anthropocentric realism is importantly different. In order to understand it, consider the following non-moral concept: "poisonous." "The respiration of pure carbon dioxide is poisonous" is true for all humans. But it is not true for plants. Furthermore, the very notion of "poison" is meaningful only in the context of living organisms. From the perspective of pure physics, nothing is poisonous. Nonetheless, it is true or false that something is poisonous (for humans), whether a particular individual or a culture is aware of this fact or not. We might say that poisonous-for-humans is an anthropocentric quality. It is useful and meaningful only because humans exist, but since humans do exist there are objective facts about what is poisonous for them. Similarly, the anthropocentric realist about values claims that evaluative properties and judgments are meaningful and useful only because humans—with their distinctive needs, potentials and limitations—exist. Nonetheless, there are facts about values that do not depend upon the beliefs or endorsements of any particular individual or culture.

Kupperman draws the contrast between Platonic and anthropocentric realism in this way:

> In sorting out the issues of value realism, we need to decide between two starting points. One is putative value facts. . . . If this is our starting point, then we will need to train, as it were, our value telescopes to find out whether there was something we were talking about. The other is our talk and thought about values, including the standards of evidence and logical relations that are implicit in these practices. If this is our starting point, then we will need to inquire into justification of judgments of value, and in particular whether there is justification for claiming that some judgments are authoritative (telling us what really is of value).[7]

Kupperman recommends that we reject the first approach, along with its associated "images of [values as] spectral furniture of the universe."[8] Instead, we should focus on

> . . . the structure of our discourse about values, [which] includes standards (for being in a position to be confident of judgments of value) that sometimes are met. Hence, we are in a position to say that it really is the case that some things have high value and that others have low or negative value.[9]

Kupperman is one of several Western philosophers to offer versions of anthropocentric realism.[10] However, given Kupperman's interest in Chinese thought, I am particularly intrigued by the possibility that the Confucian Xunzi may also be seen as an anthropocentric realist.[11]

In contrast with most earlier Chinese philosophers, Xunzi is at pains to insist that Heaven is morally indifferent. Heaven does not reward the virtuous (with long lives or good harvests) or punish the vicious (with illness or natural disasters): "The activities of Heaven are constant. They do not persist because of sage-king Yao. They do not perish because of tyrant Jie."[12] In fact, Heaven endows humans with a nature that is largely self-centered and will lead us into conflict with one another if unchecked:

> Humans are born having desires. When they have desires but do not get the objects of their desires, then they cannot but seek some means of satisfaction. If there is no measure or limit to their seeking, then they cannot help but struggle with each other. If they struggle with each other then there will be chaos, and if there is chaos then they will be impoverished.[13]

Furthermore, ritual activities such as funerals do not, Xunzi insists, influence Heaven or any spiritual entities. "One performs the rain sacrifice and it rains. Why? I say: There is no special reason why. It is the same as when one does not perform the rain sacrifice and it rains anyway."[14] But if Heaven is morally passive, where do human values and ethical practices come from? Xunzi explains that they are artificial constructs invented to meet human needs:

> In ancient times, the sage-kings saw that because people's nature is bad, they were deviant, dangerous, and not correct in their behavior, and they were unruly, chaotic, and not well-ordered. Therefore, for their sake they set up ritual and standards of righteousness, and established proper models and measures.[15]

For example, mourning rituals express and shape the feelings of loss that accompany the death of a loved one, and standards of righteousness provide guidelines for how to distribute goods so that everyone has enough. Despite the fact that ethics is artificial, it is objectively justified because it achieves the goal of bringing humans into a harmonious relationship with each other and with their environment:

> For Heaven can give birth to creatures, but it cannot enforce distinctions among creatures. Earth can support people, but it cannot order people. In the world, the ten thousand things and human beings all must await sages, and only then will they be appropriately divided up.[16]

Although Xunzi regarded the rituals as artificial, he seems to have thought that the particular formulation of them by the former sage kings was the one best version. For example, Xunzi states that,

> [f]or the ritual sacrifices, one engages in divination and determines the appropriate day. One fasts and sweeps out the site, sets out tables and food offerings, and has the "announcement of the assistant," as if the deceased were attending a banquet. The impersonator of the dead takes the goods and from each of them makes a sacrifice, as if the deceased were tasting them.[17]

Xunzi says of specific practices such as these: "Is not ritual perfect indeed! It establishes a lofty standard that is the ultimate of its kind, and none under Heaven can add to or subtract from it."[18] Consequently, someone like me, who does not honor his ancestors in the particular way described above, would be dismissed by Xunzi as one of those "foolish, ignorant, perverse men" who has not learned the proper way to express sufficient love and respect for his predecessors.[19] From a contemporary perspective, this seems like a significant limitation of Xunzi's thought. Surely my own "rituals" for honoring my deceased parents (visiting their grave, putting flowers on it, pretending to tell them what has happened in our family since my last visit, etc.) are just as good. As a pluralist, Kupperman will certainly agree that (contrary to Xunzi) there are multiple sets of rituals that can serve the same functions of shaping and expressing human emotions. Nonetheless, it seems to me that Kupperman and Xunzi share the general view that values depend for their existence on human needs, capabilities and practices, but are nonetheless "real" (not simply a matter of individual or cultural opinion). Now, Kupperman has written a very fine article on Xunzi's conception of human ethical cultivation, in which he notes that Xunzi is similar to Jean Piaget in holding that humans must go through distinct levels of development in order to become mature ethical agents.[20] However, to the best of my knowledge, Kupperman has not commented on Xunzi's meta-ethics. Consequently, I will be interested to see whether he finds my interpretation of Xunzi as an anthropocentric realist about values plausible.

Just as moral realism comes in more than one form, so does anti-realism. (a) Moral relativism is the view that the truth of moral claims depends upon the perspective from which they are evaluated. This perspective can be either that of an individual (subjectivism) or that of a group (cultural relativism). (b) Non-cognitivists typically regard moral claims as expressing and encouraging attitudes of some kind. Since they are expressions rather than descriptions, moral claims are neither true nor false. (c) Error theorists agree with realists that moral language is intended to be descriptive, but they argue that there are no objective values for our moral terms to refer to.

Theory	**Moral Statements Are . . .**	**Level of Objectivity**
Realism	descriptive and can be true or false.	Platonic
		Anthropocentric
Relativism	descriptive and can be true or false.	Intersubjective (cultural relativism)
		Subjective
Non-cognitivism	expressive rather than descriptive, so neither true nor false.	
Error Theories	descriptive but none are true.	

Moral anti-realism (particularly in its relativist form) seems to have become the dogma among many college students and their professors. Consequently, my two-part project in this paper is to challenge one of the standard arguments for anti-realism and to sketch an argument for a particular form of anthropocentric realism.

The Argument from Disagreement

The argument from cross-cultural disagreement is the anti-realist argument most likely to captivate students taking their first philosophy course. However, it is an argument that is both easy to misunderstand and difficult to establish. Indeed, I have sometimes been surprised to discover that even some philosophers are persuaded by what are demonstrably inadequate formulations of this argument. Consequently, it is best to begin by reviewing why it is fallacious to go directly from the premise that there is ethical disagreement to the conclusion that there are no objective ethical facts. Pick any topic (T) about which there is disagreement. Indeed, let there be sustained and seemingly intractable disagreement over T: each party to the disagreement is firmly convinced of his own views, and his efforts to convince the other parties seem to fail repeatedly. Can we infer directly from this sort of disagreement to the conclusion that there are no facts about T? We cannot. At least, we cannot make this inference without succumbing to an extreme and ultimately self-undermining ant-realism about all facts. Consider evolutionary theory. I assume that most of my readers believe that it is true and applies to humans. However, 40 percent of the current U.S. population believes that "God created human beings pretty much in their present form at one time within the last 10,000 years or so."[21] This percentage has varied since Gallup started asking the question in 1982, but it has always been at least 40 percent. Consequently, if persistent disagreement over T shows there is no fact about T, we must conclude that there is no fact about whether evolutionary theory is true. I anticipate at least three rebuttals to this argument. (1) "Whether people believe it or not, evolutionary theory has been proven to be true." However, "prove" is a weasel word, whose ambiguity allows it to suggest more content than it actually has. If we take "proof" to be synonymous with strict logical deduction, then no scientific theory is ever proven. (This is a commonplace of the philosophy of science, in which it is recognized that scientific theories are interesting and informative precisely because they go beyond the evidence that supports them, and hence cannot be deduced from that evidence.) In contrast, if "prove" means something weaker, such as convincing everyone of a conclusion, then the Gallup poll shows that evolution has not been proven in this sense.

This leads to a second potential rebuttal. (2) "Although not everyone accepts evolutionary theory, the only reason that people reject it is ignorance of the evidence." This reply does not hold water, because a number of people who have been exposed to the evidence, including some with legitimate scientific credentials, reject evolutionary theory.[22] I assume this will induce the following counterargument: (3) "Only a dogmatic bias prevents those who have been exposed to the evidence from accepting evolutionary theory." But we could say the same thing to explain why a man as obviously intelligent as John C. Calhoun defended slavery, or why well-educated and seemingly informed attorneys in the Justice Department of the Bush administration endorsed torture. The anti-realist will insist that there is still some difference between the case of the informed Creationist and Calhoun, but we see now that disagreement (even seemingly intractable disagreement) is insufficient by itself to establish that there is no fact about a topic. It is the precise nature of the disagreement that establishes this (if anything does).[23]

While we cannot *logically deduce* anti-realism about values from simple disagreement about them, some have argued that the *best explana-*

tion for the nature and extent of ethical disagreement is that there are no objective facts that we are disagreeing about.[24] However, no one has ever developed this argument in anywhere near enough detail for it to be compelling. In order to establish that the ethical disagreement we find is best explained by there not being ethical facts, it is inadequate to trot out vague anecdotes about how "some people think infanticide is perfectly fine." One must look in detail at what people believe, giving thick descriptions of their practices, their own accounts of those practices, and their sociohistorical contexts. Only then can one even begin the process of arguing for an explanation for their beliefs.[25]

I cannot prove that it is impossible to construct an inference to the best explanation argument for anti-realism. However, I would like to identify a few hurdles that any such argument must overcome. First, as Hume noted long ago, superficial disagreement over ethical matters may mask a fundamental agreement. "The Rhine flows north, the Rhone south; yet both spring from the *same* mountain, and are also actuated, in their opposite directions, by the *same* principle of gravity."[26] Similarly, a positive evaluation of perseverance in the face of danger (courage) may manifest itself very differently in a culture at war as opposed to a culture at peace. Second, there may be a variety of legitimate ways to express the same underlying human value. Herodotus was impressed with the starkly different attitudes of the Greeks (who cremated the remains of their parents) and of the Callatians (who supposedly ate the bodies of their deceased parents). Each was horrified at the practices of the other.[27] However, both rituals express the human sense that we must honor the memory of our parents by disposing of their remains in a respectful way. Third, the variety we find in ethical views may be best explained by pluralism about values. Not all values can be instantiated in any one form of life, so individuals and cultures must choose which values to promote. There is much to commend in the sort of intimate community life portrayed in Thornton Wilder's *Our Town*. Everyone knows everyone else, everyone trusts everyone else, everyone cares for everyone else. However, a community like this requires a great deal of homogeneity. As Wilder suggests with the suicide of "Simon Stimson," many would find this life claustrophobic. Conversely, the fragmented life of our modern cities provides much more room for individuality, but also a much greater danger of alienation.[28]

Fourth, let us not forget that a thoughtful examination of cultural disagreement may lead to what seems like deeper (and nonrelative) ethical insight. Although I cannot vouch for its accuracy as anthropology, Montaigne's essay "Of Cannibals" is useful as a model of what it would look like to use thick description of another culture as the basis for a critique of one's own. Many of Montaigne's contemporaries had concluded that the natives of "Antarctic France" (what is now Brazil) were "savages," because they practiced cannibalism. However, Montaigne arrives at a more nuanced view through a discussion of the role of cannibalism in the native culture as a whole. He notes that "Their warfare is wholly noble and generous, and as excusable and beautiful as this human disease can be," because (unlike European warfare) it is not motivated by greed, the desire for conquest, or religious intolerance. Rather, participation in warfare seems to be voluntary, and "its only basis among them is their rivalry in valor." Prisoners of war are treated generously, "so that life may be all the dearer to them," but are also warned of the fate that awaits them. "All this is done for the sole purpose of extorting from their lips some weak or base word. . . ." However, the natives display "the grandeur of an invincible courage," because there is "not one who would not rather be killed and eaten than so much as ask not to be."[29] When the time comes, prisoners are quickly executed, and their bodies eaten as a symbolic indication of conquest. Montaigne concludes with a nuanced evaluation of his own culture in comparison with that of the cannibals: "I am not sorry that we notice the barbarous horror of such acts, but I am heartily sorry that, judging their faults rightly, we should be so blind to our own." Mentioning such cruel tortures as racking and live dismemberment, which Europeans of his era had subjected one another to "on the pretext of piety and religion," Montaigne opines, "I think there is more barbarity in eating a man alive than in eating him dead."[30] Montaigne's exploration is intriguing precisely because he does not throw up his arms and announce, "Who's to say?" but instead looks for a deeper insight.[31]

Finally, it is worth noting that cultures are not as dissimilar as some would have us believe. Much of twentieth-century anthropology has stressed cross-cultural variety, to the point of sometimes suggesting that there is no such thing as human nature. This has been valuable as a corrective to the ethnocentrism that civilizations sometimes succumb to.[32] However, many of the paradigmatic studies that claimed to show practices and beliefs radically different from those in the West have been discredited. Margaret Mead's account of how adolescent sexuality in Samoa is unfettered, relaxed, and happy has been shown to be, at best, dubious. Benjamin Whorf's claim that the Hopi language lacks any way of expressing discrete units of time is demonstrably false. Colin Turnbull's report of the complete lack of compassion among the Ik tribe turned out to be fiction. Bronislaw Malinowski's alleged counterexample to the Oeidipus complex among the Trobriand is also quite questionable. Even the favorite cocktail party example of cultural difference, the claim that Eskimos have 22 words for snow, has turned out to be a myth.[33] In contrast with these approaches, anthropologist Donald E. Brown (a recovering relativist himself) argues that we find a set of characteristics that are nearly universal among human societies, including the use of narrative and poetry, facial expressions such as smiling and crying, marriage, incest taboos, rituals to mourn the dead, prohibitions against theft and the wanton use of violence, and many others.[34]

Are the similarities that we find among cultures best explained by a Mengzian or a Xunzian account of human nature? Consider the fact that we find some form of the institution of marriage in every human culture. Mengzi would say that, as part of our shared human nature, we all find certain things ethically shameful: even a beggar will be offended if you offer him a handout with contempt (*Mengzi* 6A.10). However, our innate sense of shame is merely incipient, like the sprout of a plant (2A.6). Like a sprout, our incipient sense of shame can either mature or wither, depending upon both our social environment and our individual effort (6A.8, 6A.9). If our sense of shame is allowed to follow its natural course of development, we will disdain to furtively satisfy our sexual desires (3B.3). Consequently, marriage rituals exist because they provide a social sanction for our sexual desires, allowing us to satisfy them without shame. In contrast, Xunzi would argue that we innately have the desire for sex but not even the incipient sense of shame. For us to come to regard the furtive satisfaction of sexual desires as shameful, our emotions must be reshaped, as arduously and artificially as "steaming and bending" a piece of lumber that is as "straight as a plumb line into a wheel."[35] This transformation is justified, Xunzi would argue, because unrestrained sexual desires would lead us to harm one another. The fundamental differences between the views of Mengzi and Xunzi are reflected in their metaphors. Mengzi's favorite metaphors for ethical cultivation are agricultural (like nurturing the sprout of a plant until it grows into maturity). In contrast, Xunzi prefers technological metaphors, which involve reshaping a passive and perhaps recalcitrant material (like grinding metal or carving wood). Mengzi would no doubt have said to Xunzi what he said to Gaozi (who proposed that "to make human nature benevolent and righteous is like making a willow tree into cups and bowls"):

> Can you, sir, following the nature of the willow tree, make it into cups and bowls? You must violate and rob the willow tree, and only then can you make it into cups and bowls. If you must violate and rob the willow tree in order to make it into cups and bowls, must you also violate and rob people in order to make them benevolent and righteous? If there is something that leads people to regard benevolence and righteousness as misfortunes for them, it will surely be your doctrine, will it not?[36]

It is beyond the scope of this paper to fully adjudicate the disagreement between Mengzi and Xunzi. However, I think it is clear that Mengzi, like Xunzi, fails to do justice to pluralism: there are a variety of distinct but equally adequate forms of marriage ceremonies, funeral rituals, etc.[37] Kupperman's comments on this general topic are, as usual, judicious. He encourages us to

> reject two extreme (and I think untenable) sorts of positions. One is to insist that a worthwhile account of human nature must be definite and hold true of people at all times and in all social conditions. The other tempting extreme is to hold that there could not be such an account or anything even remotely like it. Human nature is various, and that is the last word on the subject. . . . It is not unreasonable, though, to think it possible to arrive at an account of human nature that is largely true. This would be an account that captured ways in which a great many people, in various cultures, tend to think and behave at most times.[38]

Whatever our specific view on human nature, it seems quite clear that we do not find human cultures as wildly divergent as some advocates of the argument from disagreement suggest. In addition, no one has yet given a sufficiently detailed account of why the disagreement we do find is "best explained" by anti-realism. The argument from disagreement is at best a promissory note that anti-realists have yet to make good.

The Case for Anthropocentric Realism

The Why Question

As I explained earlier, Xunzi argues that "rituals and righteousness" are artificial constructs that are objectively justified by their role in rescuing humans from their natural state of selfishness and intemperance, which (if unchecked) will lead to mutually destructive competition for scarce resources. This line of argument is anthropocentric, because it attempts to provide a justification for values that is objective, yet ultimately grounds value in human needs and agency. As Eric Hutton has noted, there are plausible ways of interpreting Xunzi and Aristotle according to which there are some broad similarities between their approaches. However, the differences between them are also quite significant. The emphasis in Xunzi is on the "the Way of human community, where this is understood as organized society."[39] In contrast, Aristotle "seems to concentrate more on the notion of *eudaimonia* [living well] as the individual's good."[40] In the remainder of this paper I shall offer an anthropocentric argument inspired by Aristotle's account of human practical reasoning.

In attempting to understand Aristotle's justification for ethics, readers often focus on the controversial "function argument" of *Nicomachean Ethics* I.7. Here, Aristotle suggests that just as what it is to be a good sculptor depends upon the function of a sculptor, so does being a good human depend upon the function of a human. Aristotle identifies this with what is distinctive of humans as a species, and thinks this is our rationality. For a contemporary audience, this argument is problematic on several grounds, which we do not have to rehearse here. However, readers often overlook the fact that the function argument is a detour (one of Aristotle's famous digressions) from an alternative justification for ethics based on practical reasoning (*Nicomachean Ethics* I.1–5). Indeed, Thomas Aquinas focuses on this alternative account in his own discussion of the human good (*Summa Theologiae* II-I, Q. 1).[41]

For Aristotle and those who follow him, the primary ethical question is whether our actions and motivations are rational. Words like "rational," "logical," and "reasonable" sometimes arouse negative reactions, especially when applied to actions and motivations. As a pop song from the 70s whines,

> When I was young, it seemed that life was so wonderful,
> a miracle, oh it was beautiful, magical.

And all the birds in the trees, well they'd be singing so
happily,
oh joyfully, oh playfully watching me.
But then they sent me away to teach me how to be sensible,
logical, oh responsible, practical.[42]

So it is perhaps worth explaining that the starting point of this approach is nothing sinister or esoteric; it is the simple recognition that "Why are you doing that?" is always a legitimate question to ask of a human being. Sometimes this question is looking for a causal answer. "Why are you sweating so much?" "I just came from the gym." But Aristotelians are particularly interested in cases where the question seeks a justificational answer (the "final cause"): "Why are you going to the gym?" "I'm training for a marathon." So practical rationality is really just concerned with justificational answers to the question "Why are you doing that?"

This might seem to land us in relativism, though. Our answer to "the why question" depends upon what our goals are, and these are often assumed to be subjective. Such was the opinion of David Hume, who famously denied that our actions and motivations can be rational or irrational:

> 'Tis not contrary to reason to prefer the destruction of the whole world to the scratching of my finger. 'Tis not contrary to reason for me to chuse my total ruin, to prevent the least uneasiness of an *Indian* or person wholly unknown to me. 'Tis as little contrary to reason to prefer even my own acknowledg'd lesser good to my greater, and have a more ardent affection for the former than the latter.[43]

This is a provocative suggestion, but why should we assent to it? If I did prefer "my own acknowledg'd lesser good to my greater," it would seem natural (both as a matter of common sense and of ordinary language usage) to say that I was being "foolish," "stupid" and, yes, "unreasonable." However, Hume is confident about his claim because it follows from his particular philosophical psychology. The contents of the human mind, Hume asserts, consist solely of "impressions" and "ideas." Impressions are "all our sensations, passions and emotions, as they make their first appearance in the soul."[44] Ideas, in turn, "are deriv'd from impressions, and are nothing but copies and representations of them."[45] Truth and falsehood consist in the agreement or disagreement "of ideas, consider'd as copies, with those objects, which they represent."[46] Given these assumptions, Hume's conclusion follows fairly directly:

> Whatever, therefore, is not susceptible of this agreement or disagreement, is incapable of being true or false, and can never be an object of our reason. Now 'tis evident our passions, volitions, and actions, are not susceptible of any such agreement or disagreement; being original facts and realities, compleat in themselves, and implying no reference to other passions, volitions, and actions. 'Tis impossible, therefore, they can be pronounced either true or false, and be either contrary or conformable to reason.[47]

In other words, only certain kinds of "ideas" can be true of false, because only they, being copies (of either sensory impressions or other ideas), can correspond or fail to correspond to their objects. A "passion," as Hume calls any motivational state, "contains not any representative quality, which renders it a copy of any other existence."[48] Therefore, no passion (and by the same reasoning, no action) can be rational or irrational. Unfortunately for Hume, no informed philosopher today would accept his philosophical psychology.

Even if we did find plausible Hume's account of impressions and ideas, his claim about the nonrationality of passions and actions is stipulative and arbitrary. Motivations and actions cannot be rationally assessed, Hume claims, because reason is solely the discovery of truth and falsehood, and neither motivations nor actions can be true or false. Admittedly, if I "prefer the destruction of the whole world to the scratching of my finger," my *preference* is neither true nor false. But it is question-begging to assume that rationality is only about truth and falsity. Consequently, unless we accept Hume's outmoded account of impressions and ideas, or his unwarranted stipulation that reason is only about truth and falsity, he has given us no reason to deny that the statement "You ought to prefer your greater good to your lesser good" is true.

Although we lack a good argument *against* it, we might still wonder why we need to make objective evaluative assessments of practice. (I don't have a good argument against square dancing either, but it's clearly not necessary and I don't want to do it.) My answer is that objective evaluative assessments are indispensable to anything recognizable as human agency. One type of such evaluation is captured by the Hypothetical Imperative: if you choose goal, G, then you ought to take the most efficient means, M.[49] For example, if Bloggs (a novice runner) chooses to run in a marathon, then Bloggs ought to train four days a week for 18 weeks prior to the event. This statement is surely not a pure description of what Bloggs *will* do: Bloggs might choose to run in a marathon, but fail to train adequately. One might object that, if Bloggs doesn't train adequately, he really didn't "choose" to run in the marathon. Admittedly, if Bloggs didn't train for the marathon at all and didn't even show up, we could legitimately question whether he had actually chosen to participate. But there might be plenty of reasons to think that Bloggs *had* chosen to participate in a marathon (he signs up for the marathon, he trains intermittently, he shows up and runs in it) even if his preparation was inadequate. Perhaps Bloggs wants to run in a marathon but doesn't care if he does well? But it seems quite possible that someone like Bloggs wants and hopes to do well in the marathon, but succumbs to weakness of will by skipping too many practices and eating badly. So if Bloggs chooses to run in a marathon (really chooses, as would be evident not just from his words but from some of his actions), and if he wishes to do well in it, and if he is a novice runner of average health, then he ought to train for four days a week for 18 weeks prior to the event.

If this example (or any other instance of the Hypothetical Imperative) is true, then there is at least one objective evaluative claim. Let us consider a potential objection: "The 'ought' in this example is a subjective evaluation, not an objective one, because Bloggs's choice to run in a marathon is a matter of personal preference. Surely you don't think that Bloggs is objectively obligated to run in a marathon?" This objection fails to distinguish between the Hypothetical Imperative and its constituent propositions. The consequent of the hypothetical ("Bloggs ought to train four days a week for 18 weeks prior to the event") is not objective, because it only follows from the truth of the antecedent ("Bloggs chooses to run in a marathon"), which is dependent upon a contingent and subjective choice. However, the truth of the hypothetical as a whole is neither contingent nor subjective. If training four days a week for 18 weeks is in fact the best means for a human of Bloggs's physical condition to prepare for a marathon, then the complete hypothetical, "If Bloggs chooses to run in a marathon, then he ought to train four days a week for 18 weeks prior to the event," is true, and true independently of what any individual believes, true independently of what any group of people believe, and true independently of whether Bloggs does in fact choose to run in a marathon.[50] Instances of the Hypothetical Imperative are central to our ordinary agency and practical reasoning. Consequently, we are committed to objective evaluations.[51] Although this is a very specific and limited conclusion, it is nonetheless important. Once we acknowledge the necessity of even one objective evaluation, we see that there is nothing in principle implausible or philosophically promiscuous about accepting them.

Although he does not use the phrase "Hypothetical Imperative," Hume was aware that this principle was a prima facie counterexample to his claim that motivations and actions are never irrational. He grudgingly admits that "by an abusive way of speaking, which philosophy will scarce allow of,"[52] we might say that an action or motivation is unreasonable "when founded on a false supposition, or when it chuses means insufficient for the design'd end."[53] Hume's response was to attempt to naturalize the Hypothetical Imperative by making it descriptive rather than prescriptive:

> The moment we perceive the falsehood of any supposition, or the insufficiency of any means our passions yield to our reason without any opposition.[54]

It is easy to miss what a stunning (and implausible) suggestion this is. If Hume is correct, there has never been anyone who, like Bloggs, planned to run in a marathon, but then skipped practice too many times; there has never been anyone who knew that having "just one more cigarette" would sabotage her efforts to quit smoking, yet smoked it anyway; there has never been anyone who continued to love someone after her illusions about him were shattered. Would that people were as practically rational as Hume assumes!

Although instances of the Hypothetical Imperative are objective evaluations, the "ought" of the consequent only applies to someone who satisfies the antecedent of the conditional. If I don't plan to run in a marathon, I have done nothing wrong by failing to train for one. Some philosophers would concede that there are facts about what we ought to do given what our goals are, but no facts about what our goals ought to be. In other words, one might concede that there are objective answers to the why question when it comes to means, but no objective answers when it comes to goals. I shall approach the issue of whether there are any objectively valuable goals in two steps. First, I shall argue that there are goals that actually motivate some human beings that can be seen to be rationally indefensible. Second, I shall propose some goals that are not only defensible, but could only be challenged via moot or fantastic objections.

Four Inadequate Answers to the Why Question

Let us imagine that Bloggs seems to dislike his job as an attorney. We ask him, "Why are you working as an attorney when you don't enjoy it?" Bloggs can refuse to answer, but he cannot deny the legitimacy of the question. Perhaps he will respond, "I make more money as an attorney than I could make any other way." We persist by asking, "Why do you need so much money? There are other jobs that would give you enough to survive comfortably." Bloggs replies, "I need money for the sake of money." This fails as a rational justification, because money is only a means to other ends. If money were intrinsically valuable, then the best strategy would be to collect something like Confederate currency; it is much easier to get than U.S. dollars. Of course, you cannot buy anything with Confederate currency. But this just shows that what makes money desirable is the things other than money that you can get with it. Despite this fact, there are many people who, like Bloggs, act as if money were an intrinsically valuable goal: they struggle to accumulate far more money than is needed to ensure their physical comfort and security, without any clear conception of some other goal their money will help them achieve. But insofar as people do act like Bloggs, we can see that their behavior is irrational.

In reality, Bloggs is more likely to give a different answer, such as, "I work as an attorney because I hope to get a big case that will make me famous." Fame is one of the most valued goods in our celebrity-obsessed culture, so we know that people have motivations like the one Bloggs expresses. Indeed, there are people who seem to want fame at any cost. In 356 BCE, Herostratus set fire to the Temple of Artemis at Ephesus (one of the Seven Wonders of the Ancient World) simply because he believed that this gratuitous act of destruction would ensure his eternal fame. (Obviously, he was right.) However, it seems plausible to diagnose such an extreme craving for attention as a mental illness, perhaps brought on by a lack of personal validation earlier in life. If Herostratus had the talent and opportunity to be admired as a talented poet or skillful general, he would have preferred that to the choice he made. So suppose we press Bloggs further, asking, "Do you just want to be famous, or do you want to be famous for being good at something? If I offer you a choice between being famous because your incompetence resulted in an innocent person going to prison, or being famous because of your skillful handling of a challenging case, which do you prefer?" Presumably, Bloggs would greatly prefer to be famous for being a skilled attorney. We might describe this by saying that what Bloggs really wants is not simply fame, but prestige.

Prestige is very plausible as a part of the reason why we do what we do. All of us want to be admired for our good qualities. This is not inconsistent with humility. To paraphrase C. S. Lewis, humility is not about smart people pretending they are stupid, or attractive people pretending that they are ugly.[55] Humility is about recognizing that our excellences are simply small parts of the big picture. Thus, I am entitled to enjoy the prestige that comes when students tell me they have gotten a lot out of my classes, or when colleagues tell me that they found something insightful in one of my papers. I just need to remind myself that my class is a very small part of any student's life experience, and all of my scholarship does not amount to a single brushstroke on the canvas of world civilization. As these examples suggest, one has to be prestigious *for* something good. Thus, while it is not completely inaccurate to state that one's goal is prestige, it is incomplete. Furthermore, fame and prestige are problematic goals, because they are so dependent upon the whims of others. Bloggs will undoubtedly get a certain amount of prestige as an attorney. However, many other people share the view expressed by one of Shakespeare's characters: "The first thing we do, let's kill all the lawyers."[56] The same will be true of any career Bloggs chooses.[57]

In our initial account of Bloggs, we stipulated that he does not enjoy being an attorney. Some would say that this shows he has already failed in his choice of goals, because pleasure is the only reasonable goal of human action. We can certainly agree that it should be part of our goal. But pleasure is similar to prestige in that both are incomplete goods. Just as one must get prestige *for something*, so must one take pleasure *in something*. There is the pleasure I get from scratching an itch. There is the pleasure I get from watching Bergman's *Hour of the Wolf*. There is the pleasure I get from making love with my wife. There is the pleasure I get from watching *The Simpsons*. There is the pleasure I get from a good workout at the gym. There is the pleasure I get from a fine meal at a gourmet restaurant. There is the pleasure I get from a greasy bacon double cheeseburger at a diner. There is the pleasure I get from writing this academic paper. There is the pleasure I get from talking and playing with my children. Notice that the singular word "pleasure" masks a huge diversity in states of consciousness, which sometimes have little in common besides the fact that we feel positively about them. There is really no such thing as pleasure simpliciter; there is only the pleasure-of-X or the pleasure-of-Y.[58]

"Be that as it may," the hedonist replies, "our goal is still to maximize pleasure in some form." There are at least three arguments against the hedonist, though. (1) All of us can imagine pleasures that we would prefer not to have. David Cronenberg's 1996 film *Crash* explores the possibility of people who are sexually aroused by viewing and participating in fatal or crippling car crashes.[59] I think most of my readers would be horrified to discover that they had developed such a fetish (and would seek therapy to overcome it should it develop) even if it turned out to be an intense source of pleasure. If this example seems too fanciful to have any bite, use your own imagination, and be honest with yourself about your gut reaction to certain pleasures. (2) Kupperman discusses another counterexample to the thesis that pleasure should be our only goal: the happy clam.[60] Imagine our mental life reduced to its most basic functions, such as the pleasures of relieving hunger and eliminating waste (like a mollusk perhaps experiences). Let us stipulate that we will have no awareness of the kinds of pleasure that we have lost, so we will have no occasion for regret. Since we will only know about the simple pleasures we still have, they will seem the peak of delight to us. Nonetheless, almost all of us would be unwilling to trade our current lives (with their complex but often difficult-to-satisfy preferences) for that of a simple but satisfied clam. The best explanation for our sense that there are shameful pleasures and that one can maximize certain kinds of pleasure yet still be missing something is that pleasures differ not only in quantity and kind, but also in value. (3) Once we acknowledge that pleasures are of fundamentally different kinds, we see that maximizing pleasure is not intelligible as a goal in itself. In order for the concept of "maximizing X" to have content, there has to be a metric for X that allows us to choose between alternatives based upon how much X each offers. However, since pleasures are so different, there can be no common metric by which they can be measured and compared. Consider a concrete example. I sometimes have to choose between spending quality time with my children and working on scholarly projects. Should I spend an extra hour with my children that I would have spent working on a book? Interacting-with-my-children pleasure simply feels different from writing-a-book pleasure, so I cannot directly compare one to the other, and make the choice based on which would maximize pleasure in some neutral sense. (Sometimes we hear talk of "hedons" of pleasure, but this is at best a vague metaphor, and at worst a Procrustean quantitative fetishism with no basis in actual experience.)

Does this mean that the choice of how to combine pleasures in a life is irrational? No. Not all reasoned judgments can be settled numerically. Any of Rembrandt's self-portraits is better than any of C. M. Coolidge's paintings of dogs playing poker, even though we cannot quantify the difference. Furthermore, in ordinary practical reasoning, pleasure is normally not the first thing that comes into our consideration. In thinking about how to balance my role as a father with my role as a scholar, I am much more likely to start with assessments of the values I assign to the activities themselves, and of what kinds of time commitments I need to reach goals central to those values. I might be concerned that my child is having problems with school, so I spend more time helping with homework. Alternatively, perhaps I think I have a distinctive scholarly contribution to make with a particular article, but I have had trouble completing it, so one weekend I forgo a trip with my children to a Renaissance Faire in order to spend more time writing. I will get pleasure from either activity, but the pleasure is not the focus of the deliberation. Pleasure becomes the focus only in special cases, like when we are trying to decide what to do on our vacation ("Going to the beach would be nice, but I also like skiing. Which one would I enjoy more?"). I want to stress again that *pleasure is an important component of living well.* Perhaps someone could rationally choose a life in which there was little pleasure, but at the very least we would seriously question that choice. But there is a world of difference between saying, (1) it counts strongly against the rationality of a choice if it does not bring pleasure of some kind (true), and (2) the maximization of pleasure can and should be the sole determinant of all our choices (false).

I hope to have made two points in the preceding section. First, the choice of human goals cannot be completely subjective, because there are some (even ones that motivate many humans) that are simply unintelligible as ultimate goals. For example, wealth is rational as an intermediate goal, a means to achieving some further end, but it is simply unintelligible to suggest that wealth is an ultimate goal in itself. Second, we have seen that some things are reasonable to pursue as aspects of our ultimate goals (like prestige and pleasure), but they are conceptually dependent on some other goal to give them concrete form. In the next section, I shall argue in favor of six candidates for ultimate goals.

Six Adequate Answers to the Why Question

We have been discussing a variety of unsatisfactory answers that Bloggs could give to our question, "Why are you an attorney?" but now let us approach from the opposite direction and consider what an adequate response would be. Suppose Bloggs says, "I am a defense attorney because I think it is important to protect the innocent. Even when I know my client is guilty, I feel like I am serving the community because I am a bulwark against the indiscriminate exercise of government power." At long last, we have an intelligible, defensible answer. Bloggs has told us what he finds valuable in his career, and we can sympathetically understand it as an intrinsically valuable goal. When we imagined Bloggs saying that he is an attorney because it makes him the most money, it was legitimate for us to ask what he wants all that money for. In contrast, if Bloggs says that he is an attorney because he wants to help others and serve the community, it makes no sense for us to challenge him, "But why would you want *that?*" The difference is due to the fact that money is merely an instrumental good, while helping others is intelligible to us as an ultimate goal.

How does it affect the adequacy of Bloggs's answer that he seems not to enjoy being an attorney? Tortured geniuses like Ludwig Wittgenstein (in real life) or Dr. Gregory House (in fiction) have a sort of romantic appeal to them. My intuition is that their lives can be worthwhile, even though racked with pain and sadness. However, I am not certain of this, and even I admit that their lives would be better if they were more pleasant. But the case of Bloggs need not be so extreme. Let us suppose Bloggs explains, "Being a defense attorney is very stressful and frustrating, so I often seem to not be enjoying myself. However, I get immense satisfaction when I successfully defend the rights of a client. At the moment I can't imagine being satisfied by any other career." Not only does this answer make sense, but we might think that Bloggs gets more satisfaction out of his work precisely because it is so challenging. Not everyone would concur, but for many of us a life without the stresses and pains that come from surmounting challenges sounds horrific. This perspective is illustrated in the *Twilight Zone* episode in which a criminal, "Rocky Valentine," dies and awakens in a world where his every wish is instantly met: he has unlimited amounts of cash, he wins every time he gambles, police are powerless before him, and he is surrounded by beautiful women (who lack any personality that might lead them to resist his whims). After a month, Rocky is almost insane with boredom, and tells the person whom he thinks is his guardian angel, "If I gotta stay here another day, I'm going to go nuts! I don't belong in Heaven, see? I want to go to the other place." The angel replies, "Heaven? Whatever gave you the idea that you were in Heaven, Mr. Valentine? This *is* 'the other place!'"[61]

Being a defense attorney is an example of what Aristotelians call a "political" life (in a broad sense of that term). While we should heed Kupperman's admonition that "it would seem doctrinaire to claim to be able to limit in advance the number of major types of very good lives,"[62] it would be potentially useful to many true "lovers of wisdom" if we could categorize some of the more plausible candidates. Three kinds of goods have been serious contenders for intrinsic value in the pre-modern Western tradition: (1) theoretical understanding and inquiry (as might be exemplified in the life of the theoretical physicist, the pure mathematician, and the academic philosopher); (2) practical activity with others for the good of one's community (as could be seen in the life of a senator, a bureaucrat at the FDA, and a defense attorneys like our friend Bloggs); and (3) religious devotion (as might be found in the life of a monk, hermit, or monastic nun). These goods can be combined in certain kinds of lives. No matter how "pure" our research, most of us in academia have to walk back down into "the Cave" and take our turn as chair or dean. Similarly, Jesuits like Frederick Copleston famously combine religious devotion with theoretical inquiry.

In addition to the traditional three candidates, there are other kinds of goods that have been proposed as intrinsically valuable. (4) G. E. Moore suggested that it is "universally admitted that the proper appreciation of a beautiful object is a good thing in itself."[63] He was perhaps overoptimistic about how universal this view is, but it is certainly a common and plausible one. It is rare that one will be able to organize one's entire life around just the appreciation of beauty; however, it is undoubtedly a valuable component of a good life. (5) Because we value the appreciation of beauty in art, most of us would acknowledge that the production of art also has intrinsic value. The appreciation and production of art are related activities, but not identical. I could have very good taste in music without being able to create it. In addition, artists are not always insightful about other arts or the work of other artists. But someone who said that she is working to produce beautiful paintings, sculptures, pieces of music, poems, or novels would not have to provide a further justification for her actions.

I think most of my readers will appreciate the value of the preceding categories. However, I want to argue now for a more controversial type of intrinsic value: (6) skillful activity in a practice. I am here appropriating Alasdair MacIntyre's specific notion of a "practice," by which he means a "cooperative human activity through which goods internal to that form of activity are realized."[64] "Internal goods" are those that can only be obtained through a specific practice. External goods can in principle be obtained in other ways; the activity is only a means to external goods. We can illustrate the distinction with the practice of teaching. An external good of teaching would be earning a salary. An internal good would be the experience of finally "reaching" a student who was initially resistant to learning.[65]

Not every human activity has internal goods. Changing the bulb on my headlight is not a practice, because the only good that results is external (even though important): I can see when I drive at night. Nothing will be lost if I achieve the same goal in other ways (as by hiring a mechanic to fix it). Internal goods arise at least in part because practices present challenges to humans of potentially infinite complexity. Because practices are complex in this way,

> . . . human powers to achieve excellence [in a given practice], and human conceptions of the ends and goods involved, are systematically extended. Tic-tac-toe is not an example of a practice in this sense, nor is throwing a football with skill; but the game of football is, and so is chess. Bricklaying is not a practice; architecture is. Planting turnips is not a practice; farming is.[66]

Let's consider the example of Western chess in more detail. Playing chess well is obviously a challenging activity. This is part of the reason that chess aficionados are intrigued by and admire especially good moves or ingenious solutions to chess problems. Chess is also an endless source of fascination because, although the basic rules have not changed since the nineteenth century, the tactics of chess continually evolve. One test of whether an activity is a practice is whether it is appropriate to say of at least one practitioner, "Not only was she really good at it, but she revolutionized the way we do it." For example, Wilhelm Steinitz, the first World Chess Champion, revolutionized the game with his subtle positional approach.[67]

Some of MacIntyre's examples of practices—including physics, chemistry, biology, painting, music, and "politics in the Aristotelian sense"—are consistent with the valuable ways of life we discussed above.[68] However, MacIntyre's examples of chess and football fall outside our categories (1) through (5), as would similar practices like playing poker, cooking, bonsai, pumpkin carving, and jiu-jitsu. I would further expand the list of practices in directions not suggested by MacIntyre. I have no doubt that Plato and Aristotle, at least, would find accountancy a vulgar and banausic activity. I would argue, though, that being an accountant could be a practice. Because the business world is always changing, accounting procedures are always in flux, and it requires a thoughtful approach to determine what are legitimate and illegitimate ways of measuring revenues, expenses, assets, liabilities, retained earnings, etc. (Luca Pacioli's *Summa Arithmetica* of 1494 revolutionized accounting by publicizing and standardizing the method of double-entry bookkeeping.) Similarly, the various forms of engineering have not surfaced on traditional lists of intrinsically valuable activities, but the complex and ever-changing challenges presented by engineering problems make solving them a practice.[69] If engaging in practices is intrinsically valuable, chemical engineers, CPAs, and poker players who are devoted to their respective crafts and do them well can take their place alongside philosopher-kings and saints as paradigms of lives that are well-led.[70]

Conclusion

Let's return to an example I used at the beginning of this paper: the claim "pure carbon dioxide is poisonous" is true. This claim is only true because there are animals like human beings; there would be no content to the notion of "poisonous" in a universe without animals. However, the claim is not, for that reason, subjective. Long before any human being or culture knew that there was such a thing as CO_2, it was true that inhaling pure carbon dioxide would be lethal. I have argued in this paper that claims like "Producing beautiful works of art is a worthwhile goal" are similarly anthropocentric. This claim is true only because humans exist, and because humans have the needs and capacities that we have; however, its truth is not relative to either individual whims or cultural fads. Producing beautiful works of art is intelligible as an ultimate goal in a way that the mere accumulation of wealth is simply not.

There are far more potential questions and objections to the theses of this paper than I can answer here or even anticipate. But I want to conclude by addressing one counterargument that I suspect will have particular urgency for many readers: "You seem to expect everyone to justify themselves to others and to their standards of rationality. Suppose Bloggs *did* insist that he wanted money for the sake of money? Suppose Herostratus *did* say that he preferred fame to prestige? Suppose someone said that his overarching goal in life is to count the blades of grass in various geometrically shaped plots?[71] Why should it carry any weight that these answers seem incoherent or unsatisfactory to you or to anyone else?"

To answer this objection, we need to take a step back and consider the nature of philosophy itself. For centuries, people have gone out of their way to denounce Descartes and accuse others of being Cartesians. But many of these same critics accept without reflection the fundamental subjectivism of Descartes's approach. To really exorcise the ghost of Descartes, we must reject his view of philosophy as a solitary monologue, in which each person is answerable only to his own standards. As both the *Analects* of Confucius and the dialogues of Plato show (in their distinctive ways), philosophy is a discussion between humans attempting to reach a shared understanding. The attempt is not guaranteed to be successful, and understanding is not identical with agreement. In our individual lives and human history we increasingly recognize the extent to which others disagree with our view of the world. But we are able to recognize this only because we understand the values and perspectives that we do not agree with. To give up on understanding others is not to respect them; it is to objectify them, to treat them as we do rocks, plants, or hurricanes, whose "actions" can be causally explained, but not justified. To treat others as humans is to treat them as beings whom you can potentially ask, "Why are you doing that?" and expect an intelligible answer. Their answer may surprise you, challenge you, or disturb you, but until you have understood it, you have not done justice to your shared humanity with them.

And if you don't agree with that, tell me "Why?" and we will begin a dialogue aimed at achieving a shared understanding.

Acknowledgments

I am grateful to Chenyang Li and Peimin Ni for their hard work in putting this volume together. Professor Ni was generous in providing many thoughtful comments on this paper, resulting in some significant improvements (though neither he nor Professor Li is responsible for any faults that remain). Of course, I am especially grateful to Joel Kupperman for his outstanding work on both Western and Chinese philosophy, as well as providing a living example of how to be a Confucian gentleman in the contemporary world.

Notes

1. "People often have a sense of having experienced how much value, or lack of value, various things have. In some of these cases, it looks reasonable to suppose that they have got it pretty much right; that what they value really does have value, or that what they disvalue really is boring, empty, or abhorrent" (Kupperman 2006, 143). Elsewhere, Kupperman remarks, "there seems no harm in speaking of value facts, as long as we bear in mind that to speak of the fact that X has high value . . . is equivalent to saying that X really does have high value" (Kupperman 1999b, 81). Formulations like this simply "draw a contrast between what Smith or Bloggs or a casual onlooker might take the value of some experiences to be, on the one hand, and some more authoritative judgment, on the other" (Kupperman 1999b, 80).

2. "Broad general rules provide a useful starting point and core of any morality; but there should be more to a morality than a core. . . . There is no requirement in logic or in the nature of moral thought that maxims take the form of general rules. Nor, if we do rely on rules, can we infer that for any given morally problematic case there is a single general rule that clearly and incontrovertibly is appropriate to that case" (Kupperman 1991, 77–78).

3. "Even if one accepts Aristotle's favorable evaluation of the highly intellectual contemplative life, surely it is also true that lives that center on aesthetic creation, aesthetic experience, effective political and social activities, or on styles of personal relations can be very good. . . ." (Kupperman 1991, 134. See also 144–145.)

4. Kupperman notes both that "It is easy to jump to conclusions about someone else's life because we have missed nuances that are important to its value," but also that "No one has ever advanced a coherent and convincing set of reasons for saying that judgments of this sort are nonsense or have to be false" (Kupperman 1991, 133).

5. Kupperman advocates what he describes as "a modest skepticism" about our knowledge of value, which "can be conducive to keeping an open mind." However, he quickly adds that "complete skepticism would be unwarranted" (Kupperman 2006, 138).

6. My typology of realism and anti-realism in this paper is not meant to be exhaustive. I am simply focusing on what I think are some of the more common and plausible positions.

7. Kupperman 1999b, 81.

8. Kupperman 1999b, 81. Kupperman also notes: "It is natural to speak of 'values' in connection with our thought about and experience of what is or is not of value; and then it is easy to go from that to thinking of values as like things, furniture of a peculiar sort among the other furniture of the universe. But the objects of our thought and experience, even when they are empirical features of the real world, are not always things. In this respect it is healthy to compare values to the rate of inflation or to magnetic fields. Neither seems particularly furniturelike, and each is an interpretative construct related to (less conspicuously interpreted) underlying phenomena" (Kupperman 1999b, 74).

9. Kupperman 1999b, 82.

10. See Wiggins 1987; McDowell 1998; Putnam 1992.

11. For a defense of the interpretation of Xunzi I sketch here, see Van Norden 2011, Chapter X, 163–183; Van Norden 2000; Van Norden 1993.

12. Ivanhoe and Van Norden 2005, 269. (Translation slightly modified.)

13. Ivanhoe and Van Norden 2005, 274.

14. Ivanhoe and Van Norden 2005, 272.

15. Ivanhoe and Van Norden 2005, 299.

16. Ivanhoe and Van Norden 2005, 281–282. (Translation slightly modified.)

17. Ivanhoe and Van Norden 2005, 284.

18. Ivanhoe and Van Norden 2005, 276.

19. Ivanhoe and Van Norden 2005, 283.

20. Kupperman 2000. Kupperman also makes passing reference to Xunzi in Kupperman 2001, 37, 77 and Kupperman 1999a, 101.

21. Gallup Poll, conducted December 2010 <http://www.gallup.com/poll/145286/>. In 2010, only 16 percent of those polled believed that a purely naturalistic view of evolution accounts for the human species.

22. In 2004, Nathaniel Abraham, who holds an MS in biology and a PhD in philosophy from an accredited university, was hired by Woods Hole Oceanographic Institution on the basis of his credentials, but he was dismissed when he revealed to his superior that he is a Creationist (Boston Globe, December 7, <http://www.boston.com/news/local/articles/2007/12/07/biologist_fired_for_beliefs_suit_says/>). In addition, Benjamin Stein (a law professor and former New York Times columnist) co-wrote and starred in *Expelled: No Intelligence Allowed*, a film criticizing evolutionary theory and championing intelligent design (Frankowski, Miller, Stein & Ruloff 2008).

23. Kupperman asks, "What logic connects the claim that very often we cannot expect consensus in judgments of value with the conclusion that such judgments cannot be correct? There surely is no logical contradiction in the notion of correct propositions about which, nevertheless, people cannot entirely agree" (Kupperman 2006, 140–141).

24. Charles Sanders Peirce was the first to emphasize that inference to the best explanation (or "abduction" as he called it) is a form of argument distinct from deduction. See Fann 1970.

25. Mackie 1991, sketches an inference to the best explanation version of what he labels (somewhat misleadingly) the "argument from relativity." However, he simply asserts that moral disagreement is best explained by the absence of moral facts, without discussing any detailed examples to make his case.

26. Hume 1983, 113. (Emphasis in original.)

27. Herodotus, *History*, Book III.

28. David Wong 1986, has argued that the disagreements between Western and East Asian cultures over individualism and filial piety are sufficient to support "relativism." However, he has confirmed (in conversation) my sense that what he means by "relativism" is much like what I would label "pluralism."

29. Montaigne 1958, 156.

30. Montaigne 1958, 155.

31. Kupperman's extensive and insightful work in comparative philosophy is a further illustration of this approach to cultural differences. See, for example, Kupperman 1999a and Kupperman 2001.

32. For a thoughtful discussion of how contemporary anthropology has helped challenge narrow views of human nature, see Clifford Geertz 1973.

33. See Freeman 1986; Malotki 1983; Grinker 2001; Spiro 1992; Martin 1986.

34. Brown 1991, Chapter 6.

35. Ivanhoe and Van Norden 2005, 256.

36. *Mengzi* 6A1. Translation from Ivanhoe and Van Norden 2005, 144–145.

37. Some philosophers interpret Mengzi and Xunzi as being much more similar in their views of human nature than I suggest here. For one such account, see Ni 2009. Ni also presents a provocative account of Mengzi as holding a noncognitivist view of human nature, according to which the claim that "human nature is good" is neither true nor false, but is rather a "performative" recommendation. For my own (cognitivist) account of Mengzi, see Van Norden 2011. In addition, I argue in Van Norden 2007, that, although traditional Confucians were not pluralists themselves, the core insights of Confucianism can be incorporated into a pluralistic philosophy.

38. Kupperman 2010, 189–190.

39. Hutton 2002, 373.

40. Hutton 2002, 374.

41. I hasten to note that neither Aristotle nor Aquinas was an anthropocentric realist about values. This is reflected in the important role that "final causes" play in Aristotelian physics and in the "function argument" of the *Nicomachean Ethics*. What I am doing in this paper is appropriating a particular aspect of Aristotle's approach that does not in itself require anything beyond anthropocentric realism about values.

42. Supertramp 1979.

43. Hume 1978, 416 (Book II, Part III, Section III). (Emphasis in original.)

44. Hume 1978, 1 (Book I, Part I, Section I).

45. Hume 1978, 19 (Book I, Part I, Section VII).

46. Hume 1978, 415 (Book II, Part III, Section III). For example, if I have a "complex idea" that consists of a mental image of the Space Needle in Seattle, my idea is true, because it is an accurate copy of a sensory impression of the Space Needle; however, if I have an idea of the Space Needle in *Portland*, my idea is false, because it does not accurately copy any sensory impression.

47. Hume 1978, 458 (Book III, Part I, Section I).

48. Hume 1978, 415 (Book II, Part III, Section III).

49. In order to be fully adequate, any account of the Hypothetical Imperative would have to be much more complex, and could not treat our goals in isolation. However, all I need for my argument is the acknowledgement that we cannot do without some version of reasoning about the best means to achieve our goals.

50. The truth of the claim *is* anthropocentric, though. If there were no human beings, there would be no fact about how long humans have to train for them (and also no truth about how long a "marathon" is).

51. Another potential objection is that the "ought" of the Hypothetical Imperative is non-moral. If I choose to run in a marathon but fail to adequately train, I am guilty of a failure of practical rationality, but not guilty of a moral failure. This is accurate, but I am not attempting to defend a distinction between moral and other kinds of value. It is sufficient for my purposes if I establish that there are objective values of some kind.

52. Hume 1978, 459 (Book III, Part I, Section I).

53. Hume 1978, 416 (Book II, Part III, Section III).

54. Hume 1978, 416 (Book II, Part III, Section III).

55. Lewis 1992, Letter XIV, 73.

56. "Dick the Butcher," in *Henry VI, Part II* (Act IV, Scene 2).

57. Does Bloggs aim at genuine prestige or specious prestige? In other words, would he rather be admired for a good quality that he actually has, or for a quality people mistakenly think he has? Here I think we should say the same thing we said about fame: we can imagine someone seeking specious prestige, but we cannot imagine them rationally preferring specious prestige to merited prestige.

58. Aristotle puts this rather poetically by saying that the pleasure that accompanies an activity is like the bloom upon the cheek of a healthy youngster (*Nicomachean Ethics* X.5, 1174b30). Aquinas puts it more technically by saying that pleasure is not the "essence" of living well, but rather a "proper accident" of it (*Summa Theologiae* II-I, Question 2, Article 6).

59. Cronenberg, Thomas, & Lantos (1996) is not to be confused with the film of the same name by Paul Haggis (2005).

60. Kupperman 2006, 3–4.

61. Beaumont 1960.

62. Kupperman 1991, 134.

63. Moore 1903, §114, 189.

64. MacIntyre 1984, 187.

65. The internal goods of a practice can be ignored, as is illustrated by the character "Elizabeth" in the film *Bad Teacher*: "When I first started teaching, I thought that I was doing it for all the right reasons: shorter hours, summers off, no accountability . . ." (Kasdan, Eisenberg & Stupnitsky [2011]). MacIntyre would say, I think, that teaching is a practice, but "Elizabeth" does not treat it as such.

66. MacIntyre 1984, 187.

67. In a comparison of Steinitz to one of his leading opponents, someone said, "Kolisch is a highwayman and points the pistol at your breast. Steinitz is a pickpocket, he steals a pawn and wins a game with it" (Anderssen 1887).

68. MacIntyre 1984, 187–188. It might seem that any human activity (other than the most mindlessly simple and repetitious) counts as a "practice." However, some engaging human activities will fail. Stamp collecting may be fun, but I do not think that it is challenging (except insofar as one needs money to buy certain rare stamps) or complex enough (because the standards and techniques of stamp collecting do not evolve).

69. A classic defense of the value of engineering, both for its internal and its external goods, is Florman 1994.

70. It will be evident to students of Confucianism that there is much more that can be said about the similarities and differences between the Aristotelian and Confucian views of the legitimate goals of human life. I explore these in more detail in Van Norden 2013.

71. The example is borrowed from Rawls 1971, 432.

References

Anderssen, Adolf. (1887). "Steinitz, the Chess Champion." *The New York Times* (January 23).

Beaumont, Charles (Writer). (1960). "A Nice Place to Visit" [Television series episode]. In Rod Serling (Creator/Narrator), *The Twilight Zone*, Season 1, Episode 28 (originally aired on CBS, April 15, 1960).

Brown, Donald E. (1991). *Human Universals*. Philadelphia: Temple University Press.

Cronenberg, David (Producer/Director/Writer), Jeremy Thomas (Producer) and Robert Lantos (Producer). (1996). *Crash* [Motion Picture]. Los Angeles: New Line Cinema.

Fann, K. T. (1970). *Peirce's Theory of Abduction*. The Hague: Martinus Nijhoff.

Florman, Samuel C. (1994). *The Existential Pleasures of Engineering* (2nd ed.). New York: St. Martin's Press.

Frankowski, Nathan (Director), Kevin Miller (Writer), Benjamin Stein (Writer/Narrator), and Walt Ruloff (Writer). (2008). *Expelled: No Intelligence Allowed* [Motion Picture]. Salt Lake City: Rocky Mountain Pictures.

Freeman, Derek (1986). *Margaret Mead and Samoa: The Making and Unmaking of an Anthropological Myth*. New York: Penguin Books.

Geertz, Clifford. (1973). "The Impact of the Science of Culture on the Concept of Man." In Geertz, *The Interpretation of Cultures*, 33–54. New York: Basic Books.

Grinker, Roy. (2001). *In the Arms of Africa: The Life of Colin Turnbull*. Chicago: University of Chicago Press.

Haggis, Paul (Writer/Producer/Director). (2005). *Crash* [Motion Picture]. Santa Monica: Lion's Gate Entertainment.

Hutton, Eric. (2002). "Moral Reasoning in Aristotle and Xunzi." *Journal of Chinese Philosophy*, 29.3 (September): 355–384.

Hume, David. (1978). *A Treatise of Human Nature* (2nd ed.). L. A. Selby-Bigge and P. H. Nidditch (eds.). New York: Oxford University Press.

———. (1983). "A Dialogue." In J. B. Schneewind (Ed.). Hume, *An Enquiry concerning the Principles of Morals*. Indianapolis: Hackett Publishing.

Ivanhoe, Philip J., and Bryan W. Van Norden, (eds.). (2005). *Readings in Classical Chinese Philosophy* (2nd ed.). Indianapolis: Hackett Publishing.

Kasdan, Jake (Director), Lee Eisenberg (Writer), and Gene Stupnitsky (Writer). (2011). *Bad Teacher* [Motion Picture]. Los Angeles: Columbia Pictures.

Kupperman, Joel J. (1991). *Character*. New York: Oxford University Press.

———. (1999a). *Learning from Asian Philosophy*. New York: Oxford University Press.

———. (1999b). *Value . . . And What Follows*. New York: Oxford University Press.

———. (2000). "Xunzi: Morality as Psychological Constraint." In T. C. Kline III and Philip J. Ivanhoe (eds.). *Virtue, Nature, and Moral Agency in the* Xunzi. Indianapolis: Hackett Publishing.

———. (2001). *Classic Asian Philosophy*. New York: Oxford University Press.

———. (2006). *Six Myths about the Good Life*. Indianapolis: Hackett Publishing.

———. (2010). *Theories of Human Nature*. Indianapolis: Hackett Publishing.

Lewis, C. S. (1992). *The Screwtape Letters* (reprint). Book-of-the-Month Club.

MacIntyre, Alasdair. (1984). *After Virtue* (2nd ed.). Notre Dame: University of Notre Dame Press.

Mackie, J. L. (1991). *Ethics: Inventing Right and Wrong*. New York: Penguin Books.

Malotki, Ekkehart. (1983). *Hopi Time*. Berlin: de Gruyter.

Martin, Laura. (1986). "Eskimo Words for Snow: A Case Study in the Genesis and Decay of an Anthropological Example." *American Anthropologist*, 88.2: 418–423.

McDowell, John. (1998). "Values and Secondary Qualities." In McDowell, *Mind, Value, and Reality*. Cambridge, Mass: Harvard University Press.

Montaigne, Michel de. (1958). "Of Cannibals." In Donald Frame (trans.). *The Complete Essays of Montaigne*. Stanford: Stanford University Press.

Moore, G. E. (1903). *Principia Ethica*. Cambridge: Cambridge University Press.

Ni, Peimin. (2009). "A Comparative Examination of Rorty's and Mencius's Theories of Human Nature." In Yong Huang (ed.), *Rorty, Confucianism, and Pragmatism*. Albany, NY: State University of New York Press.

Putnam, Hilary. (1992). *Realism with a Human Face*. Cambridge, MA: Harvard University Press.

Rawls, John. (1971). *A Theory of Justice*. Cambridge, MA: Harvard University Press.

Spiro, Melford. (1992). *Oedipus in the Trobriands*. New Jersey: Transaction Publishers.

Supertramp. (1979). "The Logical Song." On *Breakfast in America*. Santa Monica: A&M Records.

Van Norden, Bryan W. (1993). "Hansen on Hsün-tzu." *Journal of Chinese Philosophy*, 20.3 (September): 365–82.

———. (2000). "Mengzi and Xunzi: Two Views of Human Agency." In Thornton C. Kline and Philip J. Ivanhoe (Eds.). *Virtue, Nature and Agency in the Xunzi*, 103–134. Indianapolis: Hackett Publishing.

———. (2001). "Mencius and Augustine on Evil: A Test Case for Comparative Philosophy." In Bo Mou (ed.), *Two Roads to Wisdom? Chinese and Analytic Philosophies*, 313–336. Chicago: Open Court Press.

———. (2007). *Virtue Ethics and Consequentialism in Early Chinese Philosophy*. New York: Cambridge University Press.

———. (2011). *Introduction to Classical Chinese Philosophy*. Indianapolis: Hackett Publishing.

———. (2013). "Toward a Synthesis of Confucianism and Aristotelianism." In Stephen Angle and Michael Slote (eds.), *Virtue Ethics and Confucianism*. New York: Routledge.

Wiggins, David (1987). "Truth, Invention, and the Meaning of Life." In Wiggins, *Needs, Values, Truth: Essays in the Philosophy of Value*. Oxford: Blackwell.

Wong, David. (1986). *Moral Relativity*. Berkeley: University of California Press.

4

The Different Faces of Love in a Good Life

DAVID B. WONG

The question of how one ought to live occupied the center of the classical Greek and Chinese philosophical traditions. Contemporary philosophy has remained comparatively silent on what is arguably the first question of philosophy and has focused on the narrower question of what one morally ought to do. Joel Kupperman and a handful of other contemporary philosophers have been notable exceptions to this silence. Acceptance of a plurality of valuable and justifiable ways to live has served as the major factor in why silence has been the rule. Too many contemporary philosophers have nothing to say on a subject if they cannot hope to identify the singular truth. Alternatively, most of what they have to say is that there is no final word or singular truth, as if that were all that was left to say. Joel Kupperman has been at the forefront of a resurgence of interest in the question of the ancients, and in a way that is compatible with the contemporary acceptance of pluralism about the good life. The tone of much of Kupperman's work is that of a gentle and wise interlocutor who refrains from lecturing to us on what the good life is, but rather assists us in our individual and collective endeavors to live a good life by articulating much good advice and well-taken cautions. This essay on the place of love in the good life is meant as a contribution to the kind of project that Kupperman has done so much to renew in a contemporary setting.

A second characteristic of much of Kupperman's work that I hope to reflect in this essay is the deft way that he ranges over different philosophical traditions from which to draw insights into the problem at hand. This is not quite comparative philosophy in the traditional sense of being focused on better understanding of the philosophy of one tradition by juxtaposing it with that of another tradition. The focus is the philosophical problem, and the idea is that one is more able to address that question by drawing from a richer array of insights. A philosophizing that draws from multiple traditions might *involve* comparative philosophy in the traditional sense, because properly bringing to bear the insights of another tradition to the problem at hand will often necessitate locating them within the larger framework of that other tradition and relating that framework to that of one's "home" tradition. One might have to deal with obstacles to the idea that insights from another tradition are really relevant to the philosophical problem as posed within one's home tradition. I have always admired the way in which Kupperman has managed to move over and around these obstacles in the course of doing his sort of cosmopolitan philosophy. In a similar way, I shall try to draw insights from early Chinese philosophy and work on Buddhist meditation.

I have always admired Kupperman's use of empirical and theoretical work from the human sciences such as psychology. Thankfully, we are past the idea that the proper province of philosophy is pure conceptual analysis, with the implicit understanding that others will refrain from poaching on our territory as we will refrain from poaching on theirs. Philosophers and psychologists risk showing themselves to be amateurish in venturing into each other's traditional territories, but those who take the risk can enrich their disciplines and increase their explanatory power. Psychology and neuroscience have recently produced intriguing if inconclusive empirical work bearing on the nature of love, some of which I shall try to incorporate here.

Does Love Answer to Reasons?

To start, I would like to pose the question of whether one loves for reasons, and if so, what kinds of reasons. Let me pose the question in a personal way. At a time that doesn't seem that long ago, but objectively is many years ago, the woman I love asked me why I loved her. I was totally flustered by this question. I don't remember exactly how I answered her, but it was an awkward attempt to affirm my love while declining to give reasons. It was not for lack of wonderful qualities such as her multifaceted intelligence, warmth, emotional honesty, and beauty that drew me to her and changed my life. But I resisted giving these qualities as an answer to why I loved her. Part of this was a reluctance to express my feelings, but I was also motivated by an inchoate sense that identifying those wonderful qualities as reasons for my love would have been a reductive answer. The descriptions of qualities that came to mind seemed too generic. Moreover, it seemed that naming any set of qualities as the reasons for my love made my end of our relationship seem static. It did not convey the sense of open-endedness I had about our future. She might change, and so might I. That didn't mean, and I hoped and intended that it would not mean, the end of our love.

The kind of thought this story suggests has prompted some philosophers to argue that love of a person is not love of her nonrelational qualities, and that if it were love of such qualities, it would fail to hold constant against change in qualities, would fail to be non-fungible as love can be.[1] This line of thought might lead to the understanding of love as requiring no reasons, that is, no normative reasons that make love wise or reasonable or just a good idea, or not. Harry Frankfurt has put this thought by claiming that love is not a response to the perceived intrinsic worth of the beloved but rather that it is the other way around: that the beloved has worth because one loves her.[2] For Frankfurt, love for one's children seems to be the purest paradigm for the kind of love he has in mind. One does not love one's children because of some value inherent in them independent of one's loving them; in fact, Frankfurt states, he loved his children before they were born. For Frankfurt, love that does not answer to reasons but rather creates them is neither essentially affective nor cognitive: it is volitional—being motivated in certain ways toward the beloved.

There are ways we talk and think about love that suggest a different way to understand it. To return to my own case, my declination to give reasons for my love did not cause the woman I love to reject me. In fact, she went so far as to marry me, and Laura and I have a daughter, Liana. And now, I, like many fathers, occasionally find myself thinking about what sort of person my daughter might come to love and perhaps make a life with. If my daughter asks of the person who loves her for the reasons he loves her, I would not be disappointed if he affirms his love but declines to give reasons. So far, I am consistent. But I believe myself to be quite a conventional father in hoping that she will be *discerning* in love. I am not so conventional, to my daughter's credit, in confidently *expecting* her to be discerning in love. I hope and expect that she will find someone worthy of her love. Going one step further, I might find myself hoping and expecting that she loves someone *for good reasons*.

Unsurprisingly, I hope for kindness and responsibility in someone she loves. So now I seem to have become inconsistent. Though I thought that reasons for my love of Laura were somehow inappropriate, the kind of love I wish for my daughter is love on the basis of nonrelational qualities her beloved should possess. This is the kind of thought, at any rate, that gives rise to a competing conception of love as answering to reasons, to nonrelational qualities the beloved possesses.[3]

As reflected by my example, the nonrelational traits in question are usually conceived as personal traits that vary from person to person but also as ones that can be possessed by more than one person, and so the conception of love for reasons seems vulnerable to the objection that it makes love fungible. If love answers to reasons of that sort, why can't it be transferred to someone else who better instantiates those reasons? J. David Velleman's Kantian conception presents a surprising remedy for this problem. On that conception, love answers to what is worthy in all persons—their rational nature. Of course, Velleman grants that love cannot be merely such a response, for otherwise we would love everyone and that would be indistinguishable from moral respect, and so he ingeniously adds that in love we perceive the worth of some persons through their personal qualities. This perception makes us emotionally vulnerable to them, in such a way that our defenses against being hurt are drawn down. What makes love non-fungible, according to Velleman, is not that is purely conative in a Frankfurtian sense, but the fact that it responds to a Kantian worth that is beyond price, beyond comparison to the worth of another.[4]

The downside of such a conception is that it does not make love discerning in the way I want my daughter's love to be discerning. I wish for her a love of an admirable person, at least partly on the basis of his admirable qualities. But on Velleman's account the explanation for her loving one person and not another is her being struck by that person's particular ways of expressing his rational nature such that she becomes emotionally vulnerable to him. But to say that she responds to that person's rational nature is not to show that she is being discerning between rational persons. To say she becomes emotionally vulnerable to a particular rational person because of the particular ways he expresses his rational nature is not to show she is being discerning either. The explanation of why she becomes vulnerable is purely causal and not justificatory. Thus, conceptions of love based on the beloved's nonrelational qualities either run up against the reluctance to make love fungible (where the justifying qualities are personal ones) or fail to sustain one of the original motivations for such conceptions, which is to acknowledge the desire for love to be selective in a normative sense (where the only justifying quality is one that every person possesses).

There is a third possible answer to the question of whether love is grounded in reasons. Alongside the answer of "no reasons" and "reasons that are nonrelational qualities of the beloved," there is the answer that the reasons for love are the relationships between lovers. Such a characterization squares with some things we think and feel about romantic love, friendship, and familial love. Sometimes we think of these kinds of love as being grounded in the history of the relationship: how friends have shared important experiences, how they have influenced each other, and how they have come to trust each other. Sometimes the relevant feature of relationship is the fit between those who love each other. In the case of romantic love, for example, I want for my daughter not only that she love and be loved by a kind and responsible person, but also a person who "fits" with who she is in a way that I cannot presume to describe in advance.[5] Matchmakers tend to see fit in terms of similarity of likes and dislikes, temperaments, and goals in life. Sometimes fit is spelled out in terms of the complementarity of contrasting qualities: one likes to talk; the other likes to listen. Similarly, such qualities of "fit" between friends can be all important.

So far, I have spelled out reasons of relationship in terms of the history between two individuals or the ways in which their personal qualities may mesh in a felicitous fashion. But reasons of relationship can also encompass relationship to the other based on biological and social role, as in love between parents and children or between siblings.[6] Sometimes the social/biological role is regarded as a sufficient basis for familial love. I may say that I love my daughter simply because she is my daughter, even if I also love her independently of her being my daughter. As has been pointed out by Niko Kolodny, a contemporary defender of love as based on relationship, one advantage of such a relational conception of reasons for love is that it enables love to be more constant in the sense of being more secure against changes in personal qualities or changes in the relationship such as shared interests and activities.[7] Making relationship the basis for love may secure the kind of greater constancy that we believe love is capable of displaying.

Sandra Day O'Connor retired from the U.S. Supreme Court to spend more time with her husband John who had entered into an advanced stage of Alzheimer's disease. Later the family found it necessary to place John in a care facility where he fell in love "like a teenager," as his son put it, with another resident. Justice O'Connor is reported to have been "thrilled" and "relieved" that her husband had found happiness.[8] Though this is all we know from news reports, it is entirely plausible that Justice O'Connor still loves her husband despite the fact that the person she had loved for many years was no longer there. It is plausible that her *continuing* love for the person John O'Connor is now explains why she welcomed his newfound love. Such constancy seems within reach through love based on relationship. O'Connor may continue to love her husband because he is her husband; she may continue because she wants to honor the history of their relationship and to continue it though it will have to undergo radical changes in its character.

Another advantage of a relational conception of reasons for love is that it provides greater security for the bonds of love between creatures as greatly flawed as we human beings are. It is commonplace but still very significant to observe that we do not choose our parents or our children. For familial bonds to be secure, it is necessary for human parents and children to love each other even if they do not score highly on desirable personal qualities, and indeed familial love is expected to involve forbearance of flaws and unlikeable qualities in the beloved.[9]

How literal are we prepared to be if we say that someone's being one's parent or one's child is a sufficient reason to love that person? There is frequent talk about the unconditional love of parents for their children, and the argument is that it makes them more psychologically secure and better able to do what is right for reasons other than fear of losing love. There is less talk, at least in American culture, about the unconditional love of children for their parents even when the asymmetry in power and responsibility is reversed as parents age and children become middle-aged adults. On that score there may be important cultural differences in the reasons of relationship that people take seriously and act upon. In the next section, I want to explore a case that poses the issue of cultural differences. I shall also use this case to get deeper into the issues of why constancy of love might be important for human beings and of how to deal with conflicts of value that love gets us into.

Shun's Love for His Family

In the Chinese Confucian tradition, the legendary figure of sage-king Shun (舜, purported to be a ruler of China in the later twenty-third and early twenty-second centuries BCE) is celebrated for his familial love that persisted in the face of three attempts by his father, stepmother, and half-brother to kill him. The story of Shun is a particularly spectacular example of love based on relationship and most definitely not on admirable personal qualities. To many Confucians, Shun's filiality toward his family is heroic and exemplary. To critics of Confucian conception of filial piety, the stories about Shun and his family constitute a reduction ad absurdum of the Confucian conception.

Indeed, continuing to love and protect one's family members even if they try to kill one is an extreme form of filiality many of us would be unable to find acceptable. However, we might see Shun's filiality as an exemplification of the need for forbearance in love, hyperbolic and mythical in the extremity of Shun's filiality, but an exaggeration of something we all need to do in love. If parents are expected simply to love their children, whoever they turn out to be, it is reasonable to ask for some reciprocity to help sustain that love. This is not to deny that parents can give without asking for return in the form of love and forbearance from their children, and it is certainly not to deny that unreciprocated giving is worthy of praise. But we may require reciprocation all the same if it is unreasonable to predict that most parents will do what is worthy of high praise.

At the same time, many of us do place boundaries on love. There are few if any ways of shunning a person that are more final, and either colder or angrier than to say, "You are not my son anymore. You are not my daughter anymore. I disown you." Many of us cannot imagine saying that to our sons or daughters, but perhaps that is because we cannot imagine what they could do or become that would prompt a sincere utterance of those words. Or if we can imagine that, it would mean that our sons or daughters would have become totally different people than we know them to be. But of course, that is also said sometimes, at the end of a love: "You've become a different person. I don't know you anymore." I believe my daughter loves me because I am her father, but I can imagine becoming a different kind of person than I am now, perhaps even a different person than I am now but one continuous with my worse tendencies, and I think that she should not love that person. I would not want her to love that person.

The thought that love requires forbearance of flaws in the beloved but there must be limits to that forbearance is actually addressed by the legends about Shun. As Sarah Allen has pointed out in her perceptive book, *The Heir and the Sage*,[10] there is a potent set of conflicts embodied in the set of legends that concern King Yao 堯 picking a commoner named Shun to assist him in governing the kingdom, Yao's making Shun his son-in-law by giving his two daughters in marriage to him, and Shun's ascension to the throne after Yao despite Yao's son having a hereditary claim to the throne. These legends interweave with those concerning Shun's relationship to his father, his stepmother, and his half-brother. Shun is treated horribly by his father, his stepmother, and his brother. No redeeming personal qualities are attributed to these family members. Yet they have a claim to Shun's filiality. The legends concerning Shun's relationship to Yao and the legends concerning Shun's relationship to his family, as Allen points out, all contain conflicts between the principle of according priority to heredity and the principle of according priority to personal virtue that enables exemplary rulership. Shun is the worthy successor to Yao, rather than Yao's son, but the son is the rightful heir to the throne on the hereditary principle. By giving his daughters in marriage to Shun, Yao has in effect made Shun his son on the basis of Shun's personal qualities. Shun, in assisting Yao's rule of the Empire, has made his own father a subject and replaced him as a father with Yao. These actions exemplify creative ways of resolving conflicts between the imperative to honor family and the imperative to award rule to those who merit it.

As Allen points out, different Chinese texts of the ancient period present different versions of this set of interwoven legends. Each version contains a different way of playing out and resolving the conflicts between heredity and virtue. It is the *Mencius*' telling of these legends that shall interest us here, for his version also exemplifies creativity in resolving the conflicts. Unlike other versions of the legends, neither does Shun succeed Yao by violently overthrowing him, nor does Yao voluntarily abdicate his throne to Shun and pass over his son; rather, Shun administers the Empire for Yao until Yao dies. He does not take the throne but rather gives way to Yao's son. He only becomes King when Heaven appoints him through the people's acceptance of him as ruler rather than Yao's son (5A.5). The effect of the *Mencius*'s version is that Heaven relieves both Yao and Shun from facing the conflict between virtue and heredity.

In Shun's relationship with his family, there is a parallel relief from conflict between filiality and virtue. Shun continues to love his brother Xiang 象 or "Elephant" even after Elephant has conspired with his father and mother to kill Shun. Shun enfeoffs his brother, but gives him territory at a distance from the seat of the throne, and appoints an administrator to govern his brother's fiefdom (5A.3). My reading of

Shun's action is that it reconciles filiality with virtue. Shun continues to act as loving brother to Elephant while protecting himself and the subjects of Elephant's new fiefdom from Elephant's wickedness. Similarly, when Shun marries Yao's two daughters, he does not tell his father, knowing that he would not receive permission to marry. This apparent violation of filiality is justified in the *Mencius* in one place (4A.26) by the claim that it was Shun's overriding filial duty to provide an heir to his father, and in another place (5A.2) by the claim that to let his father prevent his marriage would have prevented Shun from having the most important of human relationships and therefore would have engendered bitterness in Shun, the implication being that such bitterness would have poisoned the filial relationship between father and son. Here the actions that enabled Shun to assist Yao in ruling the kingdom and to attain greater fulfillment are justified as filial acts, even if not in accord with conventional conceptions of filial requirements.

I will not pause to evaluate the plausibility of such justifications, though I have defended them elsewhere. The point of interest here is the attempt to address the tension between heredity and virtue. This tension parallels the tension between loving someone on the basis of worthy personal qualities and loving someone on the basis of relationship. Yao was not the only father to have been disappointed in his son and moved to treat a worthier person as if he were his son. Shun is not the only son who continues to love his father in spite of his father's lacking any admirable personal qualities. Shun is not the only son who hoped to win his father's love through the constancy of his own love. The *Mencius* even places Shun in a hypothetical situation in which his father murders a man. Shun as the King, says Mencius, would have refrained from interfering with his father's arrest, but in the end he would have abdicated the throne and fled with his father. This again is a kind of balancing between filiality and virtue, I would argue, because Shun would not be able to protect his father while he was King, and can only perform his filial duties by relinquishing his kingly duties and casting aside the Empire as if it were an old shoe (7A.35). Each version of the Shun legends conveys a distinctive understanding of the conflict between heredity and virtue, filiality and virtue, and of the possibilities for resolving that conflict. The *Mencius* conveys an allegiance to heredity and filiality but assures us of the possibility for resolution of their conflicts with virtue. In one case, Heaven as the source of order assures us that things will be made whole in the end; in the other cases, Shun's sagacity, which tracks Heaven's order, assures us of a dissolution of the conflict or if the situation makes dissolution impossible, the best way to deal with tragic conflict. The story of Shun is instructive for its acceptance of and attempt to deal with plurality and conflict, and it is this sensibility I want to bring to the task of understanding the plurality in the faces of love I have attempted to describe thus far.

Keeping the Different Faces of Love in Play

I want to argue that the three forms or faces of love—the kind that answers to no reasons, the kind that answers to reasons grounded in personal qualities of the beloved, and the kind that answers to reasons grounded in relationship, must all be kept in play. Accounts that make one of these faces the only or primary kind of love sooner or later display strains that reveal their partiality as accounts.

By singling out parental love as the "purest" form of love, Frankfurt acknowledges that there are other forms of love such as romantic love, but simultaneously demotes them as not "very authentic or the most illuminating paradigms of love as [he] is construing it."[11] This is because romantic love or relationships that are primarily sexual contain "vividly distracting elements" that do not belong to the essential nature of love. Besides not being based on a perception of the intrinsic worth of the beloved, the essential nature of love as Frankfurt construes it includes a "disinterested" concern for the beloved: one does not love someone as a means to getting something else one cares about. One loves that person for her own sake.

Joel Kupperman has discussed a similar aspect of love he describes as a kind of selflessness, a desire for the happiness and well-being of the beloved; but he notes that romantic and parental love also has a self-concerned aspect such as a desire that the beloved reciprocate one's love. Kupperman notes that these two aspects sometimes pull apart from each other. In romantic love, one might regretfully conclude that the well-being of one's beloved requires one's withdrawal from the relationship.[12] His example brings out another aspect of love that could be described as self-concerned, which is the desire to be "with" the beloved. One may not only desire one's beloved's well-being for her own sake, but want also to be an active agent in promoting her well-being. One might also want for one's relationship with her to become part of her well-being, and part of one's own. From my own case I know that loving parents can go from intense and active involvement in a child's life to seeing that kind of involvement steadily diminishing as she ventures into different worlds outside the family. Embracing this change as inevitable and desirable, as necessary for the flourishing of one's child, is compatible with a keen sense of personal loss. Whether one approves of such self-concerned aspects of love, I see no good reason to exclude them as somehow less authentic than purely disinterested forms. The fact that need can distort love does not justify eliminating any role for need in love.

Indeed, when one's own needs as a lover coincide with one's ultimate desire for the well-being of the beloved, it explains how love can be so intense and ecstatic and so deeply satisfying. That congruence of needs can create new needs that involve an "us," since a loving relationship comes to include what "we" do together: our joint pursuit of ends that may go well beyond the relationship itself, that have to do with our social and political values, for example; or how "we" love and try to bring up a child as well as possible, such that "our" love comes to include another; and of course that other can profoundly alter the character of that love.

Frankfurt's desire to elevate a purely conative disinterested form of love as the most authentic form seems unmotivated until one places his theory of love in the context of his theory that normative reasons arise from our own psychologies, and in particular from the special structure of desire he calls caring: not just desiring but also desiring to desire (i.e., to desire that one's first order desire continues); and not just desiring to desire but identifying with this desire as expressing what one really wants.[13] Ultimate caring thus construed is the source of reasons, and love is a special form of caring that is disinterested. Frankfurt goes on to attribute two more characteristics to love. The second is that it is particular in that one does not love something merely as a member of a class; and the third is that, unlike some other forms of caring, it is nonvoluntary. The different aspects Frankfurt attributes to love make sense as a bundle when placed in the context of a theory that attempts to identify the ultimate source of normative reasons in the individual's psychology and not in some feature of the world independent of the individual. One does not love for reasons, but rather love is the source of reasons; it is disinterested because satisfaction of interest would be a reason for love; it is particular because properties defining the class would constitute reasons; and it is nonvoluntary because voluntariness typically brings with it choosing for reasons.

I do not want to so much criticize this theoretical appropriation of love as I want to point out its dangers. When an account of something so multifaceted and central to human life is incorporated into a developed and sophisticated theoretical framework dedicated ultimately to explaining something other than love—the source of normative reasons—there is bound to be strain and de-emphasis of some phenomena that could plausibly be taken as revealing what is typical of love. One such phenomenon, as I observed earlier, is the sense that love can be discerning. Love such as this would have to be relegated to a less authentic, less pure form of love, but if the ultimate criterion for authenticity and purity is goodness of fit within a larger theoretical framework designed to explain the source of normative reasons, one might justly worry about losing touch with forms of love that play central roles in human life and that might seem to be necessary for living what seems to be, at least at the pre-theoretical level, a good human life. If these forms are de-emphasized as less authentic and pure, one might pay less attention to the question of why these forms have loomed large in human life.

Velleman's very different and opposing Kantian theory of love de-emphasizes the same phenomenon of discerning love, but in his case this is for the sake of construing love as a response to the worth that is possessed by all rational beings. His claim that "love is a moral emotion" likewise seems unmotivated until it is placed within the larger theoretical project of explaining agency toward persons in terms of value and valuation, and respect. As love is a purely volitional form of care for Frankfurt, love for Velleman is a form of respect, an emotionally arresting awareness of value existing independently of the perceiver's psychology and possessed by the beloved. Where love is a kind of ultimate caring or desire for Frankfurt, love is a kind of disarming vision of independent value for Velleman. The result of this theoretical appropriation of love is again strain and de-emphasis of some prominent phenomena concerning love in everyday life.

Besides being unable to account for discerning love, Velleman is led to dismiss conative accounts of love as expressing "a sentimental fantasy—an idealized vision of living happily ever after."[14] To support this criticism, Velleman has to identify conative accounts with the desire to share and to be with. But to take one example, Frankfurt's account requires no such desire for love. Essential for Frankfurt is the disinterested concern that, as I pointed out earlier, may require under certain circumstances that one remove oneself from the beloved's presence. The same example shows that the desire to do good for the beloved is not necessary under a conative account. One might nevertheless desire the beloved's good without conceiving oneself as an "agent of that person's interests," in Velleman's terminology. Thus conative accounts of love *can* emphasize disinterestedness in their own way as much as an account that founds love on appreciation for the rational natures of persons. With that said, however, it seems arbitrary to limit all love to disinterested forms. Forms of "interested" love that include the desire to be with and to share cannot be dismissed as the sentimental desire to live "happily ever." One can desire to be with and to share and know that one's desire cannot be fulfilled, and one can love in this sense while accepting one's own deep misfortune.

To take another example of strain in Velleman's account, it entails that we cannot truly love animals because we cannot regard them as having rational natures. To think, therefore, that one loves one's dog or cat, for example, is to be confused. Some support for this position might derive from the way many of us anthropomorphize the animals in our lives. We dubiously attribute to them thoughts and feelings and concerns as if they were our children. But this anthropomorphizing does not necessarily indicate confusion—maybe we don't have to be convicted of false beliefs that our dogs and cats are furry children with four legs and a tail. Perhaps it is rather that we naturally turn to the language of love for our children to metaphorically express the love we have for our animals. Perhaps this is why much of our anthropomorphizing of them is playful in tone, even deliberately absurd and self-mocking.

One solid basis for love of animals, I would think, is that they can fulfill needs for an elemental giving and receiving of affection without the judging gaze of the other. It is precisely the uncomplicated nature of the affectionate relationships between humans and animals as compared to relationships between human beings that can make the former deeply satisfying. In his book, *The Philosopher's Dog*, Raimond Gaita tells of his love during his troubled childhood for the family dog named Orloff, a dog that provided unfailing affection and satisfied his deep need of physical comfort, protection, and security. None of this, Gaita tells us, required him to think that Orloff was a person or that Orloff had capacities he did not possess.[15] If I had to choose between regarding the young Gaita's love for Orloff as genuine and love as restricted to Kantian regard for persons, I would without hesitation choose love for the dog.

Again, this is not so much as to criticize Velleman's account but to point to its dangers. Undoubtedly, love can take the form of a moral emotion in the way Velleman so articulately describes. And it would be unfair to say that the theoretical accounts given by Frankfurt and Velleman are cut off from forms of love that we encounter in everyday life (well, maybe not *every*day life). Franfurt's love for his children is obviously a powerful source of his intuitions about love, as is Velleman's sense that "Love does not feel (to me, at least) like an urge or impulse or inclination toward anything; it feels rather like a state of attentive suspension, similar to wonder or amazement or awe."[16] If we are fortunate, we have had moments such as Velleman describes. What does seem true to me, however, is that theoretical agendas and frameworks designed to promote those agendas drive Frankfurt's and Velleman's choices of which forms of love are to be regarded as primary and which are to be demoted as less authentic, impure, or associated with sentimental fantasy. This has happened in much of the philosophical literature on love because two projects concerning love have been merged. One is the project of explaining and clarifying exactly what love is and this involves philosophers drawing from their own experiences and from what they believe is commonly thought and said about love. The other is the project of incorporating love into a philosophical theory with a separate agenda such as identifying the source of normative reasons or incorporating love into a theory of moral agency. Frankfurt's and Velleman's very different philosophical commitments in the second project lead them to different theories of what love is, and to draw selectively from the mixed and wide range of things people feel and think and say about love.

Yet I think there is a fundamental problem that the debate between these different philosophical accounts of love brings out. In discussing each conception of love—love that answers to no reasons, love that answers to nonrelational reasons, and love that answers to relational reasons, we have seen their advocates argue that their favored conception is based on things that people do feel and think and say about love. But none of these conceptions fully satisfy because these various phenomena associated with love don't seem to hang together coherently. It is not just that the different philosophical theories are based on very different theories of the source of normative reasons. It's that love is plural in form, and the forms can come into conflict with each other. That is why philosophers are led to elevate some forms of love and to demote other forms.

It might be thought about Velleman's Kantian account of love that it is not a representative theory of loving a person on the basis of her nonrelational qualities. The usual suspects for nonrelational qualities are personal qualities, not rational nature. Recall, however, that personal qualities do not yield non-fungibility. It might be thought that relational qualities, i.e., one's relationship to the beloved, provide non-fungibility or something very close to it. Moreover, it might account for the constancy and plasticity of love we desire.[17] However, sometimes one has to make certain decisions about the future course of a relationship which cannot be based on the way the relationship has been in the past or is in the present. There can be a volitional element that can propel one into that future course that need not be based on reasons of relationship. On this matter I think Frankfurt is close to the truth. Of course, depending on how that future course works out, one might be provided with new reasons to love, of either the relational or nonrelational kind. But sometimes one must want to take that leap in order to get the reasons one eventually will have.

Thus, I propose that each of the kinds of reasons to love, and no reasons at all, can play a role in the flow of love. I propose that the phenomena of love do not hang together coherently because we do love in different ways—at different times, in several ways at the same time—because these different forms of love answer to different and compelling needs. The plurality and internal conflict within love answers to the plurality and internal conflict of the human psyche. To make this proposal plausible, I will sketch a naturalistic picture of why love appears in human life, and from this naturalistic picture, I believe we will see why the different faces of love answer to different needs. By a naturalistic picture, I mean one that draws from the human sciences, from evolutionary theory, psychology, and neuroscience. I do not mean to give a reduction of love in terms of scientific theories. I use these theories only to help us to identify what needs the different faces of love answer to. In arguing that each face of love is important and central to human life, I ultimately appeal to certain generalizations about features that a good life has. I stress that these will be generalizations about what goes into *a* good life, not *the* good life. As indicated at the beginning of this essay, I accept that there is a plurality of good lives that are significantly different from each other.

Why Love Has Different Faces

Let me begin with a possible evolutionary explanation of romantic love. Compared to their closest relatives, human beings take far longer to develop their brains and to reach sexual maturity after they are born. One plausible hypothesis is that this prolonged immaturity required pair bonding that lasts at least long enough for partners to cooperate and raise children. In trying to understand why we love as we do, it does not hurt to remind ourselves that our biology gives us the basis for performing these functions even as they are elaborated and developed differently by culture and personal experience, and even when we choose not to perform these functions for reasons that have nothing to do with contributing to the gene pool. Psychological and anthropological studies of love identify the component of attraction, which motivates choice and preference for a mate.[18] This is the phrase of romantic love in which it is good to be discerning, at least when this is permitted by feelings of euphoria when love is reciprocated or forlornness when it is not.

From an evolutionary perspective, it is unsurprising that we should try to be discerning in love. Our human ancestors were equipped with motivations that made it more likely to find mates with good genes. "Fitness indicators" point to an animal's general health and well-being which in turn indicate evolutionary fitness. Large, bright, many-eyed tails function as fitness indicators of peacocks for peahens, precisely because having such tails requires a lot of energy to grow, to preen, and to carry around. Unhealthy and unfit peacocks cannot afford them, and that is why the cost reliably indicates the fitness of a peacock that has one. What is physically attractive about human beings to other human beings might be based on what is a sign of good genes. But it has been argued that sympathy and kindness can function as fitness indicators for human beings, again because of the potential costs to the individual bearing them. Of course, traits that are incompatible with altruism might also function as fitness indicators because of the cost they impose on their bearers, but the advantage of an other-regarding trait is that it benefits the group containing its possessors in ways that other fitness indicators might not.[19] Strikingly, the evolutionary psychologist David Buss found that "kindness" was the single most important feature desired in a sexual partner by both men and women in every one of the thirty-seven cultures he studied.[20] The possible evolutionary explanation of romantic love supports the expectation that love on the basis of personal qualities has and will continue to play an important role in human life.

Evolutionary explanations are immensely popular these days, so it is important to try to identify how they really help us and what their limits are. The evolutionary explanation of the "attraction" element of romantic love does help us to realize that love for reasons, whether these reasons are personal qualities or relational ones, is deeply rooted in psychological processes that lie at the center of human life. The explanation I have presented does not show that loving on the basis of personal qualities is part of a good life. Perhaps we do want healthy children and viable partners in childrearing if we want children at all; but if we do, it is because we endorse those ends as contributing to a good life for ourselves or for others, and not because we want to maximize our contribution to the gene pool. The desire for kindness in a partner, of course, is something we can endorse on very good grounds having nothing to do with having and raising children. That we should look for partners who are a good fit for the sort of people we are and how we go about doing things perhaps has similar evolutionary roots in the choice of a partner for rearing children, but looking in this way is a good idea even if the tasks are supporting each other in demanding careers or the pursuit of causes that go well beyond the welfare of one's own family.

With that caution sign held up, let me next note that psychological and anthropological studies identify another distinct component of love that is often called "attachment" or "companionate love" which prompts pairs to stay together and raise children. In contrast to the tumult of attraction that may involve euphoria or forlornness depending on reciprocation or its lack, attachment typically involves feelings of calm, security, and emotional union with the beloved. Some psychologists have theorized that the kind of attachment between adult pairs that prompts them to work together in raising children has a great deal in common with the attachments they form to those children.[21] For example, in both kinds of attachment, security and tending to one's needs is sought in the other (this relationship is highly asymmetrical in the parent-child case, though may become less so as the child grows toward adulthood), and when attachment is successfully forged, one feels less defensive and more exploratory toward the rest of the world. Brain-imaging studies suggest that some of the same neural systems underlie both romantic attachment between adult pairs and attachment between parents and their children. These overlapping neural systems include the reward circuitry of the brain that activates in response to food, drink, sex, drugs, and money. Furthermore, the brain receptors for the neuro-hormones oxytocin and vasopressin appear to be activated during both romantic and maternal love. These neuro-hormones also seem implicated in social bonds outside the family. Oxytocin facilitates a temporary attachment between strangers, increasing trust, reciprocity, and generosity.[22] Anonymous charitable giving based on moral beliefs has also been linked to networks that control the release of oxytocin and vasopressin.[23]

Areas of the brain associated with negative emotions and with critical social judgments of others showed suppressed activity in both romantic and maternal love.[24] When in love, we may feel as if our beloveds are unique, and we resist comparative judgments that disfavor them. This may be part of what makes the attachment secure (recall my discussion of the need for forbearance in love), and may partly account for reluctance to say that we love on the basis of personal qualities, and even for any reasons at all. Frankfurt's argument that love is a kind of ultimate unreasoned care may be drawing its intuitive appeal from this very deep well in our natures. Kolodny's sense that love on the basis of relational reasons provides constancy may also point us in this direction to the idea that love, at least sometimes, needs relief from judgment and comparison to sustain itself.

As pointed out earlier, on the other hand, change in personal qualities of one's beloved can bring about an end to love, and there are times when none of us could argue that an end isn't for the better. That love at times also turns on reasons might also be expected if we are primed by our biology to seek out suitable partners for an ongoing project, even if we choose to make that project something more or something other than making and raising children. Our biology, I suggest, prompts us both to be discerning and accepting in love, and there are good reasons to continue acting on each imperative that go beyond our biology.

To make everything logically neat, we might try arranging these conflicting tendencies in stages. Perhaps we look for a suitable person with whom to *fall* in love, and then, once *in love*, we do not look for reasons to continue loving even while celebrating what is good and even wonderful in our beloveds. Alternatively, after falling in love, we might still have reasons for love, but these turn into reasons of relationship, as has been suggested by Niko Kolodny.[25] But these neat separations seem artificial and untrue to the dynamic nature of love. As Amélie Rorty has pointed out, love can have a history, a narrative structure.[26] The basis of the relationship can change over time, and while that often happens without lovers consciously deciding it, sometimes the change must be marked, discussed, and negotiated.

Sometimes reconsideration of a relationship involves reconsidering one's conception of the other person. Being in a relationship for a while gives one more information about the other person's tendencies than one has at the beginning, and it can correct an initial conception that was based more on hopefulness than experience. Getting clearer about the other person's personal qualities and getting clearer about the nature of the relationship, both its weaknesses and strengths, are interwoven. I am not saying that how people feel can be decided on the basis of discussion. But each can influence how the other feels through his or her expression of feeling and commitment to the relationship or lack of such commitment. Each can consider how the relationship could continue or change in response to a better view of who the other person is. We must be discerning in love not just at the beginning but also at times when it is necessary to decide how and whether to continue. Love without reasons and love for reasons of either kind cannot be sequenced as earlier and later but alternate in a love with history and mutual adjustment.

As indicated earlier, there is evidence that attachment involves a dampening of negative and comparative judgment of the beloved, along with the feeling that one's beloved is unique. This makes the relationship more secure and may be the source of intuitions people have that love answers to no reasons. Perhaps this form of love plays one of its most critical roles at times in a relationship where things have changed so much that the reasons for loving that one once had no longer apply, but love as ultimate caring sustains a process in which one can come to see and appreciate the beloved in a new light and within the context of a changed relationship that gives one new reasons to love. Seen in the light of what helps to sustain a relationship, loving for no reasons at all is compatible with loving for reasons. If we are fortunate, love can vary according to what is most needed at the time.

We might get a better view of how love can vary and take different forms if we view it as a complex emotion. Complex emotions involve several layers. Love as a complex emotion involves bodily changes, the awareness of which provides the "feeling" of love. Attraction and attachment, along with sexual desire in many cases of romantic love, correspond to different types of bodily changes: attraction involves adrenaline rush, and sometimes a fixation on the beloved that is comparable to the brain processes of those with Obsessive Compulsive Disorder. Attachment, by contrast, is associated with reductions in stress and feelings of calm (the calmest moments of my life have stemmed from my infant daughter sleeping on my chest).

Love as a complex emotion also involves appraisals of the beloved. As has been observed in the burgeoning literature on emotion in psychology and philosophy, initial appraisals in an emotion can be fast, automatic, and nonconscious. They may involve no judgment or belief about the object of emotion but rather a perceptual or quasi-perceptual seeing the object as such-and-such, in the case of love, seeing the beloved as wonderful, desirable, as someone to be protected or as someone who will protect, and so on.

An additional layer of complexity is that appraisals can become reflective and involve judgments. One may fall in love and not have any reasons, be attracted to personal qualities of the beloved, or there may be something that feels right about the fit between oneself and the beloved. But the feeling of the changes wrought in us may prompt an attempt at greater self-understanding of one's own response, or greater understanding of the beloved. Reflection may lead to the recognition of reasons when before we had none, or new reasons in addition to or in place of the old ones. This can lead to a change in how we perceive the beloved and our relationship to that person. Our appraisals—what this person is like to whom we are so drawn and what the relationship is like—could become richer and more detailed. And of course these changing appraisals could both guide and change in response to interactions with the beloved. All this could feedback into how we feel—that is, could prompt the sort of bodily changes that constitute the transition from attraction to attachment. Jenefer Robinson has produced some of the most compelling philosophical work on emotion, and she has emphasized that emotion can be a complex process extended over time in which fast automatic appraisals, the feeling of bodily changes, and reflective appraisals interact and feedback upon one another.[27] This model of a complex process over time is particularly suited, I think, to love, and helps us to see how the three faces of love could each have a basis in what happens during this process.

It might be objected that switching back and forth between competing attitudes is psychologically untenable, somehow impossible, or perhaps psychologically unhealthy. Whether it is untenable or unhealthy might depend on how fast the switching occurs, but I find it difficult to generalize about this. A personality dimension on which people have been found to differ significantly is tolerance of ambiguity. On one end of the spectrum sit people who experience stress and desire avoidance of ambiguous situations that involve unfamiliar, complex, or incongruent cues. On the other end sit people who perceive such situations as desirable, challenging, and interesting.[28] It could well be that that a high degree of tolerance of ambiguity is connected to the ability to tolerate or accept the need for love to change its faces.

What we feel can be so complex, fluid, and elusive that any attempt to label it is inevitably reductive, and the manner in which we reduce it is heavily influenced by the emotional concepts provided by our cultures. But if such concepts are the language of our reflective appraisals, the emotional concepts provided by cultures can influence what we feel through self-fulfilling feedback loops. Culture influences the relative roles of love with and without reasons. Some cultures emphasize that love is something we cannot control, and the dominance of this belief in American culture may contribute to Frankfurt's attribution of nonvoluntariness to love. But this is not a dominant belief in other cultures.

Consider the practice of arranged marriages. There are in fact many different practices that fall under this heading and that tend to get reduced in the West to a stereotypical cluster of characteristics: being arranged by parents without regard to the wishes of their children; being arranged purely for the sake of practical considerations such as maintaining or increasing the financial and social status of the families; and being "arranged" as opposed to "marriage for love." In fact, we find practices of arranged marriage that fit none of these descriptions. Within these practices, parents or other family members look for a suitable match for children and arrange for meetings between "candidates." The purpose is to accomplish marriage if things go well between the couple. In a recent study based on interviews of Beiruti Muslims who were either engaged or married through the arranged marriage system, all the participants deemed love essential to marriage. However, they thought of love as something that could be cultivated after a level-headed assessment of the other person's suitability. When couples meet in an arranged encounter, they already intend to marry if things go well, and in their view it is the intention that fosters love rather than independently growing feelings of attraction and attachment resulting in the decision to marry. A mother of one of the interviewed couples was also interviewed, and she said that couples in arranged marriages were expected to go through two stages: "first they use their reason to check for the right conditions then they let go of their emotions. This is the benefit of an arranged marriage. The man and woman have time to study each other before they start getting attached."[29]

There is not much scientific work on how such arranged marriages work out over time as compared to marriages "for love," but a study of 50 Indian couples, half of whom married for love and half of whom had arranged marriages, were surveyed with questions designed to assess the level of romantic love that existed in the marriage. The couples who married for love and who were married less than a year scored higher than the couples who had arranged marriages who had been married less than a year (70 points for the "love" marriages compared to 58 points for the arranged marriages on a scale of 91). However, the level of romantic love declined steeply for couples in love marriages who had been married 10 years or longer, whereas the level for couples with arranged marriages rose (40 points for the "love" marriages compared to 68 points for the arranged marriages).[30]

Going back to the Beiruti study, level-headed assessment on the basis of personal qualities gets the ball rolling in Beiruti practice of arranged marriage, but the mother's statement also reveals belief that attraction and attachment can come later, when attraction to personal qualities and/or the relationship itself become reasons for loving, or perhaps when a love grows that needs no reasons. The nature of complex emotion allows any of these possibilities and allows them to morph into each other. The Beiruti practice is premised on the assumption that one can deliberately cultivate love if the right person and the right conditions of fit are in place. A similar assumption underlies the Chinese Confucian emphasis on rituals that express reverence, respect, and care for the ancestors and parents who have made one's life possible. If one is receptive to the emotions such rituals are meant to express, one is more likely to feel them through practice, especially if the others with whom one is practicing are feeling them.

If complex emotions are indeed processes extended over time in which fast and automatic appraisals, bodily responses, and reflective appraisals can all interact, such practices might be tapping into the real possibility that we can exercise some control over love. But to confidently assess this possibility, or its denial, we need to know a lot more about the nature of emotion than we do now, and what affects the course of its development. So far, I have argued that switching between loving for reasons of different kinds and loving for no reasons has an important place in a good life for human beings. I have said nothing yet as to whether we can cultivate the ability to deliberately execute such switching in response to the perception that the situation calls for it.

Someone who consistently has this ability, it strikes me, is extremely fortunate or very powerful. This ability requires a high degree of self-knowledge and awareness of what one is feeling as well as knowledge and awareness of the others in relationship are feeling. And then it requires control of one's emotions in light of such knowledge and awareness. Most of us, myself included, could hope only for intermittent flashes of awareness and control, and if we are very fortunate indeed, at the times when it matters to have these things.

Love as a Virtue

Let me make clear what has been implicit in my discussion. I am talking not only about the way love *is*, but also about the way it *should* be. In arguing that love does indeed take on different faces that are irreducible to each other, I have been arguing that it does so because it fulfills important needs in our lives, needs that can change as a relationship evolves. Of course, to do good for the persons involved, a change in the face that love takes on needs to answer to what is needed, and I have been discussing the difficulty of cultivating the ability to accomplish that timely change. In talking about the possibility of cultivating this ability, I have therefore begun talking about the ability to love well and wisely, about love, that is, as a virtue. Some of the most interesting philosophical and scientific work on cultivating emotion has to do with empathy and compassion and not specifically love, but recall that some of the same neurological mechanisms underlying attachment to particular others also underlie our commitment to causes backed by moral beliefs, such as anonymously donating to charities. The apparatus of human practical reasoning is built on top of the oldest layers of the motivational system that were selected during the evolution of the species. Some neuroscientists speculate that the capacity to feel attachment to social causes emerged from a co-evolution of genes and culture that allowed primitive reward and social attachment systems to operate beyond the immediate spheres of kinship and thus enabling human beings to directly link motivational value to abstract collective causes, principles, and ideologies.[31] Our love for particular others, then, may share a motivational base with our care and respect for humanity or human beings as such.

Chinese philosophy, the Buddhist literature on compassion meditation, and the psychological literature on ways to increase self-control are very promising areas to explore in conjunction with each other. In all three bodies of work the ability to shift attentional focus is regarded as important for self-control. In the *Mencius* the necessity to *si* 思 or to reflect upon manifestations of inborn moral impulses, feelings, or intuitions is regarded as crucial for moral self-cultivation. In one crucial passage of the text, Mencius attempts to persuade the king of a Chinese state, King Xuan, that he can become a true king who brings peace to his people. To show Xuan that he can become a true king, Mencius reminds the King of a time when he spared an ox being led to ritual slaughter. Having reminded the King of this moment in way that gets him to recall how he felt compassion (the King remembers that he was led to compare the ox's manifest fear with an innocent man being led to execution), Mencius reminds him that he could similarly spare his people suffering (1A.7).

In Buddhist compassion meditation, the idea is to expand the scope of one's compassion through focusing, typically in the beginning, on wishing for the wellbeing or freedom from suffering of a loved one and then later in training trying to generate a similar state of mind toward everyone in general and no one in particular. Lutz and Davidson conducted a brain-imaging study of master meditators (who had practiced meditation for at least 10,000 hours) as they practiced compassion meditation and found that in comparison with novice meditators performing the same meditation, they showed marked response to emotional vocalizations of distress in the insula region of the brain, important for detecting emotion in others and specifically in mapping bodily responses to emotion such as heart rate and blood pressure and making that information available to other parts of the brain. Activity also increased in the temporal parietal juncture, particularly in right hemisphere, which has been implicated in processing empathy, especially in perceiving the mental and emotional state of others. Lutz and Davidson think that this study suggests the possibility of cultivating compassion through meditation, and are interested in teaching compassion meditation to children as they approach adolescence.[32]

It is often said that compassion involves the ability to regulate one's thoughts and emotions. One way to understand why this might be so is that unmodulated distress and anger can feed a self-preoccupation and defensiveness that obstructs openness to others. This lack of modulation is reflected in activation of the amygdala, which initiates a cascade of bodily changes in preparation for self-defense or attack. In a brain-imaging study in which people were shown photographs of angry or fearful faces, Lieberman and his colleagues found that the amygdala was less active when subjects named their feelings, calling them "anger" or "sadness," for instance. That labeling corresponded to greater activity in the right ventrolateral prefrontal cortex, which is associated with thinking in words about emotional experience and also with inhibiting behavior and processing emotions.

Creswell conducted a survey of participants in Lieberman's brain-imaging study and rated them on their disposition to "mindfulness," a concept from Buddhist meditational practice which involves paying attention to one's present feelings, thoughts, and bodily sensations without passing judgment or reacting. As the mindful meditator is typically instructed, one takes note of these internal events and "lets them go."

Creswell and his colleagues found that subjects in Lieberman's study who were more mindful in disposition had more activation in the right ventrolateral prefrontal cortex and less activation in the amygdala, suggesting that the more mindful bring more prefrontal resources to turn down the amygdala.[33] In other words, the effect of mindfulness may be similar to the effect of "naming" emotions—distancing the self from them and dampening their effects.

I earlier suggested that tolerance of ambiguity might be related to the ability to switch back and forth between the different faces of love in accordance with which face is most needed to occupy the emotional foreground. I wonder, but can only so wonder, if this ability is related to forms of self-regulation that are based on a high degree of emotional self-awareness. To be able to have a distanced perspective on what one is feeling at the present moment (perhaps representing one of the faces of love) might be related to the ability to tolerate that the emotion is in tension with other feelings (perhaps representing the other faces of love) about the same person.

All we have now with this kind of evidence is an interesting set of clues. It is not clear how much self-regulation that emotional self-awareness can confer, or what other psychological, social, and cultural conditions need to be in place if it is to be effective. Mencius's attempted intervention with King Xuan to try to get him to feel compassion for his subjects was in the end not very successful. The King, like many present-day political leaders, might have politely listened to Mencius and then turned to the next prestigious academic who advised him as to when to draft his subjects to make war on a neighboring state. Lutz and Davidson's experiment does not show that 10,000 hours of meditation will make you more likely to respond to real-life cry of distress. And the paired Lieberman-Creswell experiments may show a way toward a kind of self-regulation, but that is at best a necessary condition of compassion, certainly not a sufficient one. What I hope to have made, however, is the case for further exploration of the different faces of love as they play their irreducibly different and apparently contradictory roles in human life, and of the possibilities for the cultivation of such love as a virtue.

Acknowledgments

I hit upon some of the main ideas for this essay in writing a short presentation, "Can Love be Reasoned," for a symposium on love at the

Eastern Division Meetings of the American Philosophical Association on Dec. 28, 2008 in Philadelphia. I am grateful to the other speakers for their stimulating discussions: Harry Frankfurt, Rae Langton, Michal Stocker, and J. David Velleman. The chair and organizer of the session was Ruth Chang, to whom I must give my thanks for prompting me to write about this subject. I must thank Amélie Rorty for a very helpful discussion about the nature of love when we were both fellows at the National Humanities Center in 2007–2008. The present essay is a revision of "Love and Its Place in a Good Life," for presentation at the conference, "Character: East & West, in honor of Joel Kupperman's 50th year at the University of Connecticut," on May 21, 2011. I am grateful to Paul Bloomfield, who led the organization of the conference, and to the audience of that talk, and to those who subsequently engaged me in much stimulating conversation and correspondence about love. It brought home to me what a special philosophical community Kupperman has done so much to create and sustain. Sin Yee Chan and Peimin Ni have generously provided comments that have prompted me to further defend and clarify some critical points.

Notes

1. Neera K. Badhwar accepts that love can be or is non-fungible, but rejects the idea that love can be purely volitional and without reasons. She holds that love involves taking pleasure in the existence and well-being of the beloved, and that this emotion must be based on appreciation of the value in the beloved. This valuing, she further holds, must be based on qualities of the beloved. To reconcile the idea of love of a person for her qualities with the non-fungibility of love, she suggests a "thick" conception of the person that would include a person's concrete style of expression of abstractly specified qualities such as being honesty or generous or optimistic. This concrete expression would be colored by and expressed in that person's particular historical encounters with the world (Badhwar 2003, 64). My reservation about accepting this suggestion is that it seems like more of a rationalization of the volitional attitude that I believe Frankfurt has gotten right. If I love a friend's particular way of being warm and generous, as it has been colored by his past encounters with the world, it seems to leave out the open-endedness of love that can survive a deep change in his way of expressing these qualities, given further encounters with the world.

2. Frankfurt 2004, 39.

3. Here I use the term "nonrelational" in the limited sense of referring to qualities regarded as character traits and that are not specifically qualities of relationship between the lover and the beloved. There may be very few if any

psychological traits that are strictly nonrelational in the sense that they are specifiable independently of any conditions that elicit the relevant attitudes, emotions, or patterns of behavior.

4. Velleman 1999.

5. This point was suggested to me by Amélie Rorty in conversation.

6. Thanks to Sin Yee Chan and Peimin Ni for suggesting that I clarify the difference between kinds of reasons of relationship.

7. Kolodny 2003, 140.

8. Biskupic 2007.

9. I owe the word "forbearance," which seems to me exactly right for capturing this aspect of love, to Amélie Rorty.

10. Allen 1981, 27–54, 131–133.

11. Frankfurt 2004, 43.

12. Kupperman 2007, 55.

13. Frankfurt 2004, 16.

14. Velleman 1999, 353.

15. Gaita 2005, 161–79.

16. Velleman 1999, 360.

17. Thanks to SinYee Chan for raising this point to me.

18. Fisher et al. 2002.

19. For a statement of the sexual selection theory and its application to moral traits, see Miller 2000.

20. Buss 1989. The extent to which sexual selection itself played a role in the evolution of other-regarding emotions and desires remains a highly contested and uncertain issue, of course. Some theorists will even persist in maintaining that the other-regardingness of emotions such as kindness is not basic and always has a self-interested psychological base. Others, while not denying the psychological reality of basic, other-regarding emotions and desires, may not accord sexual selection any large role in the evolution of these motivations but rather point to other selection mechanisms.

21. Shaver and Hazan 1988.

22. Zak 2005, 2008; Zak et al. 2004, 2005, 2007; Kosfeld et al. 2005.

23. Moll et al. 2006, 2008.

24. Bartels and Zeki, 2000, 2004.

25. Kolodny 2003, 140.

26. Rorty 1993.

27. Robinson 2005.

28. Furnham and Ribchester 1995.

29. Nasser and Dabbous 2008.

30. Gupta and Singh 1982. The level of romantic love was scored on the Rubin Love Scale, designed to assess three elements of romantic love: attachment, caring, and intimacy. It was also designed to distinguish "liking" from "loving."

31. Moll et al. 2006, 2008.

32. Lutz et al. 2008.
33. Lieberman et al. 2007, 2011; Creswell et al. 2007.

References

Allen, Sarah (1981). *The Heir and the Sage: Dynastic Legend in Early China.* San Francisco: Chinese Materials Center.

Badhwar, Neera K. (2003). "Love." In Hugh LaFollette (ed.) *The Oxford Handbook of Practical Ethics*, 42–69. Oxford: Oxford University Press.

Bartels, Andreas, and Semir Zeki (2000). "Neural Basis of Romantic Love." *Neuroreport*, 11: 3829–34.

———. (2004). "The Neural Correlates of Maternal and Romantic Love." *NeuroImage*, 21: 1155–66.

Biskupic, Joan (2007). "A New Page in O'Connors' Love Story." *U.S.A. Today.* November 13. At <http://www.usatoday.com/news/nation/2007-11-12-court_N.htm>.

Buss, David (1989). "Sex Differences in Human Mate Selection: Evolutionary Hypotheses Tested in 37 Cultures." *Behavioral and Brain Sciences*, 12: 1–49.

Creswell, J. D., M. Baldwin, M. Way, N. I. Eisenberger, and M. D. Lieberman, "Neural Correlates of Dispositional Mindfulness During Affect Labeling," *Psychosomatic Medicine*, 69 (2007): 560–565.

Fisher, Helen E., Arthur Aron, Deborah Mashek, Haifang Li, and Lucy L. Brown (2002). "Defining the Brain Systems of Lust, Romantic Attraction, and Attachment." *Archives of Sexual Behavior*, 31.5: 413–9.

Frankfurt, Harry G. (2004). *The Reasons of Love.* Princeton, NJ: Princeton University Press.

Furnham, Adrian, and Tracy Ribchester (1995). "Tolerance of Ambiguity: A Review of the Concept, Its Measurement and Applications." *Current Psychology: Developmental, Learning, Personality, Social*, 14.3: 179–199.

Gaita, Raymond (2005). *The Philosopher's Dog.* New York: Random House. Kindle edition.

Gupta, Usha, and Pushpa Singh (1982). "An Exploratory Study of Love and Liking and Type of Marriages." *Indian Journal of Applied Psychology*, 19.2: 92–97.

Kolodny, Niko (2003). "Love as Valuing a Relationship." *The Philosophical Review*, 112.2: 135–189.

Kosfeld, M., M. Heinrichs, P. J. Zak, U. Fischbacher, and E. Fehr (2005). "Oxytocin Increases Trust in Humans." *Nature*, 435: 673–676.

Kupperman, Joel J. (2007). *Classic Asian Philosophy: A Guide to the Essential Texts.* New York: Oxford University Press.

Lieberman, M. D., N. I. Eisenberger, M. J. Crockett, S. M. Tom, J. H. Pfeifer, and B. M. Way (2007). "Putting Feelings into Words: Affect Labeling

Disrupts Amygdala Activity to Affective Stimuli." *Psychological Science*, 18: 421–428.

Lieberman, M. D., T. K. Inagaki, G. Tabibnia, and M. J. Crockett (2011). "Subjective Responses to Emotional Stimuli During Labeling, Reappraisal, and Distraction." *Emotion*. Advance Online Publication. Doi: 10.1037/a0023503.

Lutz, A., J. Brefczynski-Lewis, T. Johnstone, and R. J. Davidson (2008). "Regulation of the Neural Circuitry of Emotion by Compassion Meditation: Effects of Meditative Expertise." *PLoS ONE*, 3.3: e1897. doi:10.1371/journal.pone.0001897.

Miller, Geoffrey (2000). *The Mating Mind*. New York: Anchors Books.

Moll, Jorge, Frank Drueger, Rolansd Zahn, Matteo Pardini, Ricardo De Oliveira-Souza, and Jordan Grafman (2006). "Human Front-Mesolimbic Networks Guide Decisions about Charitable Donation." *Proceedings of the National Academy of Sciences of the United States of America*, 103: 15623–628.

Moll, Jorge, Ricardo De Oliveira-Souza, and Roland Zahn (2008). "The Neural Basis of Moral Cognition: Sentiments, Concepts, and Values." *Annals of the New York Academy of Sciences*, 1124: 161–180.

Nasser, Khaled A., and Yamine Dabbous (2008). "Love at 'Second Sight': The Mediation of Affection in the Lebanese Arranged Marriage Structure." Paper presented 11-20-2008 at the annual meeting of the NCA 94th Annual Convention, San Diego, CA. Online <PDF>. 2008-12-10 from <http://www.allacademic.com/meta/p259374_index.html>.

Robinson, Jenefer (2005). *Deeper than Reason: Emotion and its Role in Literature, Music, and Art*. New York: Clarendon Press.

Rorty, Amélie (1993). "The Historicity of Psychological Attitudes: Love is Not Love Which Alters Not When It Alteration Finds." In N. K. Badhwar (ed.) *Friendship: A Philosophical Reader*, 73–88. Ithaca, NY: Cornell University Press.

Shaver, Philip R., and Cindy Hazan (1988). "A Biased Overview of the Study of Love." *Journal of Social and Personal Relationships*, 5: 473–501.

Velleman, J. David (1999). "Love as a Moral Emotion." *Ethics*, 109.2: 338–374.

Zak, P. J., R. Kurzban, and W. T. Matzner (2004). "The Neurobiology of Trust." *Annual of the New York Academy of Science*, 1032: 224–227.

Zak, P. J. (2005). "Trust: a Temporary Human Attachment Facilitated by Oxytocin." *Behavioral Brain Sciences*, 28: 368–69.

Zak, P. J., R. Kurzban, and W. T. Matzner (2005). "Oxytocin is Associated with Human Trustworthiness." *Hormonal Behavior*, 48: 522–527.

Zak, P. J., A. A. Stanton, and S. Ahmadi (2007). "Oxytocin Increases Generosity in Human Beings." *PLoS ONE*, 2.11: e1128. doi:10.1371/journal.pone.0001128.

Zak, P. J. (2008). "The Neuroeconomics of Trust." In R. Frantz (ed.), *Renaissance in Behavioral Economics*. New York: Routledge.

5

On Reflective Equanimity

A Confucian Perspective

KWONG-LOI SHUN

Introduction

For the past few decades, Joel Kupperman has dedicated himself to the study of Asian and comparative philosophy, along with work in other mainstream areas of inquiry in Western philosophical thought. One such area is ethics, and in this connection, Kupperman has paid special attention to the role of character in our reflections on the ethical life. For him, such reflections can benefit in important ways by being comparative, in the sense of thinking across different traditions of ethical thought, both East and West. In a recent paper titled "Why Ethical Philosophy Needs to Be Comparative," he elaborates on this position by arguing that a broader view that results from this comparative work can help us better appreciate the importance of the transformation of character to our ethical life.[1] The paper is rich, touching on several ethical traditions, including Judo-Christian and Greek, Indian, and Chinese. In my paper, I will take as my starting point some of his comments on the Confucian tradition, or more specifically, on the *Analects* of Confucius.

Kupperman correctly points out that Confucius's central ethical concern is "with how a sort-of-good person could be transformed into a deeply (and reliably) good person," a task that he describes as the "self-conscious development of the self."[2] The kind of "deeply good person" that Confucius has in mind is described in different ways in the *Analects*, and I am interested in a certain kind of description that, on the surface, might seem puzzling. Kupperman cites Confucius's remark that such a person is "easy of mind"; conversely, someone without the relevant qualities "cannot remain long in straitened circumstances, nor can he remain long in easy circumstances."[3] The *Analects* contains several other similar descriptions of the good person, such as how the good person is free from anxiety.[4] This raises an intriguing question. Such qualities as ease of mind, remaining long in easy circumstances, and being free from anxiety seem removed from the kind of ethical considerations that are usually highlighted in contemporary philosophizing. In what way, then, are they part of an ethical ideal?

Kupperman himself hints at an answer to this question immediately after citing the two passages. According to him, the answer has to do with the fact that, whether in adversity or when things are going well, the good person "has the internal values to hold on to."[5] This is the answer I want to explore further in my paper. That is, I will show how, for Confucius and his followers, the kind of qualities we just considered are an inextricable part of the ethical ideal they espouse because these qualities are grounded in a complete orientation to the ethical standards that the Confucians uphold. While my discussion is in essence an elaboration on Kupperman's view, I will go beyond his discussion by drawing on both early and later Confucian thought to extract a more elaborate account of these qualities and of how they are grounded in a complete orientation to the ethical.

For convenience, I will use the term "equanimity" to refer to the cluster of qualities that we just considered. The notion of equanimity is often associated with connotations such as calmness of the mind, maintaining one's balance in the face of trying circumstances, and being unperturbed. For example, the *Webster's Online Dictionary* defines equanimity as "steadiness of mind under stress; evenness of mind; that calm temper or firmness of mind which is not easily elated or depressed; patience; calmness; composure." What I will do in my paper is to spell out the details of a state of mind with qualities that are akin to those just cited and that are highlighted in Confucian thought. At this stage of the discussion, I am merely using "equanimity" as a convenient but vague label to identify the state of mind that will be our subject of discussion. After presenting the Confucian view, I will describe the nature of this state of mind more systematically, and will at that point introduce the term "reflective equanimity" to refer to such a state of mind. The qualification "reflective" highlights the point that such a state of mind is, for the Confucians, grounded in a certain kind of reflective stance.

For the Confucians, that reflective stance is related to an idea central to Confucian thought which, again for convenience, I will refer to as "the primacy of the ethical." I will elaborate on this idea in a way that abstracts from the more substantive elements specific to Confucian ethical thought, and so the primacy of the ethical is an idea that can be shared by other ethical traditions with substantively different ethical ideals. As a result, my elaboration on this idea and on the state of reflectivity equanimity that follows from it has a broader relevance that goes beyond the Confucian ethical tradition.

In my discussion, I will be elaborating on Confucian ideas in a way that I believe will engage and appeal to contemporary readers. In doing so, I am assuming that the ethical concerns and experiences that underlie the ideas of the Confucian thinkers are shared to a significant degree by us nowadays. Undoubtedly, we will need to undertake a certain degree of abstraction, setting aside more specific Confucian ideas that are no longer fully intelligible or appealing to us, to extract ideas that reflect these common concerns and experiences. But my assumption is that there is still a substantive body of ideas of interest to us nowadays even after this process of abstraction.

Obviously we will need to engage in close textual analysis in order to approximate the ideas recorded in the relevant texts that reflect the ethical concerns and experiences of the Confucian thinkers. I will not be engaged in such analysis in this paper; instead, I will draw on the results of the textual analysis that I have already undertaken in other publications.[6] Using as my starting point the outcomes of these past textual studies, I will seek to relate ideas from the relevant texts to our own contemporary ethical experiences, elaborating on them in a way that makes them both intelligible and appealing to us. In doing so, I will go beyond the actual ideas that can be traced to the texts through textual analysis. Although I will refer to the account I present as a Confucian account, I do not intend it to be a faithful representation of ideas in the relevant texts in all their fine details. Instead, it is a Confucian account in the sense that it is based on certain core Confucian ideas that can be extracted from the texts, and that the way I spell out the details of the account fits in with various other ideas that can also be traced to the Confucian texts. Here, in speaking of how the account might "fit in" with ideas in the texts, I mean only that it provides a way of making sense of these ideas, not that it provides the only way of elaborating on these ideas.[7]

In the following section, I will describe an idea, which I have referred to as "the primacy of the ethical," from Confucian thought that

I will take as my starting point. With this discussion as background, I will elaborate on the different aspects of the state of mind, which at this point I have referred to as "equanimity," that follow from this idea, drawing on both early and later Confucian thought for this purpose. The sections entitled "Invulnerability and Contentment" and "Acceptance" focus mostly on ideas already highlighted in early Confucian thought, and "Detachment in Engagement" focuses mostly on ideas highlighted in later Confucian thought. But this distinction reflects only a difference in emphasis, as the ideas presented in these three sections are intimately related to each other. In the course of presenting the Confucian view on the subject, I will introduce the notion "reflective equanimity" more formally to refer to the state of mind under consideration. In the final section, I conclude with some general remarks on the Confucian view of reflective equanimity, and raise a potential problem for the Confucian view calling for further inquiry that I plan to undertake in another paper.

The Primacy of the Ethical

By the primacy of the ethical, I have in mind a Confucian view that has four components. First, the Confucians share a substantive account of an ethical ideal that concerns not just observable behavior but also various activities of the mind, including emotions and feelings, as well as the minute thoughts and other subtle activities of the mind.[8] There are inevitably differences among Confucian thinkers on specific elements of the ethical ideal they espouse, such as the extent to which they allow deviation from established ritual practices, but they do share sufficient common elements for us to speak of a Confucian ethical ideal in a substantive sense.

Second, Confucian thinkers share the belief that everyone is capable of attaining this ethical ideal. Many, including Mencius and later Confucians such as Zhu Xi and Wang Yangming who proclaim themselves Mencians, hold the view that everyone is capable of attaining the ideal through one's own effort. Some, such as Xunzi, and to a greater extent Dong Zhongshu, believe that while everyone is so capable, they might need to depend on external guidance to actually succeed. In any instance, there is at least one important trend in Confucian thought that holds the view that everyone can attain the ideal through one's own effort, though the process of so cultivating oneself might take time and effort. I will be focusing primarily on this trend in Confucian thought.

Third, all Confucian thinkers hold the view that following the ethical path is of greater significance by comparison to any other kinds of pursuit or to the external conditions of life. They do not deny that other things are important, such as life and death, or the well-being of beloved ones, but they believe that there is nothing more important than following the ethical path, and consequently that any other pursuits in life should be subject to the constraints of the ethical. This is reflected in the way they understand *yi* 義, a term that has the earlier meaning of a sense of self-regard, or a refusal to subject oneself to disgrace. From early on, the Confucian thinkers transformed the understanding of *yi* by insisting that what is truly disgraceful is not the way one is viewed or treated, but for one to fall below certain ethical standards whether in action or in one's thoughts and feelings.[9] One should conform to such ethical standards under all circumstances, and *yi* as an ethical attribute refers to a firm commitment to such standards.

Fourth, not only do the Confucians believe that upholding such ethical standards is of the utmost significance, but it is also part of the ethical ideal they espouse that one should attain a state of mind that is fully shaped in the direction of the ethical. That is, ideally, not only should one be aware of the importance of the ethical and be firmly committed to it, but all aspects of the mind's activities should be shaped in accordance with it. This complete ethical orientation of the mind they refer to as *cheng* 誠 (being real, being whole), a term also explained in terms of oneness, that is, the absence of any discrepancy within the mind.[10]

By primacy of the ethical, I refer to a reflective view that incorporates the above four elements. Specifically, it (1) works with a substantive account of an ethical ideal that has to do with not just behavior but also with various activities of one's mind, (2) regards it as fully within one's control to attain the ethical ideal, (3) regards the ethical as of greater significance than other pursuits or conditions of life though the latter may also be of significance, and (4) advocates a transformation of one's whole person so that one is completely oriented toward the ethical. This view, as I will try to show in the rest of this paper, results in an ethical ideal that includes the kind of qualities that I have referred to as "equanimity."

To give a quick summary of the overall argument, let us consider the state of mind of someone who has attained a complete orientation toward the ethical. The primacy of the ethical does not deny the significance that one may attach to other pursuits and conditions of life, and so this person would still be engaged in various kinds of pursuits and be affected by various conditions of life, whether favorable or unfavorable. He may be frustrated, feel sorrow or joy, and be subject to all kinds of emotional responses. Given his complete orientation to the ethical, he would not seek to alter adverse conditions of life by unethical means, however trying the circumstances. And being aware that he is abiding by the ethical, which for him is of greater significance than any other condition of life, he would, despite the adverse circumstances of life, take contentment in the fact that he is abiding by the ethical and would stay unperturbed by his more immediate responses. What we have is a picture of the mind operating at two levels: it is actively engaged in all kinds of pursuits and is emotionally affected by various conditions of life at one level, while it stays unperturbed and calm at another. Equanimity describes the posture of the mind at the second level, on which one keeps a distance from one's more immediate responses to situations one confronts, and maintains a balanced perspective while staying emotionally calm. In the following two sections, I will elaborate more on this posture of the mind, and in the section following those, I will discuss the relation between the two levels on which the mind operates.

Invulnerability and Contentment

One implication of the primacy of the ethical is that someone who has attained the ethical transformation it advocates will be invulnerable in two senses. He will be firmly committed to the ethical and will not be led to deviate from it by external influences. This firmness of commitment is conveyed in the *Mencius* in terms of the idea of the "unmoved mind"—as long as the mind realizes that it is holding on to the ethical, it will not be subject to fear or uncertainty as a result of external influences.[11] This firmness of commitment is beautifully conveyed in another passage in the *Mencius*:

> He cannot be led into excesses when wealthy and honored or deflected from his purpose when poor and obscure, nor can he be made to bow before superior force. This is what I would call a great person.[12]

Not only is the person not vulnerable to the potentially distortive influences of external circumstances because of this firm commitment to the ethical, but this firm commitment itself is also something that no external force can deprive one of. It is a matter of one's setting one's mind on the ethical, and what one sets one's mind on is something entirely within one's control and not subject to external influences unless one allows it to. This point Confucius conveys by saying that:

> [w]hile an army can be deprived of its commander, even the commonly clad person cannot be deprived of that on which he has set his mind.[13]

Thus, one sense in which the person is invulnerable is that, once he has set his mind on the ethical, he cannot be led to deviate from the ethical nor be deprived of this firm commitment to the ethical by any external influence.

Another sense in which he is invulnerable is that he cannot be harmed by others in a way that is of the deepest significance to him. He does attach importance to various pursuits and conditions of life other than the ethical, and so he can be affected if things do not go well. He can be frustrated if he fails in his endeavors, can feel sorrow upon the loss of a beloved one, and can feel hurt at the way he has been treated by others. In these various ways, he can still be harmed. However, he is aware that what is of greatest significance, namely, following the ethical path, is something entirely within his control and cannot be affected by external influences. Thus, he cannot be harmed in the way that is of the deepest significance to him: deviating from the ethical. Such harm can only be self-inflicted, as the only person who can lead him to deviate from the ethical is he himself. This sense of invulnerability is related to the idea that a good person cannot be harmed, at least in the way that truly matters, an idea found in other traditions that share the structural feature of what I have called the primacy of the ethical.[14] It also follows from the primacy of the ethical that it is worse to do than to suffer wrong—it is the person who commits wrong doing who has been harmed in the sense that truly matters.[15] This explains how someone who has suffered wrong at the hands of those who have been manipulated could have pity on the latter—although they have done wrong to oneself, they themselves, in having been manipulated to do wrong, are the ones who have been harmed the most.

So far, we have focused on a firm commitment to the ethical that grounds the two senses of invulnerability just described. But what the Confucians advocate is not just such a firm commitment, but a total reshaping of oneself in the ethical direction. As mentioned earlier, this complete orientation toward the ethical is conveyed through the notion *cheng* 誠 (being real, being whole), and it involves not just a reshaping of one's way of life, but also one's thoughts and feelings, including the subtle and minute activities of the mind, in an ethical direction. The state of *cheng* is often related to *le* 樂, both by Mencius and by later Confucians under his influence.[16]

The character *le* is often used in the *Analects* to describe the ethically accomplished person. In *Analects* 6.11, Confucius comments on his favorite student Yan Hui:

> The Master said, 'How admirable Hui is! Living in a mean dwelling on a bowlful of rice and a ladleful of water—others would find unbearable their anxiety, but Hui would not let this affect his *le*. How admirable Hui is!'[17]

Confucius also refers to his own *le*, and remarks how his *le* in moral learning leaves no room for anxiety; the reference to the absence of anxiety occurs in other passages in the text.[18] As I have argued elsewhere, what *le* in these contexts refers to is not a state of emotional exhilaration or excitement, but a state of moving along at ease with the flow of things, calmly and without obstruction, in the way in which one immerses oneself in and dances to the rhythm of elegant music.[19] The character *le* is the same as the character *yue* which refers to music, and in *Mencius* 4A.27, Mencius draws a connection between *le* and music:

> When *le* arises how can one stop it? And when one cannot stop it, then one begins to dance with one's feet and wave one's arms without knowing it.[20]

This understanding of *le* is stated explicitly by Zhu Xi, who explains *le* in terms of one's flowing along with things contentedly, with ease and without effort. Commenting on *Analects* 6.11, Zhu says:

> Master Cheng said, 'The mind of Yan Hui . . . is at ease and contented, and it is in a state of *le* wherever he is. It is not that he regards the Way as worthy of *le* and have *le* as a result.'[21]

And commenting on *Mencius* 4A.27, Zhu says:

> To say that *le* arises is to say that one is flowing along at ease and without the need for effort.[22]

Thus, for the Confucians, *le* in the ethical context is a state in which one is immersed in the ethical, flowing along with it at ease and without anxiety. To reflect this understanding of *le*, I will translate *le* as "contentment" when *le* is used in such a context.

Note that what I have described is the Confucians' understanding of an ideal state of mind that they refer to as *le*. My point is not that the character *le* is generally used in this sense in the classical Chinese language, only that it is used in this sense when used in Confucian texts to refer to an idealized state of mind.[23] The early Chinese do have a conception of states of mind that are more like emotional exhilaration or excitement, akin to the connotations of the English words "joy" and "delight." *Le* is sometimes used outside of the Confucian context to refer to such a state, though there are other terms, such as *xi* 喜, that are more commonly used for such purposes. There are important differences between such a state and the state of mind idealized by the Confucians. The former is a more immediate response to one's environment, such as a response to one's obtaining what one desires, and it can come and go as the way one relates to one's environment changes. It is a state more closely linked with the way one feels, and is not necessarily grounded in some reflective outlook on life. The latter, the state of mind idealized by the Confucians, is by contrast grounded in a reflective stance, namely, one's awareness that one is flowing along with the ethical and one's affirmation of such an orientation. As such, it is a more enduring state by comparison to the former. While it involves one's feeling a certain way, it is not primarily a matter of feelings as it also involves the reflective stance just described. Even the way it feels is different—rather than moments of exhilaration that come and go, it involves a more enduring sense of calm and stability, as well as a sense that things are under one's control, a point highlighted in our earlier discussion of the idea of invulnerability.

As highlighted in some of the passages cited earlier, contentment (*le* 樂) is contrasted with anxiety, where "anxiety" is a translation of the character *you* 憂. Now, even a Confucian can have worries, as when one is worried about the health of an ailing parent. There are other terms that are more typically used to refer to such a state of worry, such as *ju* 懼, though the character *you* can also be used for such purposes. But when the Confucians use *you* by contrast to *le*, where *le* refers to an idealized state, they are using *you* in the sense of a disturbed or unsettled state of mind, a state in which one dwells on one's worries in a way that one loses control of oneself and is led along by one's emotions. For the Confucians, *le* as an idealized state of mind is compatible with worries of the former kind, which are directed to specific aspects of one's environment, but not with anxiety of the latter kind. One's awareness that one is flowing along with the ethical, along with one's affirmation of such an orientation, anchors oneself so that one does not lose control of oneself to one's more immediate responses to the environment.

This discussion of contentment (*le*) and anxiety (*you*) suggests the picture of the mind working on two levels. At the level of immediate responses to specific situations in one's environment, one will exhibit emotional responses of all kinds, including joy and worry, such responses changing with the way one relates to one's environment. At another level, one's state of mind exhibits a stability, characterized by contentment and an absence of anxiety, which is grounded in the kind of reflective stance described earlier. We will return to this two-tiered picture of the mind in the section on "Detachment in Engagement." For now, let us consider another related quality also highlighted in early Confucian thought.[24]

Acceptance

The idea of invulnerability described above provides a sense in which the truly good person transcends the adverse circumstances of life—the latter cannot lead him to deviate from the ethical, and cannot harm him in the sense that truly matters. The idea of contentment complements the idea of invulnerability by describing how the good person flows along, contentedly and at ease, with the ethical. In addition to these two ideas, there is another idea that concerns how the good person relates to the adverse circumstances of life, not just in the sense of being unaffected by them, but in the sense of willingly accepting them. This posture is conveyed by the early Confucians through the use of the term *ming* 命.[25] Acceptance is a posture directed to adverse circumstances of life that are either literally not within one's control, or can only be altered through unethical means that one would not adopt. One is still affected by these adverse circumstances—one feels sorrow at the death of a beloved one, is disappointed by the lack of appreciation by others, or laments the ethical corruption of the times. But one would not be bitter and resentful, and would not devote energy to complaining about the outcome. One might think about what has happened to learn from it and to find a way of responding to it, but one would not dwell on thoughts about how things could have been different nor seek to alter things by improper means. Furthermore, one would redirect one's energy in a positive direction, as when Confucius turned to teaching after realizing the inevitable futility of his political endeavors. Realizing that the desired political transformation was not possible during his lifetime, he turned to teaching his students in preparation for change in a future generation.

To better understand the Confucian notion of acceptance, let us contrast it with other ways of viewing the external conditions of life that it should not be identified with. The posture of acceptance is not based on a general belief about how things could not be otherwise, and in that sense is not a fatalistic attitude. Instead, it is a posture taken up in response to particular situations that are of significance and that go contrary to one's wishes. The posture is not one of resignation in the sense of losing hope and seeing all action as pointless, as when a prisoner of war resigns to his imprisonment. Nor is it a matter of inertia in the sense of unreflectively flowing along with the circumstances, as in the case of a slave unreflectively going along with the fact that he was born enslaved. In these other instances, the posture involved is one of subordination to the environment.[26] By contrast, the posture of acceptance that the Confucians advocate enables one to transcend the environment in a certain sense. While being aware of the unavoidability of what has transpired and while being emotionally affected by it, one at the same time distances oneself from it in that one does not fixate on what has happened and is not overwhelmed by one's emotional responses. One does not lose control of one's life; instead, one redirects one's energy to other pursuits in areas in which one can make a difference. That acceptance involves this kind of independence from external circumstances shows its linkage to the idea of invulnerability described earlier, the latter also having to do with one's transcending the influences of external circumstances. The two differ in that, though both have to do with the way one relates to the adverse conditions of life, the idea of invulnerability focuses more on one's not being influenced by them, while the idea of acceptance focuses more on how one transcends such conditions by actively redirecting one's energy.

Acceptance is also different from another way of viewing certain events in one's life that is sometimes conveyed through the notion of fate.[27] For example, an accomplished philosopher might say that it was fate that, when he was in his late teens, he read an inspiring work that turned him to the path of philosophy. In so using the word "fate," he is assigning to a certain event in his life a special purpose—the event plays a pivotal role in steering his life in a certain direction. The posture of acceptance differs in that it is directed specifically to an adverse condition of life, and is not a matter of assigning a special purpose to that condition. Instead, the posture involves one's viewing that unfavorable condition of life in a broader context, so that whatever pain or frustration one feels is mitigated, not by assigning that condition a special purpose, but by seeing that it pales in significance compared to one's commitment to the ethical.

Acceptance relates to the primacy of the ethical in that, by seeing how other pursuits and the external conditions of life pale in significance by comparison to the ethical, one relaxes the importance that one attaches to them and can transcend them in the sense just described. The relation between the two is particularly highlighted when we consider adverse conditions of life that one could have literally avoided though only through unethical means. Consider, for example, a Confucian official in a politically corrupt environment who could have defended himself against political attacks only by employing political vehicles, such as the deliberate manipulation of perception, which he finds ethically objectionable. The official would refrain from adopting such means and would instead accept the political damage that he could have otherwise prevented. He would accept the outcome in the same way he would accept other adverse conditions of life that he literally could not have prevented—he would not fixate on or be overwhelmed by what happened, and would redirect energy to seeking other vehicles of change. What makes this case different is that the outcome is not literally unavoidable, though it is viewed as unavoidable. The official regards the political harm as something that he "cannot" avoid, where the "cannot" derives from his character rather than just from the circumstances. Being experienced in politics, he knows the kind of political maneuvers that could have helped prevent the outcome, and so in a sense he has the needed political skill. Yet, by virtue of the kind of person he is, he cannot bring himself to so act; here, the inability is an inability of the heart rather than a lack of skill.

This kind of "practical impossibility" is a converse of the notion of "practical necessity" that has been well explored in the literature.

Such phenomena have to do primarily with the limiting of options, where certain options are precluded not literally, but by virtue of one's character.[28] What is special about the Confucian view is that the way in which such options are precluded involves repulsion of a certain kind. Now, one maybe pained and as a result repelled by the thought of harm happening to another whom one cares about. This sense of repulsion is related more to the ethical attribute *ren* 仁 (humaneness, benevolence), and is conveyed through the notion *bu ren* 不忍, a term meaning one's being unable to bear the thought of harm occurring to others.[29] The sense of repulsion under consideration, however, is more closely related to the ethical attribute *yi* 義 (righteousness, sense of duty). It has to do with the insistence on upholding certain ethical standards, and the sense that one's acting otherwise is below oneself and is tainting on oneself. This attitude toward acting below one's ethical standards is conveyed through the term *chi* 恥, which involves a sense of disdain toward what one regards as below oneself.[30] From the perspective of the Confucian official, the alternative to what he "cannot" avoid is viewed as something deeply repelling and much worse than the political damage that he accepts.

Thus, acceptance is a posture directed toward adverse conditions of life that one regards as something that one cannot avoid, where the "cannot" is construed broadly to include constraints coming from the external circumstances or from one's own character.[31] Acceptance, along with the sense of invulnerability and of contentment discussed in the previous section, depict a posture of the mind that exhibits the characteristics usually associated with the notion of equanimity—being emotionally calm and not perturbed, and maintaining a balanced perspective despite the trying circumstances of life. For this reason, I have introduced the term "equanimity" to refer to this state of mind at the beginning of the paper. However, as should be clear by this stage of the discussion, the state of mind we are discussing in relation to Confucian thought also has certain characteristics not adequately conveyed by the ordinary use of the term "equanimity." The state of mind we are considering is not a matter of one's immediate responses to one's environment, and is not something that comes and goes as the way one relates to one's environment changes. One does feel a certain way by virtue of being in that state of mind—there is a sense of calm, of being at rest and at peace, of not moving around or being agitated, and of being in control of oneself and not being a captive of one's environment. At the same time, the state of mind also involves a certain reflective stance, namely, one's awareness and affirmation of the fact that one is flowing along with the ethical. It is a more enduring state that is grounded in this reflective stance, and it involves a certain outlook, posture, or orientation in life, having to do not just with one's feeling a certain way, but also with the way one views and relates to the world. To highlight the point that it is grounded in a reflective stance, I will from now on use the term "reflective equanimity" to refer to such a state of mind.

Detachment in Engagement

Our discussion in the previous two sections shows that the state of mind of someone who has fully transformed himself in an ethical direction can be viewed as operating at two levels. On the one hand, he does care about various conditions of life, and would take appropriate action to pursue what he does care about, as well as respond to the outcomes in a way that engages his emotions and feelings. As mentioned in the earlier discussion of contentment (*le*) and anxiety (*you*), he may exhibit emotions of all kinds, including joy and worry, as part of his immediate responses to his environment. On the other hand, even if the outcomes go against his wishes and he responds with disappointment, frustration, pain, or sorrow, he would at the same time take on a posture that enables him to stand apart from such responses. Having done what he could within the bounds of the ethical, he would accept the outcomes in the sense described in the previous section, and would not dwell on them in a way that leads to anxiety, fear, or uncertainty. Instead, he would stay contented in the awareness that what is of greatest significance to him, namely following the ethical path, remains intact. For convenience, I will use the term "engagement" (as opposed to "disengagement") to describe the first-order responses of the mind to situations it confronts, and the term "detachment" (as opposed to "attachment") to describe the mind's second-order posture which involves a distancing of the mind from its first order responses. These two aspects of the operations of the mind may thus be described as "detachment in engagement."

This picture of the mind as having two aspects of operation, which is already implicit in the early Confucian ideas that we discussed in the previous two sections, is particularly highlighted in later Confucian thought. For example, Wang Yangming puts it in terms of a distinction between the operation of the emotions and the way we relate to these emotions:

> The seven emotions follow their natural courses of operation. . . . But we should not be attached to them. . . .[32]

That is, we should respond emotionally to the conditions of life in ways appropriate to them, and yet at the same time we should stand apart from such responses and maintain a more removed posture. This picture of the mind is often presented in terms of the metaphor of a clear mirror or still water. For example, Wang remarks that the mind

> is like a clear mirror . . . It reflects things as they come, without retaining any residue. This is what is meant by the saying that 'the sage's emotions follow the ten thousand affairs and he has no emotion of his own.'[33]

Like a clear mirror or still water, which reflects accurately without itself being affected by the reflections, the mind should also respond appropriately to what it encounters but should itself stay unaffected by such responses.

This picture of the mind has also been presented in relation to specific emotions such as anger or sorrow. For example, Zhu Xi notes how

> (the sages) are angry when they should (be), and (their anger) hits the mark. But when the affair is over, (their anger) dissipates and there is no residue.[34]

Wang Yangming also notes how, ideally:

> Although we are angry, our minds are broad and stay unperturbed.[35]

The idea is again that, while anger is an appropriate response to a situation that one finds problematic, one should at the same time keep a distance from such response and not be personally involved, so that once the problematic situation has been addressed, the anger dissipates.[36]

Let us consider sorrow as another example. Wang Yangming was once asked how contentment (*le*) can be compatible with sorrow, such as one's sorrow upon the death of a parent. His response is that

> [t]here is contentment only if the son has cried bitterly. If not, there will not be contentment. Contentment means that despite crying, one's mind is at peace.[37]

The point is that crying bitterly out of sorrow is an appropriate response to the death of a parent, and there will not be contentment unless one has responded appropriately. Again, we see a distinction between the first-order response of sorrow, and the second-order posture of contentment which is based on the awareness that one has responded appropriately to the situation.

Thus, the engaged responses of the mind reflect the fact that we do care about various things in life; there can be genuine pain at what has transpired, even if we realize that it is the ethically appropriate thing to let it transpire. So, on one level, we are vulnerable to genuine injury and pain, and are subject to all kinds of emotional responses. At the same time, the detached posture of the mind reflects the fact that, on another level, we stay anchored and unperturbed despite the first order responses. That we remain detached in this sense does not mean that we do not really care about the things to which we respond emotionally; it means only that there is something of greater significance to us, and our awareness that what is of greatest significance stays intact enables us to stay unperturbed by these first-order responses.

Although we have spoken of two different levels on which the mind operates, this is just a metaphorical way of describing two interconnected aspects of the mind's operations. The "detached" posture of the mind refers to that aspect of the mind having to do with a posture grounded in a reflective awareness that one is abiding by the ethical and a reflective affirmation of this way of life. This reflective stance enables one to stay anchored and unperturbed by one's immediate environment and one's responses to that environment. The "engaged" responses of the mind refer to one's responses to specific situations in one's immediate environment, which take into account other things that one also cares about in life. But such "engaged" responses are themselves affected by the "detached" posture, as what this "detached" posture does is to ensure that one's "engaged" responses properly reflect what we regard as important. This point is also illustrated by the metaphor of the clear mirror or still water—the clear mirror or still water still reflects, and what its clarity or stillness does is to ensure that the reflections are accurate to what has been presented. Thus, while the detachment of the mind means that it maintains a distance from its more immediate responses to the environment, the detached mind is not just serving as a mere spectator to such responses.[38] To speak of the mind as operating at two levels is just a metaphorical way of describing two interacting aspects of the operations of the mind—the direct responses to situations one confronts, and the more reflective posture one takes toward one's responses, a posture rooted in a commitment to the ethical.[39] These two aspects of its operations are part of a unified mind, and the reference to two levels of operation is not intended to suggest a segregation in the mind's operations.[40]

On Reflective Equanimity

Earlier, I characterized the primacy of the ethical as a reflective ethical view with four elements: it works with a substantive account of the ethical, regards it as fully within one's control to attain the ethical ideal, regards the ethical as more important than other conditions of life that are also of significance, and advocates a total transformation of oneself so that one is completely oriented in the ethical direction. The discussion of the previous three sections describes the state of mind of a person who endorses such a view and who has transformed himself accordingly. "Reflective equanimity" refers to the more "detached" posture of the mind described in these three sections, and in this sense the Confucian view of reflective equanimity follows from the primacy of the ethical.

Note that, in ordinary usage, the word "equanimity" can be used to describe the way one calmly responds to a specific situation. For example, one may be said to exhibit equanimity in one's calmly responding to a deliberately insulting remark. What I have been focusing on is not specific responses of this kind; instead, my focus is on an enduring state of mind that is grounded in a reflective stance. For this reason, I have deliberately introduced the notion of reflective equanimity to refer to such a state of mind. Furthermore, for the Confucians, reflective equanimity is based not just on a reflective awareness and affirmation of the significance of the ethical, but also on a total reshaping of oneself to embody this awareness and affirmation. As a result, one would follow the ethical without effort even at the expense of things of deep personal significance to oneself. Such a transformation involves a fundamental reshaping of one's outlook on life as well as one's whole mode of being, including not just thoughts, feelings, and actions, but also one's demeanor and posture. In this sense, the Confucian ideal of reflective equanimity may be described as a spiritual ideal, if the spiritual is understood in a way that is divorced from pietistic and devotional practices.

Ideals of reflective equanimity are not specific to the Confucian tradition. As we have seen, the Confucian view of reflective equanimity is grounded in the idea of the primacy of the ethical. But the four elements in terms of which we characterized the primacy of the ethical do not include a specification of what the ethical ideal is substantively like, and so they could also be shared by other ethical traditions with very different substantive accounts of the ethical ideal. Thus, our discussion of the Confucian view of reflective equanimity has a broader relevance that goes beyond Confucian thought, extending to other ethical traditions that also subscribe to the primacy of the ethical.

Furthermore, there can be other reflective ethical views that ground reflective equanimity in other ways. For example, an ethical tradition might hold the view that, while we do regard things as of significance in our day-to-day activities, at a more reflective level, we should realize that such apparent significance is just a product of the perspective that we happen to have adopted, whether through upbringing or other means. While we continue to be emotionally affected at the level of first order responses, this realization enables us to relax the importance we attach to various conditions of life, so that we stay unperturbed at another level. Such a view is like the Confucian view in advocating a reflective awareness, and an embodiment of that awareness, that leads to a relaxation of the importance we attach to various conditions of life. It differs from the Confucian view in that the reflective awareness it advocates does not involve a substantive account of the ethical, though it itself can be described as an ethical view in that it also espouses a view of how humans should live.[41]

As another example, an ethical tradition might hold the view that, while we do regard things as of significance in our day-to-day activities, everything pales in significance compared to our devotion to some deity. While we would still be emotionally affected by the adverse circumstances of life, we can at the same time take consolation and contentment in the realization that we have lived fully in the service of that deity. This view is structurally similar to the Confucian view in that it acknowledges the genuine significance of the other conditions of life while at the same time regarding them of lesser significance compared to something that has primacy in the sense that we described earlier. It differs from the

Confucian view in that what takes primacy has to do ultimately with devotion to some deity, rather than to the ethical as such.[42]

To conclude, let us consider a potential worry about the Confucian view that I hope to investigate further in another paper. Reflective equanimity is a posture toward adverse conditions of life that is grounded in the awareness that these other conditions of life pale in significance compared to the importance of following the ethical path. But what if these conditions themselves involve the frustration of the objects of one's ethical endeavors—would there not be something objectionable in a posture that regards these endeavors themselves as more important than their objects? If the object of one's ethical endeavors concerns the well-being of others, the potential worry is that, in taking consolation in the fact that one has done what is ethically appropriate despite the failure of one's endeavors, one is putting more weight on one's own ethical qualities than on the well-being of others. And if the object of one's ethical endeavors is the ethical transformation of a corrupt environment, the objection takes on a particularly disturbing form—it seems that one is putting more weight on one's own ethical qualities than on the ethical qualities of others. In either instance, it appears that the Confucian view is open to the potential charge of a form of moral self-indulgence. This charge would not arise if we share an optimistic belief, found in some Confucian classics such as the *Zhongyong*, to the effect that the ethical transformation of oneself will inevitably lead to the ethical transformation of as well as a nourishing effect on others. This optimistic belief, while potentially appealing when we are considering the transformative and nourishing effect of a virtuous ruler of a small state, does not seem realistic as a general observation about humans. We are thus left with a potential worry about the Confucian view on grounds of moral self-indulgence, a subject that I hope to address in another paper.

Acknowledgments

This paper was first presented at a Mini-Conference in Honor of Joel J. Kupperman at the Tenth East-West Philosophers' Conference at the East-West Center, Honolulu, May 16–24, 2011. I have benefitted from comments by participants at the conference. I am particularly indebted to the editors of this volume for very helpful and detailed comments, which have helped improve the paper.

Notes

1. Kupperman 2010.

2. Ibid., 189, 194.

3. Ibid., 197–198. Kupperman cites *Analects* 7.37: "The gentleman is easy of mind" (君子坦蕩蕩), and *Analects* 4.2: "One who is not benevolent cannot remain long in straitened circumstance, nor can he remain long in easy circumstances" (不仁者不可以久處約 不可以長處樂). For citations from the *Analects*, I have followed the numbering of passages in Yang 1980, and my translation of passages from the *Analects* follows, with occasional modification, Lau 1992.

4. *Analects* 9.29; cf. 7.19.

5. Ibid., 198.

6. The textual analysis has been undertaken in my *Mencius and Early Chinese Thought* (1997) and *Zhu Xi and Later Confucian Thought* (manuscript under revision).

7. See Shun 2009 for a discussion of my overall methodological approach in the study of Confucian and comparative ethics.

8. Throughout my paper, I use the word "mind" as a translation of the Chinese character *xin* 心. The character *xin* refers to the organ of the heart, which the Chinese traditionally regard as the site of what we would now call cognitive and affective functions.

9. For a discussion of the Confucian understanding of *yi*, see my "On Anger: An Experimental Essay in Confucian Moral Psychology" (forthcoming).

10. For a discussion of *cheng*, see Shun 2008.

11. *Mencius* 2A.2; for a discussion of the idea of the unmoved mind (*bu dong xin* 不動心), see Shun 1997, 72–76. For citations from the *Mencius*, I have followed the numbering of passages in Yang 1984, substituting book numbers 1A–7B for 1–14. My translation of passages from the *Mencius* follows, with occasional modification, Lau 2003.

12. *Mencius* 3B.2: 富貴不能淫 貧賤不能移 威武不能屈 此之謂大丈夫.

13. *Analects* 9.26: 三軍可奪帥也 匹夫不可奪志也. The character which I have translated as "that on which he has set his mind" is *zhi* 志; for a discussion of *zhi*, see Shun 1997, 66–68, 75–76.

14. See Griswold 2007, 11–13, for a discussion of similar ideas in relation to Socrates and the Stoics.

15. For a discussion of similar ideas, see Winch 1972.

16. See, e.g., *Mencius* 7A.4.

17. *Analects* 6.11: 賢哉回也 一簞食 一瓢飲 在陋巷 人不堪其憂 回也不改其樂 賢哉回也.

18. *Analects* 7.16, 7.19, 9.29. The character translated here as "anxiety" is *you* 憂.

19. See my "On Anger: An Experimental Essay in Confucian Moral Psychology" (forthcoming).

20. *Mencius* 4A.27: 樂則生矣 生則惡可已也 惡可已 則不知足之蹈之手之舞之.

21. Zhu Xi *Lunyu Huowen* 11.12a: 顏子之心 從容自得 而無適不樂 不待以道為可樂 然後樂也.

22. Zhu Xi *Mengzi Jizhu* 4.15a-b: 樂則生矣 謂和順從容 無所勉強.

23. I am indebted to a comment by Roger T. Ames that alerted me to adding this qualification.

24. After completing a draft of this paper, I read Griswold 1995. The way Griswold characterizes what he calls happiness is in several respects similar to the way I characterize the Confucian view of equanimity. I have benefitted from reading his discussion.

25. For a discussion of the use of *ming* in the *Analects* and the *Mencius*, see Shun 1997, 15–21, 77–83.

26. For elaboration on these other postures, see Botros 1983.

27. For an elaboration on this way of viewing the use of "fate," see Solomon 2003.

28. In Williams 1981, Bernard Williams discusses how a precluded option maybe unthinkable in one of two senses: one can edge up to it and dismiss it, or one might not even think of it as an option. While what I literally cannot do is something that I cannot even do unintentionally, what I "cannot" do because of this kind of incapacity of character is something that I could have done unintentionally out of ignorance.

29. See Shun 1997, 49–52, for a discussion of *bu ren* 不忍 and other terms related to *ren* 仁.

30. See Shun 1997, 58–63, for a discussion of *chi* 恥 and other terms related to *yi* 義.

31. Because of the two different kinds of constraints involved, I distinguished in Shun 1997, 15–21, 77–83, between a descriptive and a normative dimension of the use of *ming* in early Confucian texts. However, it is likely that, from the perspective of the early Confucians, they did not draw this kind of distinction that we would draw nowadays. Thus, according to Tang 1978, pp. 500–527, while the different dimensions of the use of *ming* were already present in early Zhou, they were not fully separate. In relation to the conjunction of *ming* 命 and *yi* 義 in *Mencius* 5A.8, he makes the point that, when one faces what we would call descriptive constraints, there is a distinction between a proper and an improper way of responding to the situation, and so there are also what we would call normative constraints on how one should respond. For him, one difference between Confucius's and Mencius's use of *ming* is that, while Confucius focuses more on the attitude of acceptance as a response to unfavorable conditions of life, Mencius focuses also on the need to cultivate oneself so that one can consistently so respond to one's environment.

32. Wang Yangming *Chuanxilu*, no. 290: 七情順其自然之流行 . . . 但不可有所著. My numbering of passages from the *Chuanxilu* follows Chan 1983, and my translation follows, with occasional modification, Chan 1963.

33. Wang Yangming *Chuanxilu*, no. 167: 皦如明鏡 . . . 隨物見形 而明鏡曾無留染 所謂情順萬事而無情也.

34. Zhu Xi *Zhuzi Yulei*, 2445: 但當怒而怒 便中節 事過便消了 更不積.

35. Wang Yangming *Chuanxilu*, no. 235: 然雖怒 卻此心廓然不曾動些子氣.

36. The Confucians idealize an "ethical" form of anger, which they contrast with a "physical" form of anger. See my "On Anger: An Experimental Essay in Confucian Moral Psychology" (forthcoming).

37. Wang Yangming *Chuanxilu*, no. 292: 須是大哭一番了 方樂 不哭便不樂矣 雖哭 此心安處即是樂也.

38. Here, I am referring implicitly to, and agreeing with, a point David S. Nivison makes in relation to Xunzi in Nivison 1991.

39. In Shun 2010, I also consider a similar picture of the mind as operating at two levels—the direct responses to the situations one confronts, and the reflective vigilance one exercises in relation to one's responses. These two aspects of the mind's operations are also interconnected, as one's reflective vigilance ensures the appropriateness of one's direct responses.

40. I am indebted to Winnie Sung for a discussion that helped my elaboration on this point.

41. On a certain interpretation of the *Zhuangzi*, the text espouses such an ethical view.

42. This view probably characterizes certain theistic traditions.

References

Botros, Sophie. "Acceptance and Morality," in *Philosophy*, 58 (Oct. 1983): 433–453.

Chan, Wing-tsit 陳榮捷 (ed.) (1983). *Wang Yangming Chuanxilu Xiangzhu Jiping* 王陽明傳習錄詳註集評. Taipei: Taiwan Xuesheng Shuju 臺灣學生書局.

———. (trans.) (1963). *Instructions for Practical Living and other Neo-Confucian Writings by Wang Yang-ming*. New York: Columbia University Press.

Griswold, Charles L. (1995). "Happiness, Tranquillity, and Philosophy," in Leroy S. Rouner (ed.) *In Pursuit of Happiness*. Notre Dame, Indiana: University of Notre Dame Press: 13–37.

———. (2007). *Forgiveness: A Philosophical Exploration*. Cambridge, UK: Cambridge University Press.

Kupperman, Joel J. (2010) "Why Ethical Philosophy Needs to be Comparative," in *Philosophy*, 85: 185–200.

Lau, D. C. (trans.) (1992). *Confucius: The Analects*, 2nd ed. Hong Kong: The Chinese University Press.

———. (2003). *Mencius*, revised edition. Hong Kong: The Chinese University Press.

Lunyu (the *Analects*). See Yang 1980 and Lau 1992.

Mengzi (*Mencius*). See Yang 1984 and Lau 2003.

Nivison, David S. (1991). "Hsun Tzu and Chuang Tzu," in Henry Rosemont, Jr., ed. *Chinese Texts and Philosophical Contexts*. La Salle, IL: Open Court Publishing Company: 129–142.

Shun, Kwong-loi (1997). *Mencius and Early Chinese Thought*. Stanford, California: Stanford University Press.

———. (2008). "Wholeness in Confucian Thought: Zhu Xi on *Cheng*, *Zhong*, *Xin*, and *Jing*," in On-cho Ng, ed., *The Imperative of Understanding: Chinese Philosophy, Comparative Philosophy, and Onto-Hermeneutics*. New York: Global Scholarly Publications: 261–272.

———. (2009). "Studying Confucian and Comparative Ethics: Methodological Reflections," in *Journal of Chinese Philosophy*, 36.3 (September): 455–478.

———. (2010). "Purity, Moral Trials, and Equanimity," in *Tsing Hua Journal of Chinese Studies*, New Series, 40.2 (June): 245–264.

———. (Forthcoming). "On Anger: An Experimental Essay in Confucian Moral Psychology," in David Jones & He Jinli, eds., *Zhu Xi Now: Contemporary Encounters with the Great Ultimate*. Albany, NY: State University of New York Press.

———. *Zhu Xi and Later Confucian Thought*. Manuscript under revision, tentative title.

Solomon, Robert C. (2003). "On Fate and Fatalism," in *Philosophy East and West*, 53.4: 435–454.

Tang, Junyi (1978). 唐君毅, *Zhongguo Zhexue Yuanlun: Daolunpian* 中國哲學原論: 導論篇, 3rd ed. Taipei: Taiwan Xuesheng Shuju 臺灣學生書局.

Wang Yangming 王陽明. *Chuanxilu* (*Instructions for Practical Living*) 傳習錄. See Chan 1983 and Chan 1963.

Williams, Bernard (1981). "Practical Necessity," in *Moral Luck*. Cambridge, UK: Cambridge University Press: 124–131.

Winch, Peter (1972). "Can a Good Man be Harmed?" in *Proceedings of the Aristotelian Society* (1965–66), reprinted in *Ethics and Action*. Routledge and Kegan Paul: 193–209.

Yang Bojun 楊伯峻 (1980). *Lunyu Yizhu* 論語譯注 2nd ed. Beijing: Zhonghua Shuju 中華書局.

———. (1984). *Mengzi Yizhu* 孟子譯注 2nd ed. Beijing: Zhunghua Shuju 中華書局.

Zhu Xi. *Lunyu Huowen* (*Questions and Answers on the Analects*) 論語或問 (*Sikuquanshu* 四庫全書 edition).

———. *Mengzi Jizhu* (*Collected Annotations on Mencius*) 孟子集注 (*Sikuquanshu* 四庫全書 edition).

———. (1986). *Zhuzi Yulei* (*Classified Conversations of Master Zhu*) 朱子語類. Beijing: Zhonghua Shuju 中華書局.

6

Individual and Rituals

Robert Cummings Neville

To be invited to contribute to this volume in celebration of Joel Kupperman is an honor I do not deserve. He is a true scholar of Chinese philosophy, distinguished in so many ways, and so are my colleagues in this volume. I am no scholar at all but rather a philosopher who uses Chinese philosophy, indeed identifies with Chinese philosophy, in order to develop a philosophy for our time. Professor Kupperman does this too, as well as pursuing frontline scholarship.

My contribution here aims to complement his approach to Confucianism in two ways. First, he has focused very much on personal "character" in Confucianism. A character is something that can be attributed to a person the way a property can be attributed to a substance. The underlying background metaphors of substance allow Professor Kupperman to make many fruitful connections with Western discussions of ethics, now often phrased in the language of virtue ethics, as in his book, *Learning from Asian Philosophy*. There is a contrary pull in Confucianism, however, that treats individuals as defined in significant ways by their participation in networks of rituals. In an important sense, for Confucius and most in his tradition, no one "has" a character as such but rather "is" an identity shared with others that includes complex ritual play. The point about ritual is not in opposition to the study of character, but is a balancing complement.

Second, Professor Kupperman has traced the Confucian lineage mainly through Mencius, to the neglect of Xunzi, the great theorist of ritual. In this he follows the orthodox line that runs explicitly through both Zhu Xi and Wang Yangming. But Xunzi is receiving renewed attention these days, and I represent that emphasis. Again, this is to complement and enrich our appreciation of the complex Confucian heritage.

In this vein I shall develop in this essay some contemporary Confucian philosophical comments on ritual and individualism. I have developed a contemporary theory of ritual in other writings that will be summarized briefly here. The general polemical context for these reflections is the old commonplace that Confucian societies are organized around group identity, whereas other societies, particularly Western modern meritocracies, are organized around individualist behavior. This context has many facets, only a few of which will be addressed here. The more particular polemical context is a reaction to *Ritual and Its Consequences: An Essay on the Limits of Sincerity* by Adam B. Seligman, Robert P. Weller, Michael J. Puett, and Bennett Simon. I have my own take on rituals and how individuals play them, which will be explained in this essay. Their book deserves a review on its own account.

In this essay I shall (1) summarize, scandalously briefly, my (contemporary) theory of ritual drawn from Xunzi and pragmatic semiotics. Then (2) I shall develop certain points about how individuals individualize rituals and thereby become individuals themselves. Part of the process of individualization is to come to appreciate the fragility, vulnerability, and perhaps plain falsity and injustice of the rituals with which one is involved. Sincerity (*cheng* 誠) is not to be contrasted with ritual, despite the tendency to do so in Fingarette's classic *Confucius—The Secular as Sacred*, as well as Seligman et al. mentioned above. Rather, they should be construed as culturally and dialectically involved in their mutual definition. Next, (3) I shall argue that rituals played by individuated persons provide an extraordinary approach to addressing the Other as Other, something problematic for Western approaches that find it hard to treat the Other as not reduced to what can be experienced by the subject. In ritual playing, the Other is not a function of the subject's experience but is simply another player. Of course, (4) we need the right rituals, or at least adequate ones, and properly individuated players for this deep respect for Others to find embodiment and practice.

Ritual

The basic Confucian themes about ritual are most efficiently developed through some of the categories of Xunzi, although he was not the first Confucian nor the last to address ritual.[1] Xunzi argued that the biological and psychological natures that human beings receive (from heaven or nature) as their natural endowment are radically underdetermined.[2] We have capacities for emotions, thoughts, and will concerning self-governance, as well as for bodily actions.

> Love and hate, delight and anger, sorrow and joy, are stored within—these are described as "the emotions given us by nature." The eye, ear, nose, mouth, and body each have the capacity to provide sense contact, but their capacities are not interchangeable—these are termed "the faculties given us by nature." The heart/mind that dwells within the central cavity is used to control the five faculties—it is called "the lord provided by nature."[3]

But there is no natural endowment for fitting the emotions to their appropriate objects, or for thinking coherently in communication with others, or for disciplining ourselves to do the right things. So, Xunzi said that ritual was needed to bring all these things together. By ritual he meant any meaning-bearing learned or learnable behavior that helps accomplish some purpose, from cultural styles of standing and walking, signals for showing respect in eye contact, the use of language, to rituals in the sense of more commonly recognized ceremonies. Without such rituals heaven and earth (or one's natural inheritance) cannot give rise to the human.[4] The human requires rituals to bring the natural endowment to the human level, which is why Confucians take such pride in the trinity of Heaven, Earth, and the Human.[5] A contemporary way of recognizing this point is to note that what distinguishes human beings from the other "high" animals is the human's advanced capacity for semiotic behavior, where the use of signs allows for complex patterns of communication and interaction. The Western approaches to semiotics have focused mainly on words and language as the paradigm ritual behavior. The Confucians generally have taken a broader view in which learning how to stand and bow, what to wear so as to be respectful, and the steady rehearsal through ceremonies of the bonds of human relationships, are as important sometimes as speaking correctly. If Western semioticians from early on had construed language use to be among a much wider range of ritual behaviors, there would have been nothing unexpected or new in Searle's discovery of the "performative."[6]

Most but not all rituals involve several people interacting in a ritual pattern like in a dance. Most rituals contain sub-rituals and themselves are part of larger ritual structures. Different rituals sometimes intersect in certain episodes, bringing together the players of the separate rituals who otherwise would not interact. Confucians have found family rituals most instructive, a complex interweaving of husband-wife rituals, parent-children rituals, brother-sister rituals, older-younger sibling rituals, nuclear family-grandparents, aunts and uncles, cousins, and distant relatives rituals. The early formation of Confucian rituals was in the context of rural life, a context that has changed many times in Chinese history and that is very different from modern urban life. Family rituals are implicated in rituals of friendship, neighborliness in one's town or apartment building, employment in various kinds of economic activities, governance at the local and most distant level, and so forth. Ritual patterns are not steady, especially when the rich implications of rituals with other rituals in changing circumstances are taken into account.

One of the most important elements of ritual that needs to be added to customary Western theories is that rituals allow for the cooperation of people whose purposes and interests might be very much opposed and in competition. Playing a ritual together accomplishes some social or personal purpose, whether it is greeting other people, putting the children to bed at night, or getting along with the neighbors. The things, behaviors, creativity, and appreciations that constitute high civilization are possible only when there are rituals, the playing of which performs the civilization. With rituals of greeting, people who hate each other can still get along for a bit, though without greeting rituals they would have resorted to violence immediately. In a competitive world where great social stakes ride on people's behavior, ritual makes possible the accomplishment of enormously important activities that otherwise would not take place because people's interests are in competition. You do not have to like your fellow workers, but if your work is properly ritualized, you can work together and get it done. The rituals of diplomacy are a hedge against war and often the alternative to war is better rituals of competition. Patterns of dancing together for the sake of the dance allows the dance to take place, even when the dancers hate one another.

Rituals are patterns of meaningful behavior, most often involving more than one person and more than one role. One common approach to ritual analysis is to focus on the pattern of roles itself and how that pattern constitutes or allows for a certain kind of social reality or function. Certainly Western cultures would benefit from being more alert to the ritual patterns that make up daily life than they customarily are, compared with Confucian cultures. Only recently have Western cultures become aware of the ritual patterns of social maladies such as racism, discrimination against ethnic minorities, diminished social expressions for women, and bigotry against gays, lesbians, and other sexual minorities. The usual Western reaction to such social maladies, when recognized, is to try to find a villain. Michel Foucault and his followers have done enormous service in pointing out how so much of what is perceived to be obvious and commonsense truth is a function of the structures of special discourses.[7] "Discourses" are a thin and anemic slice of ritual behavior, abstracted out from the richer social reality; analysis of "discourses" seems an easy way in to the issues for people whose only paradigm of ritual is language. If Foucault were to be read as analyzing ritual rather than discourse, his contribution would open up many more lines of important inquiry. Foucault shares the Western disposition to find a villain for social maladies, and for him it is the struggle for the power to control the discourses, which in turn he says reflects the parochial interests of those who seek that power. For Foucault, like Marx before him, the villain is not individuals as such but social class in a structured social situation. Surely he is right that there are important instances in which particular social interests with power determine discourses and thereby determine what roles people have to play and what happens when those discourses are played out in society. Nevertheless rituals, including their manifestation in discourses, have an inertial power simply because they are the social habits by virtue of which life goes on. Rituals can remain in force long after everyone's interests have changed and no one benefits from them. As the building blocks of social life, even when they are bad, rituals have staying power until they are changed: changing rituals puts the social fabric at risk. In some instances, rituals have an inertial staying power stronger than the powers behind the interests of any of the current stake holders in the society. The Confucian approach to rituals has far greater potential than Foucault's for discerning the natural joints and places for change in the social fabric.

Individuation

Nevertheless, the Confucian approach to ritual has focused less on analyzing the patterns of ritual behavior than on how individuals come to play the rituals. Babies learn ritual behavior by imitating parents and older siblings. But the ritual patterns are vague roles, not specific or completely determined. Like in a dance, the ritual roles are broad steps of interaction, and they need to be played in individual ways. A small child learns to walk, for instance, by stumbling forward; anything counts as walking so long as there is forward motion on two feet. Slowly the child learns to control the lurches and develop smoother ways of walking, indeed ways adapted to the child's own body-type. Cultural elements also help to individuate the walking: Chinese children learn to walk so as to put the toe and heel down almost simultaneously, whereas Western European and Anglo-American children learn the walking style of first heel/then toe. To exaggerate the cultural differences, the Chinese way is almost like shuffling, the Western way almost like a goose step. Before long, children develop individuated ways of walking so that they can be recognized by their gait alone; this individuation continues to deepen throughout life.

Walking can be done alone, although it is learned through imitation, trial and error. Dancing, however, usually involves partners, and here the individuation is more complicated because a person learns to dance differently with different partners. What begins by struggling to get one's feet and hands in the right place at the right time relative to others becomes a more personal and individuated style of dancing. The ritual outline of the steps is the same early and late, but the dancing becomes individuated to each person's style, and that relative to the styles of the others.

The rituals most frequently in focus for the two-and-a-half millennia of Confucian tradition are those associated with family life.[8] As I mentioned earlier, these rituals are complex and overlapping, defining behavioral roles among different family positions and roles and different functions such as economic, educational, life-care, and political. Some of the favorite Confucian rituals are those of boys toward their fathers, collectively constituting filial piety. At an early age, these are taught as rather abstract duties and symbolic gestures and postures of respect. But even early on, filial piety has to be individuated to this boy having to deal with his particular father. Boys slowly learn that other children's fathers are different from their own and that they are rightfully treated differently. Even more slowly, boys learn that they themselves are different from their friends and thus have different capacities for relating to their fathers. Moreover, the content of filial piety changes with stages in life. For small children, very much of filial piety is obedience to parental dictate and learning to discern when the father is pleased or displeased; it also involves learning to appreciate and bask in the father's love. Beginning with adolescence and moving through many stages, filial piety comes more and more to be taking on the skills, work, knowledge, adult social roles, and virtues of the father. In traditional Confucian households it is important for a young man to become a father so as to learn how his father did it and to prove that his father has taught him how. Later in the filial relationship, the son comes more to take over from and to take care of the father (and mother and others of the older generation). The popular image of filial piety is the grown son taking care of aging parents who have become dependent. In our time, the male gender orientation of filial piety of course is broadened to include women, and families of filial care are rarely a single household.

The point to be stressed here is that an individual comes to be his or her own individuated self through individuating the important rituals of life, according to the Confucian sensibility. A boy comes to be more and more himself as he individuates his ritual, that is, meaningful, relation with his father (and his mother, siblings, aunts, uncles, cousins, friends, classmates, fellow workers, neighbors, etc.). This individuation is always a dual process. On the one hand, it involves orienting oneself to who the others are in the ritual, one's father, for instance. The complication here is that the other is always changing in reference to oneself, as the father individuates himself as father: the other is a moving target. On the other hand, it involves the invention of the specificities of one's own self in the ritual relation. Westerners often think of this as "discovering" oneself, as if one's character were already made up waiting to be discovered. Indeed, Westerners often suspect that the ritual forms impose strictures and limitations on one's true self that needs to rebel against them in order to find itself. Rebellion is an important part of ritual behavior, but not at this point. Rather, Confucians see the rituals as providing the form for the having of a self if the individual can only individuate specific ways of playing the ritual. So individuals have to develop and transform themselves into people capable of playing well the family rituals, and the rituals enabling friendships, work relations, community roles, and the rest. Looked at from the standpoint of the individuals, this is the problem of developing character where this is defined as competence at playing the important ritual roles of life. But whereas Westerners are likely to look upon the development of such character as a function of developing individual virtue, Confucians look upon it rather as defining character in relation to others as mediated by the various ritual patterns with roles for the individual. In a very important sense, one can never develop one's character as if it were one's own property. Rather, it is developed in relation to other individuals developing their characters as connected by the dense fabric of ritual roles.

Individuation in role playing is not merely a matter of getting specific within the general outline of a ritual role. All experience in the Confucian view is shot through with *value* and there are two kinds of norms in particular that are important for individuation in ritual behavior—sincerity and probity.

Sincerity (*cheng*) is the state of having all the layers of one's inner intentions, feelings, and outer actions so aligned with one another that one's heart is transparent in one's actions. And vice versa: one's actions follow without inhibition or deviance from one's heart. For the Confucians, this kind of sincerity, which is so important for playing ritual roles rightly, is vastly more difficult to achieve than sincerity as so often intended in the West. Westerners sometimes think that one can become sincere simply by ceasing to dissemble or by developing the courage to speak and act out of one's inner convictions and passions.[9] Of course, these things are involved in the Confucian ideal, but so many other things are involved as well. For instance, one cannot be sincere in one's responses to things unless one has learned to perceive them properly and then to understand what one has perceived. And one cannot act out of the responses of one's heart unless one has learned to organize oneself so as to be able to accomplish what one intends, a rare virtue. Ritual behavior has many levels or layers moving from the heart to the external actions. The Confucians love to point out that how one dresses is crucial for revealing one's heart in respect to the others with whom one plays important rituals! One's clothing and demeanor are part of actions with reference to other people, not mere expressions of personal idiosyncrasy. Deep education is required for this complicated sincerity, although Confucians admit that some people take to this education more easily than others.

The "big problem" for sincerity on which Confucians have pondered since the beginning is selfishness. Selfishness takes many forms, distorting one's perceptions, perverting intentions to play the roles well, and distorting our actions even when based on good intentions. In the Confucian project of properly individuated ritual behavior, the cultivation of sincerity thus has two kinds of drives. One is the positive drive to become competent at making the passage from heart to outer action continuous and transparent. The other is the negative therapeutic drive to discover and eliminate the usually hidden roots and branches of selfishness.[10]

The other kind of norm for individuation in ritual roles is probity, by which I mean a capacity to discern and act on the values expressed in one's situation, especially in the people and the social structures. The Neo-Confucians elaborated the technical conception of Principle (*li* 理) to indicate how being a thing in the natural (and social) world is to have value, and how that value is also a function of the environing things, and of the environment itself. Stephen C. Angle has written about how that might be understood in contemporary terms and develops an understanding of *li* as "coherence."[11] ("Principle," the received translation of *li*, does not say much of anything.) I prefer "harmony" to "coherence," although there is another Chinese word, *he*, that is usually translated harmony. Whatever the metaphysics, the Confucians have believed since the beginning that value is a characteristic of things of the cosmos and that human society is to be conceived as constituting elements within nature. Moreover, value is not taken to be a property resident in things, like predicates in substances, but rather is a function of things as they are related to other things in their environment. The beauty of the eagle is in winging down the mountainside. The virtue of the warrior includes his place in the battle-line. The value of the father is in his roles in the family (and elsewhere). Things are valuable in context.

The other side of the Confucian approach to value is that human beings are hardwired to appreciate value when it is encountered although they have to learn how to activate that appreciation. The tradition of Mencius has emphasized the importance of preventing this natural appreciation of value from maturing and unfolding. The tradition of Xunzi has emphasized the importance of positive learning, especially through learning to play rituals, to find out what is valuable when it is non-obvious. Both sides emphasize the importance of learning and erudition in order to discover what the world is like. The ideal of the sage is to become adept in seeing and responding to the values of things in appropriate ways. So often this means discovering deeper grounds for harmony or coherence than appear among the array of warring factions.[12] The Confucian tradition has emphasized the continuity of value (*li*) in things with its presence in structuring the inner heart and its responses, and probity is the virtue of connecting these so that actions can be moral.

Individuation in probity thus raises the question of right action. Ritual roles are defined in ways that make actions possible and give them form. But what happens if one's probity reveals that a certain ritual behavior stands in the way of moral action? Confucians have been preoccupied with the problem of what happens when one's father, or the emperor, demands obedience in a wrong cause.[13] What one should do, of course, is to "remonstrate" with the authority. Remonstration is a clear part of filial piety and civil obedience. But when should one disobey if one's remonstrations are dismissed? Go into exile? If your father commits a crime, should you turn him in to the authorities (a question asked also by Plato in the Euthyphro dialogue)? Confucius was hesitant. If the emperor is incompetent or wicked, should you rebel (Mencius said, "Yes").[14]

Individuation in ritual behavior is never just playing the roles in a style suited to oneself but includes also playing the roles with probity. Therefore the ritual behavior is enormously complicated by having to navigate the individuation with the moral judgments to which one's probity gives rise. The ritual pattern by itself does not answer the questions of how to individuate the rituals with probity.

Sincerity and probity together are two crucial ingredients in becoming a true person. They would have little or no content if the person were not in a nexus of ritual role-playing positions. The rituals provide the environment in which the person can become a true individual in the sense of being individuated in interpersonal relations. Because of the need for sincerity, ritual should never be mere role-playing, as if one's heart were not in it. In fact, when one plays rituals insincerely, that is a deep vice, according to Confucians.[15] The common criticism of Confucianism as mere formalism, indeed a formalism that rigidifies hierarchical authority relations, is first to be made by Confucians themselves. One of the deep predicaments of the human condition, according to the Confucians who appreciate the social functions of rituals, is that it opens itself to insincerity and with that the loss of the true self. In this respect, Confucian culture, to the extent it is true to its philosophic roots, is individualistic, not communalistic. Of course, because of the communal character of so many of the rituals that make possible high civilization, people are never thought of outside of social relations and so often it is the ritual structure of the fabric of relations that needs moral attention. But the human meaning of ritual playing is the development of individual character, which is the individual's responsibility.

The probity side of this individual commitment to playing the rituals well places extraordinary demands on individuals to become competent and unselfish at learning what is at stake and playing the rituals so as to be observant of the norms and values at hand. This leads to a powerful sense of the tragic and to an underlying vexation at the ambiguities and compromises of life. The Confucian claim that ritual constitutes the fabric of individual life with others commonly is thought to be personally and socially painful because the rituals restrict freedom. Instead of being obliged to play ritual roles, sometimes individuals want to shuck them all and be free. What would they do if they were free? They would go "on the road" and wander like Jack Kerouac's hippies. The Confucian model for this is self-imposed exile and it stands as a complement, not a corrective, to the model of ritual role-playing. This popular view of ritual as constraining the free spirit does not pick up on the most important sense of tension and disease in Confucian culture, namely the ambiguities and tragedies of not being able to individuate roles with coherence in accord with probity. Probity is both an extraordinary achievement and a deep burden.

The Confucian virtue of humaneness (*ren*) is far more complex than sincerity and probity, but it involves them both in high measure. Rituals by themselves can be played by people without humaneness. But this is a grievous fault that prevents robust individuating of the ritual roles. And this in turn prevents the development of the individual, which is what usually motivates insincere ritual play in the first place. Two more topics need to be explored to bring home this point, the role of the Other and the importance of having good rituals—not any old rituals will do.

The Other

I said earlier that rituals allow individuals to cooperate in whatever work the ritual accomplishes while having opposing, competitive, or even contradictory interests. One of the ways to tell a good ritual is by determining whether in fact it allows for conjoint actions among people with radically different interests, a point to which we shall return later. Now, the element of ritual to notice is that understanding the human situation in ritual terms allows for understanding Others in ways that vex some Western modes of thought.

The problem of the Other in European philosophy comes about in this way. European philosophy (and here I mean to exclude the American philosophy of pragmatism) has seen the human epistemological situation to be that of interdefined subjectivity and objectivity. Experience is the activity or property of human subjects who look out onto a world. The things of the world are conceived to be objects within subjective experience; a whole host of problems that have preoccupied modern European philosophy, both Continental and analytic, follow from this, which have to do with how we, from our subjective perspective, can know things as they are in themselves. Can we know them only as they appear to us? The powerful Kantian stream goes so far as to define objectivity in terms of the conformity of outer things to the forms of the human mind, to our modes of receptivity and categories and synthesizing activities for organizing experience. An "object" is what conforms to our experience and whatever in the object does not enter experience on our subjective terms is somehow unreal, or unknowable at least. The scientific tradition has elaborated this Kantian point, which has had many variations, to say that its objectivity consists in its reduction of claims about the world to claims about what the world amounts to when expressed in the various sciences's categories, theories, instruments, and research agendas.

Needless to say, something is wrong with this. Other people are not only what they are in our subjective experience. They have an interiority and external reality of their own. They have a value and dignity of their own that might not be registered at all in the ways we experience them. Nonhuman nature is the same way, not merely a construct of our subjective experience. Experience itself bluntly shows this to be the case. We experience people as not being reducible to our experience of them. They have a resistance to being defined in our experience, they exude a sense of the More. Emmanuel Levinas and others have sharpened this point into a major philosophic project.[16] But even the most detailed phenomenological description of others persons and their Otherness is still only a description of our experience. It is of the Others as part of us.

Frustrating as this is to mere philosophers caught in the subjective/objective orientation to the world (usually blamed on Descartes), this orientation is culturally disastrous in its treatment of people. People are turned into mere objects in the experience of the people with power and are often brutalized by being treated as nothing more than what serves the interests of the powerful. Medicine has objectified patients. Colonized peoples have been reduced to the judgments made about them and their cultures by the colonizers. Enemies are reduced to people who should be eliminated because they oppose the interests of the powerful. The people lacking power do the same thing to those who have the power. No remedy for this exists so long as we understand others to have no reality except in our experience. "Our experience" can be defined as transcendentally as one might please, as in Husserl's phenomenology, but the point still holds: things are reduced to the actual or possible experience of them.

Confucians recognize something of the structure of the subjective/objective distinction, the self and world. This often is expressed in terms of the polar continuum between the inner heart and the "ten thousand things" to which individuals relate. Although Confucians insist on continuity from the inner heart to external actions on real things, a continuity that should be sincere and activated with probity, they do not see the situation as defined by the subjective/objective contrast.[17] Rather they see it as constituted by a natural standpoint within which individuals interact, most often in ritualized, meaningful, roles. An individual understands herself or himself to be one among many individuals in the dance of a ritual. The other individuals are also players in that ritual pattern. I see the Others to be players in the ritual just like myself. Moreover, I see myself to be a player in the ritual just like the Others. The fundamental reality of the ritual, or nexus of rituals, makes players of us all. Certainly, each player needs to individuate the playing, and individuation has all the dimensions already mentioned and more. But I see my individuating to be part and parcel of the ritual reality, just like the individuations being cultivated by the others.

To be sure, my own playing of a ritual has a subjective perspective as I try to play the roles well, individuating my performance, cultivating sincerity, struggling with probity and its consequences. But that subjective perspective is not the only or even primary frame within which I understand and behave. Rather, the ritual itself is the frame within which I understand my own subjective struggles. And it is also the frame within which I am oriented to the Others, who of course are understood to have their own subjective struggles. In the ritual play, we are all Others to one another, and this is the way each of us understands our own subjective issues of individuating the rituals well.

This is the truth in the common observation that people in Confucian societies identify with the group before they do with their own individual concerns. However, that contrast is too superficial. It is not that Confucians identify with the "group" first, but rather with the rituals that include the others as well as oneself and within which everyone works out individuating personal identity. Exerting oneself to play the ritualized fabric of life well is just as much an assertion of self as it is an assertion of the group, because the very self-constitution of the self has to do with becoming humane in the very particularized contexts of one's array of rituals. The group-individual contrast reflects the Western assumption that individuals are primary and collectively make up groups. The Confucian assumption (and not only assumption, but well-argued conclusion) is that individuals are already constituted by the rituals connecting them and that the questions of life have to do with learning to play those rituals well with sincerity and probity and to work through their ambiguities and tensions.

One benefit of the Confucian ritual approach is that all the players enter the ritual activities with their whole being. They are Others to one another in their mutual play, but they are not reduced to the roles they play in the rituals. To the contrary, precisely as players they are individuals individuating themselves in the roles, coping with the integration of many rituals, and suffering through the ambiguities and tragedies that come from living with some degree or other of probity and sincerity in their ritual matrix. Of course, a given ritualized interaction might be merely instrumental and superficial; but the Confucian ideal is to treat Others within our ritual engagements as themselves players individuating themselves in all the ways involved with their own "subjectivity," as Western thought would have it. The common observation that Confucian businessmen begin a meeting by drinking tea together and talking about their families before they "get down to business" illustrates the point. (Someday the anecdotes will include business women, but probably not for a generation!) Paradoxical as it might seem from Western assumptions, Confucian ritual practice makes it part of the ritual to treat others not as mere *role*-players in the ritual but as *players* who come to the ritual roles as human subjects individuating themselves through a stretch of life with many ritual interactions.

The result of this is a kind of profound deference to the Other that quasi-automatically colors Confucian ritual behavior. By treating Others as players, one does not treat them as reduced to the roles in the rituals that are part of one's life. To be sure, there are always difficulties in getting to know other people—a conversation about families over tea is sufficient only in a homogeneous society. Also, often there are pressures just to "get down to business," and these pressures occur among Confucians as much as busy Westerners. But the orientating frame of Confucian ritual playing is filled with respect and deference for what the Other might be as a player in the other's matrix of ritual connections.

Correcting Rituals

This idealized picture of the Confucian ritual approach to individuals and their treatment as Others needs a reality check. Confucian rituals have been very abusive in some situations. We have already seen some reasons for this. The players in the rituals might be relatively un-individuated stumbling novices, obsessed with the ritual roles rather than the players because they have not mastered the roles themselves. Or the players might not be very sincere and therefore cannot bring themselves into their roles with much transparency, let alone look for that in the others players. Or the players might be lacking in probity, looking at the roles only habitually or instrumentally, not being critical, not trained to look for what is good and in the overall context of the ritual behaviors. But an even more important factor in the abuse of Confucian ritual culture is bad rituals.

That a rich matrix of rituals within which to live makes high civilization possible is an important observation, as made above. But that same matrix might contain ritual structures that habituate limitations to civilization or encode evil and oppression. That the rituals of Confucian economic life place the power and principal roles in the hands of men to the relative exclusion of women is a bad thing. We are finding out now that rituals that discriminate between people on the grounds of gender distinctions are very often bad: they might enable economic activity but do so unfairly when they define participation on grounds of gender rather than, say, productivity, skill, and other criteria relevant to business. In the American context, the rituals that habituate racism are similar: distinctions according to race are rarely genuinely important to encode in rituals involving neighborly living, economic and political activity, friendship, and domesticity. The same thing is true for rituals that encode differences in sexual orientation for the various ritualized structures of society.

An extension of probity in Confucian ritual culture is the critique and amendment of the rituals at hand. In his day, Confucius was a radical critic of his culture, arguing on the one hand that it lacked many of the rituals necessary for high civilization, having descended into violent barbarism, and on the other that some of the rituals that were indeed in place were counterproductive, rewarding the unworthy. For our time, a great work for Confucian moral philosophy is, first, to point out where our society is ritualized, second, to analyze how the rituals work, what they enable, what they prevent, and how just they are and, third, to develop new rituals in place of the old.

Coming to understand, as is common today, that the rituals of many cultures are unfair to women, to outsiders of different races and ethnic communities, and to sexual minorities, leads to the important task of developing new rituals in these regards. But the situation is more complicated than this. Social and economic conditions are shifting dramatically, and the rituals that fostered justice, communication, and respect for the Other in the olden days often are not relevant in the new circumstances. New rituals are needed and they need to be seen as transitional, always in modification as changes continue. How can you share tea and stories of families through Internet transactions, especially when they are automated? A new vision is needed of engaging players in rituals as themselves individuals individuating themselves with hoped-for sincerity and probity as well as skill. Perhaps there is some merit in complaining about the Internet and what it does to face-to-face communication between players of the important rituals. But the virtue of complaining seems to be that one feels better afterward, not that it does much direct good. Rather, the merit lies in investigating new ritual possibilities that do for our changing world what the Confucians did in their best of times.

Perhaps the most immediate challenge for Confucian moral thinking today is to understand how violence might be mitigated by harmonizing rituals. Rituals allow people who otherwise are in serious conflict to work together in the ritual pattern. Just as greeting rituals are needed to make possible peaceful encounters, so diplomatic rituals are needed to enable economic and cultural conflicts to be negotiated peacefully. Of course, there are limits to what rituals can do in this regard: all parties need to be persuaded that more is to be gained by playing the rituals together than by going to war. Part of this persuasion is the exhibition of the possibility of greater harmony behind the conflict. But then, the heart of Confucian moral theory is the cultivation of the means to discern the harmonies in the heart, in things, in situations of conflict among things, and in the background in which all things, including oneself and one's culture, have value. These are among the lessons we have learned from Joel Kupperman.

Notes

1. This section summarizes my interpretation of the Confucian tradition on ritual which finds more elaborate expression in Neville 1995, Chapter 7, 2000, and 2008.

2. See, for instance, Xunzi 1994, book 17. The chapter is readily accessible in Chan 1963, Chapter 6. See also Edward J. Machle 1993.

3. Xunzi, 16; Knoblock translation.

4. For an extended interpretation and expansion of Xunzi on this point, see Neville 1995, 166–181.

5. See Xunzi, 15, for his discussion.

6. See Searle 1969, especially Chapters 2–4; Searle draws much from J. L. Austin 1962.

7. See Foucault 1970.

8. Perhaps the most famous treatise is Zhu Xi 1991.

9. This seems to be the principal focus concerning ritual in Seligman and others 2008.

10. The classic text for this point is the *Great Learning*. See Chan 1963, Chapter 4.

11. Stephen C. Angle 2009.

12. See Angle 2009, Chapters 6–11 for an analysis of the education of the sage in the depths of *li*.

13. See, for instance, *Analects* 13.18; in Chan 1963, 41.

14. *Mencius* 1B.8; in Chan 1963.

15. An important theme in Fingarette 1972.

16. See, for instance, Levinas 1969 and Jean-Luc Marion 2002.

17. Confucians differ on the extent to which they emphasize continuity, although all accept it. Wang Yangming is a striking example. See Warren G. Frisina 2002 for a study of Wang on this question in relation to a number of Western thinkers.

References

Angle, Stephen (2009). *Sagehood: The Contemporary Significance of Neo-Confucian Philosophy*. New York: Oxford University Press.

Austin, J. L. (1962). *Sense and Sensibilia*. Reconstructed from the manuscript notes by G. L. Warnock. Oxford. UK: Oxford University Press.

Chan, Wing-tsit (1963). Ed. and trans. *A Source Book in Chinese Philosophy*. Princeton, NJ: Princeton University Press.

Fingarette, Herber. (1972). *Confucius—The Secular as Sacred*. New York: Harper & Row.

Foucault, Michel. (1970). *The Order of Things: An Archaeology of the Human Sciences*. New York: Pantheon Books.

Frisina, Warren G. (2002). *The Unity of Knowledge and Action: Toward a Nonrepresentational Theory of Knowledge*. Albany, NY: State University of New York Press.

Levinas, Emmanuel. (1969). *Totality and Infinity: An Essay on Exteriority*. Translated by Alphonso Lingis. Pittsburgh, PA: Duquesne University Press.

Machle, Edward J. (1993). *Nature and Heaven in the Xunzi: A Study of the Tian Lun*. Albany, NY: State University of New York Press.

Marion, Jean-Luc (2002). *Being Given: Toward a Phenomenology of Givenness*. Translated by Jeffrey L. Kosky. Stanford, CA: Stanford University Press.

Neville, Robert Cummings (2008). *Ritual and Deference: Extending Chinese Philosophy in a Comparative Context*. Albany, NY: State University of New York Press.

———. (2000). *Boston Confucianism: Portable Tradition in the Late-Modern World*. Albany: State University of New York Press.

———. (1995). *Normative Cultures*. Albany: State University of New York Press.

Searle, John R. (1969). *Speech Acts: An Essay in the Philosophy of Language*. Cambridge, UK: Cambridge University Press.

Seligman, Adam B., Robert P. Weller, Michael J. Puett, and Bennett Simon (2008). *Ritual and Its Consequences: An Essay on the Limits of Sincerity*. New York, NY: Oxford University Press.

Xunzi (1994). *Xunzi: A Translation and Study of the Complete Works*, Volume III, Books 17–32. Edited and translated by John Knoblock. Stanford, CA: Stanford University Press.

Zhu Xi (1991). *Chu Hsi's Family Rituals: A Twelfth-Century Chinese Manual for the Performance of Cappings, Weddings, Funerals, and Ancestral Rites*. Translated, with annotation and introduction, by Patricia Buckley Ebrey. Princeton, NJ: Princeton University Press.

PART II

Moral Cultivation and Material Well-Being

7

Material Well-Being and Character Cultivation in Confucianism

CHENYANG LI

This essay is inspired by Joel J. Kupperman's work on character and the good life. Kupperman writes,

> There are certain good things—good food, comfortable surroundings, and the like—that are so widely pleasing that it is possible to talk about pleasure as the end of life and to create the impression that it really does not matter who or what you are as long as you, so to speak, get lucky in such matter as the material conditions of life, your health, your friendships, and so on.[1]

However, he reminds us,

> [to] link happiness to goals, although it matches the general human expectation that one will be happy if only one gets what one wants, is to ignore that reality of what people's lives are like when they do attain their goals.[2]

Life is of course not merely about material conditions. What is the connection between material well-being and the moral life? While the value of these two pursuits is seldom questioned, their relationship is by no means intuitive. This essay investigates the relationship between material well-being in terms of economic prosperity and the cultivation of character in Confucianism.

By "material well-being," I refer primarily to a reasonable level of physical support to a person's life, including food, clothing, shelter, and medical care. Such a level should be above the minimum for survival. Perhaps we can speak of a decent and comfortable level, even though such a level of support largely depends on the economic standards of a specific society. Obviously, a homeless person in New York City with adequate McDonald's to eat everyday may seem luxurious to those suffering from famine in Ethiopia. Running water is now a necessity for decent living in a large part of the world whereas emperors of ancient China lived without it. Nevertheless, we can speak of a reasonable level of material support such as adequate food, clothes, and shelter.

Regarding the relationship between a person's material well-being and his moral cultivation, two lines of thought can be found in pre-Qin Confucian thinkers. On the one hand, there are teachings suggesting that people need to have a decent level of material well-being before they engage in moral cultivation effectively. On the other hand, there are also indications that one can become virtuous regardless of economic conditions. There is an apparent tension between these two positions. If people can cultivate themselves morally regardless of material well-being—given that in Confucianism the most important thing in life is to become a virtuous person—why would they need to improve material well-being? Conversely, if people cannot cultivate themselves morally without taking care of material well-being first, can the economically impoverished ever be able to achieve moral refinement? In the latter case, assuming that "ought" implies "can," how is it that the economically impoverished people be subject to any moral requirement? On the basis of Confucius's and Mencius's teachings, I analyze four possible solutions to this relationship and advance the view that, whereas a small portion of people may be able to become morally cultivated without a decent level of material well-being, the large majority need to have material well-being as a foundation for moral cultivation.

I

Pre-Qin Confucian thinkers in general see people's material well-being as an important hallmark of a good society. To that end, they advocate a social policy of "letting people get rich" (*fu min* 富民). In this regard,

Confucian philosophy appears radically different from an early Christian philosophy (at least according to one reading). The Bible presents Jesus as saying that "I tell you the truth, it is hard for a rich man to enter the kingdom of heaven. Again I tell you, it is easier for a camel to go through the eye of a needle than for a rich man to enter the kingdom of God" (Matthew 19:24, Mark 10:25, Luke 18:24–25).[3] It also differs from a common understanding of Buddhist teachings which promote a reserved attitude toward material wealth.[4] In Buddhist teachings, suffering is rooted in desires, which include the craving for material gain. The ideal of non-attachment, to say the least, does not promote the pursuit of material riches. In contrast, Confucius unequivocally advocates a social policy of benefiting people materially in ways they wish to be benefitted.[5] In the Confucian view, poverty is not a good thing and should be prevented; wealth is usually considered a good thing and is thus promoted. In the *Records of Confucius's Family Teachings*, Confucius is quoted as saying that "the most urgent business for government is to make people rich and to help them live long lives."[6] Presumably, when people have adequate material means they are likely to live not only a decent life but also a long and prosperous life. Specifically, Confucius urges, "if the ruler can spare people from being drafted to labor for the state, and minimize taxes, people will become rich."[7] Becoming rich, evidently, is a good thing for Confucius.

Confucius, however, did not promote such a policy merely for the sake of material well-being. Confucianism takes the virtuous life as the highest ideal. The *Great Learning*, for instance, sets the ultimate goal to be illuminating the world with enlightening virtues (*ming mingde* 明明德, TTC, 1673).[8] The virtuous life, however, is not to be obtained in the absence of material well-being. The *Analects* records a conversation between Confucius and his disciple Ran You:

> Accompanied by Ran You, Confucius arrived in the state of Wei. He said, "this state is populous." Ran You asked, "now that there is a large population, what should be done?" Confucius said, "make the people rich." Ran You asked again, "what else should be done when people become rich?" Confucius said, "cultivate them."[9]

Here Confucius seems to imply that material well-being should be given priority before moral cultivation. He indicates that the first course of governmental business is to enrich people; after people become well-off, they should become cultivated. The *Kong Congzi* records Confucius saying that "it is rare for people suffering from hunger and cold not to behave badly."[10] Obviously, when people's basic material needs are not met, it is difficult for them to become cultivated morally. Conversely, if society wishes its people to become cultivated, it must first become economically adequate.

Mencius holds a similar idea, expressed in a more explicit way. He developed a philosophy of "benevolent governance" (*ren zheng* 仁政) and the "Kingly Way" (*wang dao* 王道). Such a philosophy contains two core ideas, namely economically enriching people and morally cultivating people. These two ideas are closely linked. Following Confucius, Mencius says, "let people farm in the field and reduce taxes, people will become rich."[11] He maintains that a good government should make people prosperous so that they have grain as abundant as the easy supply of water and fire.[12] Furthermore, Mencius suggests that when people are affluent, they can become morally good. He says, "when people have as abundant grains as they have the easy supply of water and fire, how can they not become morally good (*ren*)?"[13] We should not read him as saying that, when people have enough food (and other necessities), they will automatically become morally good. Mencius suggests that, when people are affluent, they are more ready and more likely to become morally cultivated.

In another place, Mencius proposes an even stronger connection between material well-being and moral cultivation. He says,

> Those with constant means of support will have persevering hearts, while those without constant means will not have persevering hearts. Lacking persevering hearts, they will go astray and get into excess, stopping at nothing. (*Mencius* 3A.3; Lau, 97)

The persevering heart is one with the determination toward a virtuous life. Mencius takes material means of support as a precondition for people to become morally good. Economic means is a foundation for moral refinement. According to his thinking, in order to achieve a virtuous society, government must enable people to become economically prosperous. Mencius says,

> When determining what means of support the people should have, a clear-sighted ruler ensures that these are sufficient, on the one hand, for the care of parents, and, on the other, for

> the support of wife and children, so that the people always have sufficient food in good years and escape starvation in bad; only then does he drive them towards goodness, in this way the people find it easy to follow him. (*Mencius* 1A.7; Lau, 58–59)

According to this way of thinking, when people are poor, without adequate food, clothes, and shelter, moral cultivation is out of reach. A virtuous society has to be built by prosperous people.

Mencius holds that the Kingly Way begins with letting people satisfy their material needs. He says,

> If the mulberry is planted in every homestead of five *mu*[14] of land, then those who are fifty can wear silk; if chickens, pigs and dogs do not miss their breeding season, then those who are seventy can eat meat; if each lot of a hundred *mu* is not deprived of labor during the busy season, then families with several mouths to feed will not go hungry. Exercise due care over the education provided by the village schools, and discipline the people by teaching the duties proper to sons and younger brothers, and those whose heads have turned grey will not be carrying loads on the roads. When those who are seventy wear silk and eat meat and the masses are neither cold nor hungry, it is impossible for their prince not to be a true king. (*Mencius* 1A.3; Lau, 51–52)

In this passage, Mencius expresses the desirability of a comfortable level of material well-being for ordinary people. When society is economically prosperous, elderly people do not need to engage in heavy labor and they will be able to dress and eat well. In that time, only affluent people could afford to wear silk and to eat meat. Therefore, these are indications of economic prosperity. When the philosophy of "benevolent governance" is practiced successfully, people's material well-being is satisfied. Only then can the ruler be a true king, meaning that the Kingly Way prevails.

Accordingly, the Confucian Kingly Way is not just about making people affluent, but more importantly about making people virtuous. Such a goal of virtuous society cannot be achieved without a material foundation. Material well-being is a precondition for education, which is related intrinsically to the cultivation of virtue in Confucianism. This idea is consistent with a view expressed in the *Mumin* Chapter of the

Guanzi, that when their rice granaries are full, people will follow ritual propriety, and when there are sufficient clothes and food, people will have a sense of honor and shame.[15] Since food shortage was the primary cause of social instability, ancient Chinese thinkers generally shared the belief that adequate food supply is a necessary condition for a good society. With adequate supply of food, of course, people would be able to produce other things to enhance their living conditions. And they would be able to engage in the cultivation of virtues. On the relationship between material well-being and morality, this belief translates into the view shared by many that material well-being is an important precondition for moral cultivation, including those views expressed by Confucius and Mencius presented above.

This close connection between material well-being and cultivation of virtues is an important theme in Confucius and Mencius. It is, however, not the only theme. Confucius also emphasizes the need of personal cultivation *regardless of* economic conditions. At quite a few places, Confucius seems to suggest that poverty should not deter people from acquiring moral virtues. In the *Analects*, Confucius commends his disciple Yan Hui:

> What a worthy person Yan Hui is! With a basket of food, a bucket of water, living in a poor street. Other people become distressed, but it has no effect on Yan Hui's cheerfulness. What a worthy person Yan Hui is![16]

As a good role model, Yan Hui was able to pursue the Way regardless of his poor economic circumstances. Living in poverty did not preclude him from refining his moral character and worthiness. Confucius seems to hold that economic conditions do not matter if one is determined toward moral betterment. He even says that he would not talk to those who wish to pursue the Way while they are ashamed of wearing meager clothes and eating coarse food.[17] He praises Zilu, who in ragged clothes did not feel ashamed when standing side by side with someone in a fancy fur coat.[18] For Confucius, moral determination can overpower economic obstacles.

As a matter of fact, harsh material conditions could even be conducive to a person's moral development. Confucius makes this point with a metaphor that, when the weather turns cold, we realize that the pine and the cypress are the last to droop.[19] Harsh conditions can test people's will and character. While deeply caring about people's well-being, at times Confucius does not seem to be too concerned about poverty. He seems to think that poverty is a relative notion and to believe that when wealth is evenly distributed in society, there is no problem of poverty.[20] Confucius believes in social harmony.[21] Conceivably, when there are no huge gaps in society, people are more likely to be harmonious with one another. Harmonious people are able to care about one another and to cultivate virtues together. When people are harmonious, society is stable, even if it is poor. Therefore, from this perspective, for Confucius there seems to be no necessary connection between economic conditions (above the level of survival) and moral cultivation.

Mencius also believes that one should become cultivated regardless of economic conditions. His ideal person is one who, when becoming illustrious, will bring benefit to all under Heaven, and when in poor conditions, will take good care of his own moral cultivation.[22] He holds morality to be more important than life. Mencius says,

> I desire fish; I also desire bear's palm. When both cannot be obtained at the same time, I give up fish in order to get bear's palm. Life is what I want; so is rightness. When both cannot be retained at the same time, I choose to give up life for the sake of rightness.[23]

If morality is more important than life, it must be more important than wealth and other forms of material well-being. Thus, it follows that a person can acquire moral cultivation even in poverty. Presumably, moral cultivation relies on a person's own effort. One can become morally cultivated regardless of her economic situation. Accordingly, poverty itself does not make moral cultivation impossible. Poor economic conditions should not be used as excuses not to pursue moral improvement.

From the above discussion, it appears that there is a tension between the two views identified in Confucius and Mencius. On the one hand, material well-being is taken to be a precondition for moral refinement. On the other, moral cultivation can be achieved independently of material well-being. Is this a contradiction?

2

In this section, I will examine four possible solutions to the puzzle. After examining the inadequacies of the first three, I will advance an interpretation that confirms both positions without a contradiction.

The first and perhaps the *prima facie* most appealing solution is that, material well-being is not a precondition for moral cultivation, but it improves human life in a separate dimension and, therefore, it is good on its own. According to this account, human existence is multifaceted. In addition to moral pursuit, we also have material needs. A fulfilled human life includes fulfilling both people's physical needs and moral (or spiritual) needs. Therefore, material well-being is required regardless of its effects on moral cultivation.

Confucius once said that, "if wealth could be pursued I would pursue it, even if it meant to act as a guard holding a whip at the entrance to a marketplace. If wealth cannot be pursued, then I just do what I enjoy."[24] Although we have reasons to believe that Confucius would not advocate pursuing wealth at the expense of morality, this passage seems to indicate that wealth is a good in itself.[25] Assuming wealth improves a person's material well-being, as it usually does, perhaps Confucius did take material well-being as an independent good—though the passage does not rule out the role of material wealth in facilitating moral cultivation. Perhaps, other things being equal, material well-being is good in itself.

This account separates moral consideration from material consideration in order to justify people's pursuit of material well-being. The strength of this account, as I see it, is also its weakness. First of all, it is not all that clear whether we can justifiably say that, other things being equal, material well-being is good in itself. Suppose, for the sake of argument, wealth does not affect a wicked man as far as moral behavior is concerned, would making him wealthy (hence improving his material well-being) be an independently good thing? The answer is not so obvious, to say the least. To borrow the language from Kantian ethics, it seems that material well-being is a qualified good rather than an unqualified good. A qualified good is not good in itself. Confucians see the good life as a virtuous life. Even though material well-being is good, it seems plausible that its ultimate value has to be realized in becoming an all-rounded virtuous person.

Second, the overall thrust of the Confucian view is that material well-being is not separate from the overall well-being of a person. Neither Confucius nor Mencius separates the material and moral dimensions of a person's life. While taking the virtuous society as the ultimate goal, the Confucian philosophy of government also has people's livelihood (*minsheng* 民生) as a cornerstone. Disconnecting the linkage between material well-being and moral cultivation may undermine the justification of the priority of people's livelihood in Confucian political philosophy. Confucianism promotes virtue ethics.[26] In that regard, it is radically different from Kantian ethics. Confucian ethics emphasizes developing moral character rather than moral deliberation at crossroads. The latter is usually presented in contemporary moral philosophy as a "snapshot" view of ethical decision—the decision-procedure that is "oriented toward single decisions, viewed as disconnected from other decisions, in a way which ignores or slights the moral importance of continuity of commitment."[27] Moral character matters in Confucianism. A person of character possesses moral knowledge as well as dispositions to act virtuously. In this Confucian view, virtues are acquired through cultivation. Moral cultivation always takes place in specific environments. The formation of character requires habitual practice of certain actions. This requires adequate material conditions. For example, one of the primary Confucian virtues is learning (*xue* 學), including learning about life in general and book-learning in particular. While one can always learn wisdom from others in whatever economic circumstances, book-learning requires a certain level of material provisions in society. Developing such virtues presupposes an adequate level of economic conditions. For most people, such an adequate level of material provisions would imply material well-being. Therefore, in Confucianism, material well-being and cultivation of character are not independent of each other. Although we may not rule it out exclusively, the first solution does carry some serious difficulties.

The second possible solution attempts to eliminate the other horn in the dilemma by confirming that material well-being is a precondition for moral cultivation. It holds that no one can achieve moral cultivation without a decent level of material well-being. Unlike the first answer, this answer is *prima facie* implausible. For the sake of argument, we must examine it as it is nevertheless a logical possibility. There are abundant counterexamples, however, to discredit the claim that moral cultivation is impossible without material well-being, the case of Yan Hui being an obvious one as discussed earlier. Neither Confucius nor Mencius can be said of having committed to such a view. In the end, we have to conclude that this solution clashes directly with many of the sayings by Confucius and Mencius. Therefore it is not a viable solution.

The third answer is that Confucius and Mencius may have different virtues in mind when they say that one needs material well-being in order to cultivate (one set of) virtues *and* that one does not need material well-being to cultivate (another set of) virtues. They do make comments that suggest this possibility. For instance, Confucius maintains that if a person is rich and socially elevated, he should do what a rich and socially elevated person should do, and when a person is poor and humble, he should do what a poor and humble person should do. Either way, a good person can behave virtuously in ways appropriate to his circumstances.[28] Thus, it appears that one can be a virtuous person no matter what the circumstances may be. Confucius also discusses such virtues as "no whining when you are poor" and "not haughty when you are rich."[29] Hardships in poverty tend to cause people to complain, whereas material wealth may make people arrogant. Accordingly, poverty provides an environment to develop the virtue of endurance (no whining) and richness offers opportunities for people to improve their virtue of humility. Mencius also suggests a similar point. He says that the great person is not to be corrupted in richness, nor moved off track toward goodness in poverty, nor giving in to power and force.[30] Presumably, the virtue against corruption is tested in richness and the virtue of steadfastness is proved through poverty and hardship. From here we can say that varied personal conditions provide different environments to attain and reinforce respective virtues such as resistance to corruption and steadfastness in the face of overwhelming difficulties.

The main difficulty with the third answer, however, is that it makes poverty and richness equally good for moral cultivation: while wealth is conducive to developing one type of virtues, poverty is conducive to developing a different type of virtues; neither can be said to be better than the other. But, if virtues can be cultivated equally well in either situation, and if the goal is to build a society with virtuous people, then why do we need economic prosperity? Why do Confucius and Mencius go all out in promoting economic prosperity rather than taking a stance of indifference? Furthermore, if people need poverty to cultivate certain virtues more effectively, would that imply that society should provide poverty as such an opportunity? A positive answer to the last question seems implausible.[31] Furthermore, if richness and poverty provide opportunities for people to cultivate different sets of virtues, it is difficult to see how anyone can become virtuous in an all-rounded way, which the Confucian supreme virtue of *ren* 仁 requires. Thus, this solution is not as promising as it first appears.

There is a coherent account that preserves both views in the apparent dilemma. The fourth answer differentiates two categories of people and presents a twofold account: Confucius and Mencius hold that people who are already morally cultivated well and people who are so inclined strongly do not depend on good material conditions for moral refinement, but other people, those who are not already morally so inclined, need to have their material well-being taken care of first before they can become morally cultivated.

Confucius and Mencius are realistic in assessing people's varied levels of willpower toward moral cultivation. Human society is unlike Garrison Keillor's fictional town Lake Wobegon, where "all the women are strong, all the men are good looking, and all the children are above average." In the real world, some women are strong and some are weak, some men are good looking and some are rather not so good looking, and some children are just below average. So, social philosophy needs to take into account both above-average, average, and below-average people. Confucius and Mencius are painfully aware of this social reality and have developed their philosophies accordingly.

There is textual evidence in support of this twofold account. For instance, Confucius says, "morally cultivated persons are concerned about the Way, not about poverty."[32] He also says, "morally cultivated persons may be impoverished (while still persevering), but when petty persons are impoverished, they lose all restraints."[33] For those who are already morally well-cultivated or are so inclined strongly, poverty does not alter their moral pursuit. People already with strong moral character can withstand such hardships and keep moving forward on a virtuous path. The *Tan-gong B* Chapter of the *Book of Rites* records a story about a hungry man in the ancient state of Qi. There was a famine. A wealthy man handed out charity food in the street. He saw a poor man approaching and said, in an arrogant tone, "Hey you, come here and eat!" The poor man responded, "I have ended up in this condition precisely because I refuse to eat 'hey you' food like yours!"[34] The poor man chose to starve rather than to be humiliated. Similar to Mencius's comment on choosing between fish and bear's palm, the moral of this story is that a person should retain dignity even if it means he would have to suffer the consequences, including poverty and death. It suggests that lack of living necessities like food and clothes does not mean a person would have to compromise his integrity or morality, not to mention lacking a decent level of material conditions. For this reason, Confucius says that the learned person is not affected by poverty.[35] Mencius maintains that the moral path of the great person will not be altered by poverty or meager status.[36]

However, placing morality above life is rather an unusual ability. Even for most otherwise decent people, when material conditions worsen, their moral standards for action often deteriorate. For those who have yet to form a strong character or are not so inclined, presumably it is hard to stay in line with rules of propriety when they live in poverty. When in hunger, for example, the morally vulnerable are likely to steal food; when in cold, they are likely to steal clothes or to trespass into other people's places to stay warm. Hence, the morally refined persons' indifference to material well-being may not apply to people in general. We should note that in Mencius's comments about the close connection between having constant material means and moral goodness, he specifically says that it is for the masses (*min* 民).[37] For the masses, material well-being is necessary for moral cultivation. Indeed, one may argue that, precisely because of this, Mencius strongly promotes economic prosperity even though his ultimate goal is moral attainment in society. For Confucius and Mencius, whereas morally inclined people can advance along the right path in varied conditions, average people need to have their material well-being taken care of first before they can engage in moral cultivation in a meaningful way. Thus, according to the fourth solution, when these thinkers say that material conditions do not determine a person's moral cultivation, they refer to one category of people, presumably of a small number; when they maintain that material well-being is a precondition for moral cultivation, they have in mind the large majority of people. Because they have different categories of people in mind, their various sayings, though appear conflicting, are in fact not contradictory.

This kind of apparent conflict appears common in various cultural traditions. In Christianity, for instance, there is the teaching that a person has to follow God's commandments in order to get to heaven. Those who violate God's commandments will be judged accordingly and punished in hell. There is also the teaching, however, that people cannot earn their way to heaven; only God's grace can let people enter heaven. In Buddhism, on the one hand, we find that karma regulates human actions and those doing bad things will produce bad karma and have to pay the price. On the other hand, there is also the teaching that a person can achieve Buddhahood at any time; all it takes is to change one's mindset. One way to make sense of this apparent contradiction is to see different strands of teaching as targeting different kinds of people. It is not farfetched to suppose that the threat of punishment is geared toward people who may do bad things and to prevent them from doing bad things, whereas the salvage strand is to give people with bad records hopes to reform themselves for the better. It would be counterproductive if the targeted audience were reversed, not rewarding people with good deeds entirely while telling people disposed toward bad actions that what they do does not matter. Similarly, it could be the case that Confucius and Mencius were targeting different audiences in their teaching: for example, encouraging rulers to take care of people's material well-being whereas encouraging the people for moral cultivation regardless of their material conditions. Thus, one may think that these thinkers do "double talk" to different audiences out of strategic considerations.

This "double talk" account, however, has its limitations. It contradicts with the Confucian belief that moral failure is due to a person's internal weakness rather than external conditions. Confucius says, "achieving human excellence depends on yourself. How can it depend on others?!"[38] In his eyes, whether a person becomes virtuous or not is due to her internal determination or dispositions, not on external factors such as economic conditions. Mencius seems to follow a similar line of thinking. He holds that virtues are not imposed on people from outside. They are from internal sources. If people pursue these sources, they will foster these qualities and become morally good; if they abandon their effort, they will lose these sources.[39] Accordingly, a person's moral refinement is not determined by external conditions, though it may be influenced by them. If this is true with everyone, how can we say that some people need to secure material well-being before they can become morally cultivated? I believe this difficulty can be resolved by introducing the concept of statistical necessity of different categories of people.

In society, there are morally cultivated people and uncultivated people.[40] The uncultivated group should be taken as a category based on a statistical fact. This kind of fact is statistically inevitable. Statistical inevitability is neither logical nor metaphysical. Yet, it is a strong form of inevitability. Indeed, it is so strong that we may call it statistical necessity. Let me give an example for this kind of necessity. The oxygen molecules are distributed randomly in my office. It means that, at any time, a particular oxygen molecule could move away from me out of randomness. So, could all oxygen molecules suddenly move away from where I sit in their random movement and, as a result, I suffocate? It is logically possible for this to happen, but statistically impossible. It is statistically necessary that I will have access to oxygen molecules even though they are randomly distributed. The point can also be made with a familiar case, though at a lesser degree. When someone teaches a mega-sized class, it is safe to presume that some students will receive D's and F's in their grades as a matter of statistical fact. Furthermore, it is safe to presume that the poorer the circumstances are for the class, such as poor teaching, a badly equipped classroom, and unfortunate timing, the likelier more students will receive these bad grades. Similarly, if a society has a *large* number of people living in destitution, it is statistically inevitable that some or even most of them will not become educated and morally cultivated.

Now, if most people need an economic foundation in order to become morally cultivated, would that give people in poor economic conditions excuses not to become virtuous? The Confucian response to this question, I think, is twofold. On the one hand, Confucians emphasize the importance of personal effort in moral cultivation. The inevitability of the "uncultivated" category does not mean that any particular individual is born to be in the "uncultivated" group, just as the statistical necessity of my access to oxygen molecules does not imply that any particular oxygen molecule is predetermined to be within my reach. Statistically, people growing up in ghettos are more likely to have trouble with the law and not to live a good life. It is not the case, however, that any particular individual in ghettos is predetermined to grow up in trouble or otherwise. There is an ancient Chinese story about a poor boy who loved learning so much that he borrowed light from his neighbor through a hole in the wall (*zaobi touguang* 凿壁偷光). The boy, whose family was too poor to provide light for his nightly reading, was able to read by poking a hole in the wall so he could use light from his neighbor.[41] The story has inspired Chinese students throughout history. Whether a particular person will become cultivated, regardless of material conditions, depends on personal effort. Some people become cultivated after they make such effort whereas some people do not become cultivated because they refuse to make such an effort. It is not the case that some people are preassigned into one category or another at birth and cannot change. Rather, it is because a person chooses not to, therefore he does not become cultivated and consequently fall into the "uncultivated" category of statistical necessity. In the Confucian view, no one is predetermined to be without virtue. Therefore, if someone does not become virtuous, he himself bears the responsibility.

On the other hand, Confucians hold society, and the government in particular, accountable for the failure to create an environment conducive to people's education and cultivation. In reality, few people can be as determined and industrious as the boy in the above story. Most people, after a whole day of hard labor in the field, would simply go to bed. Who can blame them? The vast majority of us need an environment more conducive to moral cultivation. We need external as well as internal forces in order to become virtuous. In the Confucian view, government has responsibility for the moral failure of the general populace under poor economic conditions. Just as more students are likely to fail in a poorly taught class and more youngsters in ghettos are likely to have trouble with the law, more people are likely to be inadequately educated and poorly cultivated in an impoverished society. Therefore, in order to facilitate people's moral cultivation, society needs to enable people to become economically prosperous.

Thus, if we understand the statistical necessity of the moral failure of impoverished people, we can make sense why Confucius and Mencius maintain that, on the one hand, individual persons can become morally cultivated even in harsh economic conditions, and, on the other, material well-being is a precondition for the moral cultivation of the general population.

In conclusion, Confucians hold that material well-being is important to people's moral cultivation. While a small number of naturally so-inclined or already sufficiently cultivated people may be able to become or remain morally cultivated independently of economic conditions, for most people, however, material well-being is a necessary condition for successful moral cultivation. Therefore, in order to foster a good society, government must help people make a decent living so they obtain the necessary material means for moral cultivation. In this view, the two ideas of Mencius's philosophy of "benevolent governance," economic prosperity and moral refinement, are closely linked.

Acknowledgments

This essay was presented at a mini-conference in honor of Joel J. Kupperman on his fiftieth anniversary of teaching philosophy, held in conjunction with the Tenth East-West Philosophers Conference in Honolulu, on May 23 and 24, 2011. I thank the audience for comments and suggestions, and especially Peimin Ni, who carefully read an early version and provided insightful comments. I dedicate this essay to Joel K. Kupperman, my former teacher at the University of Connecticut. Over these years, Kupperman has not only been instrumental in the unfolding of my professional life but also served as a role model for, as Confucians say, becoming a good person (*zuo ren* 做人). Research for this article was supported by a Nanyang Technological University Research Grant M4080394.

Notes

1. Kupperman 1991, 119–20.

2. Kupperman 1991, 120.

3. Like any other world-tradition, Christianity contains more than one version and is subject to more than one interpretation. Calvinism, for instance, takes a different position on accumulating material wealth.

4. For a recent effort to counter this common interpretation, see David Loy, "Buddhism and Poverty," accessed on 29 March 2011 at <http://www.buddhachannel.tv/portail/spip.php?article3707>. According to another interpretation, the Buddhist Middle-way is not opposed to material wealth, to an extent.

5. *Analects* 20.2; TTC, 2535. "*Li* 利" literally means profit.

6. 政之急者,莫大乎使民富且壽也 (*Confucius's Family Teachings*, 108). For the Confucian view on longevity, see Li 2010.

7. 省力役，薄賦斂，則民富矣 (*Confucius's Family Teachings*, 108).

8. Character and virtue are closely related. I follow Kupperman and see character as connected directly to the person, whereas virtues can be shared by many people (Kupperman 1991, 9–10).

9. 冉有僕.子曰:"庶矣哉！"冉有曰:"既庶矣.又何加焉？"曰:"富之."曰:"既富矣，又何加焉？"曰:"教之" (*Analects* 13.9; TTC, 2507).

10. 飢寒切於身而不為非者寡矣 (Fu, 78).

11. 易其田疇，薄其稅斂，民可使富也 (*Mencius* 7A.23; TTC, 2768).

12. Ibid.

13. 而民焉有不仁者乎？Ibid.

14. A *mu* is about 666.7 square meters.

15. The original statement appears as 倉 廩 實 ， 則 知 禮 節 ； 衣 食 足 ， 則知榮辱《管子 · 牧民》(TTM, 91). The statement suggests that abundant supply of material goods is a sufficient condition for morality. When Sima Qian quoted it in the *Records of History,* he changed the word "*ze*則" into "*er*而" (倉 廩 實 而 知 禮 節 ； 衣食足而知榮辱《史記 · 管晏列傳》; Sima Qian, 2132, making the former just one of the conditions for the latter. Sima Qian's understanding appears more in line with Confucianism.

16. 賢哉回也！一簞食，一瓢飲，在陋巷。人不堪其憂，回也不改其樂。賢哉回也！(*Analects* 6.11; TTC, 2478).

17. 而恥惡衣惡食者，未足與議也 (*Analects* 4.9; TTC, 2471).

18. "與衣狐貉者立，而不恥者，其由也與？'不忮不求，何用不臧？'"子路終身誦之。子曰:"是道也，何足以臧" (*Analects* 9.27; TTC, 2491).

19. 然後知松柏之後彫也 (*Analects* 9.28; TTC, 2491). James Legge, D.C Lau and others have translated the word "彫" as "losing leaves," which is inappropriate for the pine and cypress. "彫" stands for "凋," which the Chinese lexicon *Shuowenjiezi* defines as "injured half way 半傷." I render it as "to droop."

20. *Analects* 16.1; TTC, 2520.

21. For an account of the Confucian philosophy of harmony, see Li 2013.

22. 得志，澤加於民；不得志，脩身見於世。窮則獨善其身，達則兼善天下 (*Mencius* 7A.9; TTC, 2765).

23. 魚，我所欲也；熊掌，亦我所欲也，二者不可得兼，舍魚而取熊掌者也。生，亦我所欲也；義，亦我所欲也，二者不可得兼，舍生而取義者也 (*Mencius* 6A.10; TTC, 2752). In Chinese cuisine, a bear's palm is considered far more precious than fish.

24. 雖執鞭之士，吾亦為之. 如不可求，從吾所好 (*Analects* 7.11; TTC 2482). I thank Peimin Ni for reminding me of this reference.

25. Edward Slingerland has translated the latter part as, "Since it is not worth pursuing, however, I prefer to follow that which I love" (Slingerland, 68). Such a translation would assign Confucius the view that wealth is simply not worth pursuing. This rendering is too liberal. The "如" in "如不可求" is evidently the hypothetical "if" as most translators have followed.

26. See Philip J. Ivanhoe's essay in this volume.

27. Kupperman 1991, 74.

28. 不愿乎其外。素富貴，行乎富貴；素貧賤，行乎貧賤 (TTC, 1627).

29. 貧而無怨; 富而無驕 (*Analects* 14.10; TTC, 2511).

30. 富貴不能淫，貧賤不能移，威武不能屈 (*Mencius* 3B.7; TTC, 2710).

31. During the Cultural Revolution in China, the state did provide a similar opportunity for people to eat *yikufan* 憶苦飯, or "food for remembering the past hardship." It apparently did not produce much good.

32. 君子憂道不憂貧 (*Analects* 15.32; TTC, 2518).

33. 君子固窮，小人窮斯濫矣 (*Analects* 15.2; TTC, 2516).

34. 予唯不食嗟來之食，以至於斯也 (TTC, 2314).

35. 富貴不足以益，貧賤不足以損，此則士人也 (*Confucius's Family Teachings*, 37).

36. 富貴不能淫，貧賤不能移，威武不能屈。此之謂大丈夫 (*Mencius* 3B.7; TTC, 2710).

37. 民之為道也 (*Mencius* 3A.3; TTC, 2702).

38. 為仁由己，而由人乎哉？ (*Analects* 12.1; TTC, 2502).

39. 非由外鑠我也，我固有之也，弗思耳矣。故曰："求則得之，舍則失之。" 或相倍蓰而無算者，不能盡其才者也 (*Mencius* 6A.6; TTC, 2749).

40. For the sake of argument, here I consider only normal adults and leave out the issue with relative standards and levels of the "cultivated."

41. 鑿壁偷光：匡衡字稚圭，勤學而無燭。鄰居有燭而不逮，衡乃穿壁引其光，以書映光而讀之 (Cheng and Cheng, 69–70).

References

Aristotle (1962). *Nicomachean Ethics*. Translated with introduction and notes by Martin Oswald. Indianapolis, IN, and New York: The Bobbs-Merrill Company, Inc.

Cheng Lin 成林 and Cheng Zhangcan 程章燦 (1993). 《西京雜記》 *Collected Records of the Western Capital*. Guiyang: Guizhou Renmin Press 貴陽市: 貴州人民出版社.

Confucius's Family Teachings 《孔子家語》 (2003). Beijing 北京: China Culture and History Press 中國文史出版社.

Fu Yashu 傅亞庶 (2011). 《孔叢子校釋》 *An Annotated Interpretation of the Kong Congzi*. Beijing 北京: Zhonghua Shuju 中華書局.

Kupperman, Joel J. (1991). *Character*. Oxford and New York: Oxford University Press.

Li, Chenyang (2010). "Confucian Moral Cultivation, Longevity, and Public Policy," *Dao: A Journal of Comparative Philosophy*, 9.1: 25–36.

———. (2013). *The Confucian Philosophy of Harmony*. London/New York: Routledge.

Lau, D. C. (1970). *Mencius*. New York: Penguin Books.

Sima Qian 司馬遷 (1982). 《史記》 *Records of History*, Vol. 7. Beijing 北京: Zhonghua Shuju 中華書局.

Slingerland, Edward (2003). *Confucius Analects: With Selections from Traditional Commentaries*. Indianapolis/Cambridge: Hackett Publishing Company.

Thirteen Classics with Commentaries (TTC) 《十三經注疏》 (1985). Beijing北京: Zhongguo Shudian 中國書店.

Twenty-two Masters (TTM) 《二 十 二 子》 (1986). Shanghai上海: Shanghai Guji Chubanshe 上海古籍出版社.

8

Materialistic Desires and Ethical Life in the *Analects* and the *Mencius*

SOR-HOON TAN

Confucius lamented, "It is not easy to find students who will study for three years without their thoughts turning to an official salary."[1] His student, Zizhang, was described in the text as studying for the purpose of career advancement (2.18). Fortunately, he had at least one student who was free from materialistic motivation.

> He has a bamboo of rice to eat, a gourd of water to drink, and a dirty little hovel in which to live. Other people would not be able to endure his hardships, yet for Hui it has no effect on his enjoyment. A person of character [*xian* 賢] is this Yan Hui! (6.11)

Confucius shared with Yan Hui this ability to endure, if not enjoy, poverty, which seems to be part of the character of a Confucian *junzi* 君子, an exemplary person.

> The Master said, "Wealth and honor are what people want, but if they are the consequence of deviating from the way (*dao* 道), I would have no part in them. Poverty and disgrace are what people deplore, but if they are the consequence of staying on the way, I would not avoid them." (4.5)

In appearing to choose ethical life over wealth and honor (also 7.12), Confucius seemed to imply that ethical life and materialistic desires are incompatible at least some of the time.[2] Confucians of later dynasties, Zhou Dunyi for example, interpreted Confucius and Yan Hui's "delight" (Kong Yan *lechu* 孔顏樂處) in terms of an ethical requirement to transcend the materialistic desires that drive the average person to pursue wealth and status.[3]

Joel Kupperman argues that a strong character is a necessary though not sufficient condition for a very good life.[4] Materialistic conditions enable satisfaction of some desires, which brings pleasure, and increase the chances of achieving some goals that may be conducive to happiness, but conceptions of the good life that reduces it to pleasure or happiness in terms of goal satisfaction are inadequate. If we understand Confucian interest in personal cultivation as an interest in developing strong characters, exemplified by the *junzi*, the process is bound up with the question of what values are worth aiming at in life. For one's choices guided by how one answers that question, and resulting commitments, would determine what kind of character one develops over time. This essay is concerned only with a small part of that issue, whether and to what extent, materialistic gains and wealth are acceptable values that a Confucian may aim at, given their understanding of what counts as a very good life that is, at the same time, an ethical life.

If materialistic gains and wealth are incompatible with Confucian learning and ethical life, then is Confucianism hopelessly impractical and therefore obsolete in modern market economies driven by materialistic consumption and the profit motive? Some may have the impression that Confucianism is setting up impossible ideals that ignore facts about human tendencies, natural motivations, and social realities. Others may insist that the current obsession with wealth renders our age more in need of wisdom that counsels against neglect of what is truly of value, even if it falls on deaf ears more often than not. Or one may look for a middle way, and ask if a modern Confucian could balance her ethical commitments with prosperity in this age of global capitalism. The early Confucian texts, the *Analects* and the *Mencius*, reveal not a simple opposition but varied and more complex attitudes toward materialistic desires and pursuit of wealth. Examining their reasons for disapproving unlimited pursuit of materialistic goals, and their strategies for dealing with such motivations, that they acknowledge to be very common among people and even understandable, illuminates an important dimension of Confucian ethics in practice. It brings new insights from Confucian understanding of moral psychology, and offers a critique of the excesses of contemporary capitalist societies without being rabidly anti-capitalist, or expecting people to live up to the daunting standards of Yan Hui's and Confucius's delight in poverty.

Opposition Between Materialistic/Profitable Pursuits and Ethical Life

This section will examine some passages in the *Analects* and the *Mencius* that give the impression that materialistic desires or pursuit of profit and wealth are opposed to the ethical life, but will go on to show that this is an over-simplification in the next section. Confucius shared with Yan Hui a love of learning, something Confucius highlighted more than once.[5] This is the ideal motivation for learning just as love of the ethical is the ideal motivation for ethical conduct. An exemplary person who loves learning is not primarily concerned with physical comfort, let alone the pursuit of wealth (1.14). This ethical focus that deprecates materialistic concerns extends beyond learning to the exemplary person's entire way of life:

> The Master said, "Exemplary persons make their plans around the way and not around their sustenance. Tilling the land often leads to hunger as a matter of course; studying often leads to an official salary as a matter of course. Exemplary persons are anxious about the way, and not about poverty." (15.32)

Although the learning of exemplary persons may result in a comfortable living, even wealth, Confucius considered the deliberate pursuit of materialistic gains (*li* 利) undesirable because, among other things, it would undermine social harmony (4.12). In government, "if you see only petty gains [*xiaoli* 小利], the great tasks will not be accomplished."[6] Whether in ancient times or today, one need not look far for examples of politicians and others motivated by materialistic gains who have exploited the people and neglected the interests of the country. Such socially and politically detrimental effects of the pursuit of materialistic goals alone would explain why Confucius "seldom spoke of profit," that is, his teachings were not aimed at helping students pursue materialistic gain.

Beyond the potential for disharmony and less than effective government, Confucius was wary of materialistic pursuits because of their effects on a person's character and conduct. It is difficult to "enjoy the way" when one is poor, if one hankers after wealth, and difficult "to love the rites" when one is rich, if one's wealth leads to arrogance (1.15; also 14.10). Confucius suggested that, even though the standards for consummate persons (*chengren* 成人) were relatively lower in his day, compared with the ancients, the criteria would still include, among other things, that "on seeing a chance to profit they think of appropriate conduct (*yi* 義)" (14.12). The opposition between pursuit of profit and ethical life represented by *yi* is most stark in *Analects* 4.16:

> The Master said, "Exemplary persons (*junzi* 君子) understand what is appropriate (*yi* 義); petty persons understand what is of personal advantage (*li* 利).[7]

This passage heralds the polarization of profit and ethical motives later in the tradition. For several centuries, the common popular understanding of the Confucian teaching on *yi* and *li* was one of mutual exclusion. This began to change only with the rise of the merchant class in the sixteenth century and the mingling of the social classes of Confucian scholar-officials and merchants.[8]

Mencius agreed that an exemplary person puts virtue before satisfaction of physical desires, and being recognized for virtue is better than being admired for one's "fineries" (6A.17).[9] The contradiction between materialistic gains and ethical life was sharpened in the *Mencius*, who replied to King Hui of Liang's question about "ways to profit his state," with the declaration that, "All that matters is that there should be benevolence and rightness [*renyi* 仁義]." It is not always clear from the text whether *yi* and *li* are necessarily opposed conceptually, or it is merely the case that they *can* be opposed, and in many cases often are. Mencius seemed to be inferring from observations of people's conduct and its consequences, and therefore only claiming contingent rather than necessary opposition. While they may be compatible, which is the object on which one focuses one's attention, which motivates one's action? Mencius maintained that if everyone is motivated by profit, "the state will be imperiled. . . . if profit is put before rightness, there is no satisfaction short of total usurpation" (1A.1). The *yi-li* opposition is emphasized again when Mencius objected to Song Keng's intention to persuade Chu and Qin to end the war between the two states by explaining to their rulers "the unprofitability of war" (6B.4). Mencius equated the difference between *li* and *shan* 善—the profitable and the good—to the difference between the robber and the sage (7A.25). When advising Duke Wen of Teng that "the business of the people must be attended to without delay," Mencius cited Yang Hu, "If one's aim is wealth one cannot be benevolent; if one's aim is benevolence one cannot be wealthy" (3A.3).

Although the *Mencius* emphasizes a more often mutually exclusive opposition between the ethical and the profitable, equating the profitable to the unethical, there are occasions when "*li*" was used to refer to ethically neutral benefit, gain, or advantage, as when the term refers to geographical advantage (*dili* 地利, 4B.26), or benefitting the people (7A.13), or the world (7A.26)—the first could be sought for ethical purpose, and the latter two are clearly permissible, even desirable from the perspective of *yi*. In both the *Analects* (15.10) and the *Mencius* (1A.5), the term was used also to mean "sharpness," "sharp," or "to sharpen"—literally in reference to weapons or tools. Just as sharp tools are instruments increasing one's effectiveness in relevant activities, *li* can refer to any contribution to effectiveness or doing well (2B.1; 4B.26), both unethical (*likou* 利口 "glibness," *Analects* 17.18; *Mencius* 7B.37), and ethical (*liren* 利仁 "flourish in benevolence" in *Analects* 4.2; *min zhi suoli* 民之所利 "give the common people those benefits that will really be beneficial to them" in *Analects* 20.2). Beyond neutral or even ethical references, where "*li*" is more appropriately translated as something other than "profit"—usually "benefit" which may be materialistic or ethical—we need to examine more closely textual evidence indicating that Confucian attitudes toward materialistic desires and pursuits need not be those of total rejection and condemnation. Some degree of acceptance is necessitated by the recognition that many people are motivated by materialistic desires, and will therefore pursue the means to do so, including wealth and other forms of power.

Managing Competition and Conflict Between Materialistic Desires and Ethical Desires

Confucius recognized that the most common human motives are orientated toward profit and materialistic pursuits, which tend to be self-centered and even selfish. He was well aware of how the majority in their actions are prey to various unethical or at best nonethical distractions. "Wealth and honor are what people want . . . Poverty and disgrace are what people deplore . . ." (4.5). Desires to gratify the physical senses often lead one astray: "I have yet to meet the person who is fonder of excellence (*de* 德) than of physical beauty" (9.18; 15.13). Despite lamenting the way materialistic desires get in the way of ethical life,

Confucius was accommodating of other people's materialistic concerns, to the extent that he considered it the responsibility of a good government to enrich the people, even before educating them (13.9). For all the much touted moral idealism in Mencian thought, Mencius also acknowledged that desires of the senses and the accompanying materialistic interests are common to all human beings (5A.1; 6A.7).

Both Confucius (13.9) and Mencius are more accommodating of others' materialistic desires than they are of a person pursuing materialistic gains for himself or herself. Although Mencius disagreed with Confucius on the priority of wealth over education in government (7A.14), he nevertheless advocated government satisfying people's materialistic desires: "amass what they want for them; do not impose what they dislike on them" (4A.9; 7A.23). Mencius saw that physical deprivation often proved to be demoralizing and drove ordinary people to wrongdoing (3A.3). His idea of "benevolent government" is one whose rule ensures materialistic comforts.

> If the mulberry is planted in every homestead of five *mu* of land, those who are fifty can wear silk; if chickens, pigs and dogs do not miss their breeding season, then those who are seventy can eat meat; if each lot of a hundred *mu* is not deprived of labor during the busy seasons, the families with several mouths to feed will not go hungry. (1A.3; 7A.22)

Not only are the common people's physical desires recognized as the basis of legitimate demands that should be satisfied by a good government, even the talented and virtuous appointed to office were not expected to ignore their own materialistic interests so far as to serve without material compensation (2B.14). Mencius did not criticize the "ancient practice" of paying officials and spoke approvingly of "hereditary emolument" for officials (1B.5; 3A.3). When King Xuan of Qi tried to excuse his failure to govern with virtue by admitting to the weaknesses of being fond of money and women, Mencius did not waste his breath asking the king to ignore or eliminate those desires. Instead, he asked only that the king recognize that his people had the same desires, and he should satisfy not just his own but their desires as well (1B.5).[10]

It is clear that even though they set the highest ethical standard at the level where one should be willing to sacrifice one's own life, let alone forego a few possessions or leave a few materialistic desires unsatisfied, in pursuit of the ethical, neither Confucius nor Mencius totally excludes materialistic desires from the ethical life. They did, however, believe that we can and should desire the ethical as well. Confucius spoke of desiring and being fond of authoritative conduct (*ren* 仁) (4.6; 7.30; 17.8; 20.2), desiring what is good (*shan* 善) (12.19). It is possible to be fond of learning (1.14; 5.15; 17.8), of ritual (1.15), of appropriateness (12.20; 13.4), of trustworthiness (*xin* 信) (13.4), of courage and wisdom (17.8), and of "excellence" (*de* 德) (9.18; 15.13). Mencius described himself desiring to observe the rites (4B.27) and desiring appropriateness (6A.10), the exemplary person desiring "to find the way in himself" (4B.14), and people desiring to "rectify themselves" (7B.4). He recommended fondness for benevolence (*ren*) to rulers (4A.7; 4A.9; 7B.4). Under good rulers, "people are fond of the good" (11.6; also 12.13). Ancient kings, being ethically worthy (*xian* 賢), are "fond of goodness, forgetting their own exalted position."[11]

Both texts perceive a competition between ethical and materialistic desires, and the competition becomes more explicit and intense in the *Mencius*. For Mencius, materialistic and ethical desires are associated, respectively, with the physical senses and the heart-mind, the former being the "smaller parts" (*xiaoti* 小體) and the latter the "greater parts" (*dati* 大體) of our persons.

> The parts of the person differ in value and importance. . . . He who nurtures the parts of smaller importance is a small man; he nurtures the parts of greater importance is a great man. (6A.14)

To tread the Confucian way is to strive to raise the desire for the ethical above nonethical/unethical desires, perhaps to overpower or eclipse, even to eliminate, the latter with the former. Before materialistic desires are eliminated or at least ignored at will, how far should we go to satisfy such desires? An unethical act clearly would not be permitted for the sake of materialistic gain (4.5); on the contrary, the added desire for the latter renders the act even more unethical. What reasons do we have to expect ordinary human beings to choose the ethical over the materialistic when the two conflict directly? Unless one holds the view that whatever is not ethical must be unethical (a possible interpretation of the Confucian position), there would be a variety of actions with materialistic pay-offs that will not involve acting unethically. Are they all permissible or desirable? How do Confucians go about making the ethical more desirable given the human inclinations towards materialistic desires?

The possibility of choosing the ethical over the materialistic is implicit in both texts. Most of us have probably come across people who sacrificed some materialistic benefits in order to act ethically, accept a lower level of economic prosperity in order to pursue some noneconomic interests or ideals. Much rarer are the few who could live up to the high standard of "resolute scholar-apprentices and the authoritative persons," who "would not compromise their authoritative conduct to save their lives, but would give up their lives in order to achieve it" (15.9), or of the person who would rather starve than survive by unethical acts. Mencius believed everyone capable of this high standard (6A.10), and justified his expectation with the claim that the beginnings of ethical excellences are to be found in the human heart-mind (2A.6; 7A.21). Although Mencius sometimes claimed that one merely needs to "seek and one will find it" (6A.6; 7A.3), it is more plausible that these ethical beginnings need to be nurtured through a process of personal cultivation which, for Mencius, is a matter of "retaining one's heart-mind" (*cunxin* 存心) and nurturing (7B.35) it, to "fully realize" it (*jinxin* 盡心) (7A.1).

Materialistic desires are obstacles or distractions in the process of personal cultivation, so much so that,

> There is nothing better for the nurturing of the heart than to reduce the number of one's desires. When a man has few desires, even if there is anything he fails to retain in himself, it cannot be much; but when he has a great many desires, then even if there is anything he manages to retain in himself, it cannot be much. (7B.35)

Most desires are presumably materialistic desires.[12] We find a similar thought in the *Analects* where Meng Gongchuo, who was considered good enough "to serve the Zhao and Wei families as household steward" (14.11), was praised for being "free from desires" (*buyu* 不欲), implying that this would aid him in doing a good job as household steward for which honesty is important. Someone with many materialistic desires would succumb to the temptations of profiting unethically from the position. *Analects* 12.18 also implies that materialistic desires led to thievery, so that if Ji Kangzi were to set the example by being "free from desires," then "people would not steal even if they are paid to do so."[13] Assuming that materialistic desires directly conflict with ethical life, how does one go about reducing those desires? Mencius believed that all we need is to look into ourselves; but for those whose eyes are already fixed elsewhere, what "single good word" or "single good deed" (7A.16) would turn one's attention to "the greater parts"?

A Bird in Hand . . . ?: Uncertain Outcome of Materialistic Pursuits

How does one persuade people to choose the ethical over materialistic gains? Simply condemning the latter or exalting the former will have little effect. Confucius sometimes adopted the strategy of arguing that the outcome of any pursuit of profit or wealth is uncertain at best, and therefore as goals *per se*, an inferior choice compared with the certainty of success in the self-cultivation of ethical excellence. Efforts toward materialistic prosperity may not be rewarded, as when Confucius maintained, "[T]illing the land often leads to hunger" (15.32). Rather than being entirely dependent on human abilities and effort, there is a common saying that "Wealth and honor lie with *tian* 天" (12.5). When pursuit of wealth is rejected as "*buke*" (7.12)—is it not permissible or not possible? The term "*ke* 可" may be either prescriptive or descriptive (meaning "can" or "is possible"), or both. The descriptive meaning may not seem relevant at first glance, since it seems obvious that one *can* pursue wealth. However, while one can certainly pursue wealth, one cannot pursue it with certainty of success. One may also read this passage as implying that since the pursuit of wealth is not guaranteed success, the uncertainty renders it normatively unacceptable, and even if wealth is good, one is at most sacrificing an uncertain good in pursuing other things one loves and should love more.

Going beyond the text, but still in line with Confucian thinking, the uncertainty pertaining to the pursuit of wealth has two dimensions. First, it may not be successful. Second, as an instrumental good—wealth is generally valued for what it could purchase rather than as an intrinsic good—it is also uncertain whether wealth, when gained, would necessarily bring about goods that are valued for themselves. In contrast, the pursuit of the ethical in Confucius's view is certain of success. "How could authoritative conduct be at all remote? No sooner do I seek it than it has arrived."[14] Mencius seemed to share this view:

> Seek and you will get it; let it go and you will lose it.[15] If this is the case, then seeking is of use to getting and what is sought is within yourself.[16] But if there is a proper way to

> seek it and whether you get it or not depends on Destiny, then seeking is of no use to getting and what is sought lies outside yourself. (7A.3)

One should not exaggerate the certainty of ethical pursuits. Ethical deeds may not succeed in terms of transforming the world or even benefiting another, just as pursuit of wealth may be frustrated. However, one can at least be certain that acting ethically will improve one's character. It is, however, questionable if this is enough for Confucians, given its understanding of how every person is socially constituted.

The above argument about the relative certainty of outcomes and whether a pursuit has intrinsic value or is merely instrumental will not dissuade people from the pursuit of wealth and other materialistic ends altogether unless they are already drawn to ethical ends to some degree. Indeed, Confucius chose to "follow what he was fond of" rather than lower himself in indiscriminate or unscrupulous pursuit of wealth and honor only because he had other desires that were stronger than his desire for wealth and honor. One may not be absolutely certain of becoming rich in any endeavor, but one can always spend more time trying to earn more money and learning how to be better at accumulating wealth. If ethical desires are not even present, the argument that one may not actually have to sacrifice materialistic goods (as opportunity cost) as success of pursuing the latter is never certain is not going to convince people to pursue ethical goals instead of materialistic ones. The fact that one's efforts will not necessarily be rewarded, or that wealth might prove less useful than expected in realizing intrinsically valuable goods, will not by itself divert their attention from these nonethical goals. The probability of success of this strategy depends not only on the relative strength of desires for the materialistic versus the ethical, but also on one's attitude to risks and one's relative confidence in one's various abilities.

Mencius's Objections to Confucius's Harnessing of Materialistic Desires

The above strategy does not have to assume direct conflict between the materialistic and the ethical, although it could be used even when there is such conflict. This is an advantage if one suspects that materialistic desires are stronger than ethical desires and drawing attention to the conflict between them will reduce the chances of ethical desires winning the contest. One might even go further to argue that there is no conflict, as Confucius sometimes did when he tried to persuade people that their materialistic goals could be achieved through ethical conduct, an example being his suggestion that studying often did lead to an official salary, even as he insisted that an exemplary person set his sights on the way and did not worry about poverty (15.32). Confucius's guidance of his career-minded student, Zizhang, illustrates his approach of trying to lead others toward the ethical via their materialistic pursuits. Though he must have had reservations about Zizhang's motivations for studying, Confucius did not simply condemn him or insist that the student should give up his interest in an official salary. Instead Confucius tried to steer him toward ethical conduct by clarifying the best way to achieve "*lu* 祿."

> If you listen broadly, set aside what you are unsure of, and speak cautiously on the rest, you will make few errors; if you look broadly, set aside what is perilous, and act cautiously on the rest, you will have few regrets. *Lu* lies in speaking with few errors and acting with few regrets.[17]

While he was not explicitly advocating ethical conduct, in terms of *yi*, for example, this attempt to focus Zizhang's attention on not committing errors and avoiding regret would be a step in the ethical direction when combined with Confucius's teachings that unethical conduct is erroneous and will cause regrets.

The term *lu* was commonly used in all three pre-Qin Confucian texts to refer to the payment officials received for their service, and hence the translation of "*xue yu lu* 學于祿" into "studying in order to take office" (Ames and Rosemont) or "studying for an official career" (Lau). It is important to note that what renders Zizhang's purpose questionable is the expectation of materialistic reward rather than the desire to take office, even though it is legitimate to accept pay for taking office (as acknowledged in *Mencius* 2B.14). Confucius had no objection to the desire to take office *per se*. On the contrary, serving in government, that is taking office, is an important part of the exemplary person's ethical pursuit. However, taking office should be motivated by the desire to transform the world ethically and benefit others with one's ethical excellence and talent rather than by the desire for wealth, status, or power for oneself.[18] If a state is governed well and ethical conduct rewarded, then not to prosper would be a sign of one's lack of ability or insufficient effort to contribute to an ethical polity. Confucius therefore considered it "a disgrace to remain poor and without rank when the way prevails in the state," whereas "it is a disgrace to be wealthy and of noble rank when it does not" (8.13), presumably because in a state not governed according to Confucius's ethical ideal of government, the only ways to obtain wealth and social status would be unethical.

Confucius certainly did not condemn everyone who was rich and powerful, assuming without further proof that wealth and power were gained always through unethical actions. If materialistic gains and ethical actions are compatible, then it would be easier to persuade people to act ethically when they do not have to sacrifice their materialistic interests, at least not totally, and even better, when they can actually advance those interests through ethical actions. In adopting this strategy, the hope is that, even though what initially motivates a person is a materialistic goal, if she could be persuaded to seek this through ethical actions rather than unethical ones, then over time, ethical actions could become habitual and she would acquire a disposition toward ethical actions, as well as an appreciation of the ethical that will transform their motivations, so that the ethical becomes more important than and eventually supplants the materialistic, which becomes dispensable. However, this reversal is by no means automatic, and may be highly unlikely—this has to be determined empirically. There is a danger that such a strategy of trying to lead people to value the ethical by leveraging their materialistic desires merely acquiesces to an instrumentalization of the ethical and furthermore risks the corruption of the ethical means. Mencius was certainly conscious of this danger in his tendency to polarize the contest between ethical and materialistic pursuits.

Some passages indicate that Mencius would object to any strategy that suggests a less than ethical path toward ethical ends. When Chen Dai hinted that Mencius should "bend" to serve the feudal lords, as the goal of "straightening" such people seemed worthy of a little compromise, Mencius rejected the suggestion that one could reach an ethical goal via inappropriate or unethical paths. He illustrated his point with the story of Wang Liang, a charioteer who refused to drive for someone who was unable to catch any bird when Wang "drove according to the proper rules," but caught ten birds when Wang "used underhand methods" (3B.1). While a petty person uses or even requires improper means to reach his or her goals, both means and ends of an exemplary person should be appropriate. A similar message is found in Mencius's account of how Yi Yin came to take office under the emperor Tang, denying that Yi Yin "tried to attract the attention of Tang by his culinary abilities"

(5A.7). The pursuit and acceptance of office must follow appropriate ceremony and the proper motivation for taking office is a sense of social responsibility that emulates Yi Yin's: "When he saw a common man or woman who did not enjoy the benefit of the rule of Yao or Shun, Yi Yin felt as if he had pushed him or her into the gutter."[19] For Mencius, conduct is ethical only if its motivation itself is ethical and one seeks one's goals in an ethically appropriate manner. Whether such conduct is advantageous or profitable is a matter of *ming* that an exemplary person should leave to the dictates of heaven (7B.33).

The implication of these stories in the *Mencius* is that unethical means, including materialistic motivations, taint a pursuit and render the goal ethically suspect. Mencius (6B.4) explicitly rejected Song Keng's attempt to persuade Qin and Chu to act ethically—stop an unethical war—by appealing to their materialistic concerns. He saw in materialistic desires a tendency to expand and spread, almost always at the expense of the ethical. Besides eroding the ethical value, if there was any to begin with, of the agent's own goals, conduct motivated by profit motive also often had widespread undesirable and corrupting effects in the community.

> In antiquity, the market was for the exchange of what one had for what one lacked. The authorities merely supervised it. There was, however, a despicable fellow who always looked for a vantage point and, going up on it, gazed into the distance to the left and to the right in order to secure for himself all the profit there was in the market. The people all thought him despicable, and, as a result, they taxed him. The taxing of traders began with this despicable fellow. (2B.10)

The desire for profit tends to keep expanding and become insatiable so that seeking advantage or profit quickly becomes profiting at others' expense or taking advantage of others. This pushes others into retaliation that directs their attention to the materialistic, and before we know it, we have a situation with everyone vying for advantage and profit, with no thought for social harmony or ethics, and then coercive regulation becomes necessary to curb the conflicts, exploitation, and mutual harm that inevitably result. Despite Mencius's archaic language, this is a situation all too recognizable to us today.

Even when pursued through outwardly ethical actions, materialistic goals are less likely to move one toward ethical motivations than they are to blind us to the distinction between the ethical and unethical. Materialistic pursuits are driven by desires of the senses, such as hearing and sight, which "are unable to think and can be misled by external things" (6A.15). Preoccupation with materialistic concerns greatly reduces the probability that one's heart-mind, which "can think," from finding the answer to how one should act. When one focuses on goals identified by one's physical senses—be it food, an attractive sexual partner, or any objects one wishes to possess—one's mind engages in instrumental calculation of how to obtain those objects or gratify one's physical desires. Such mental activity obscures ethical concerns about both ends and means of one's conduct, concerns that would otherwise have arisen from one's "basic heart-mind" (*benxin* 本心) that desires the ethical, what is *yi* 義, even more than life itself. Materialistic desires therefore cause one's basic heart-mind to stray. According to Mencius, it is my basic humanity that "there is something I want more than life . . . and something I loathe more than death," so that "there are ways of remaining alive and ways of avoiding death to which a person will not resort" (6A.10). Unfortunately, many people lose this basic humanity, so much so that what one "would not accept when it was a matter of life and death," had one retained that basic humanity, one then becomes willing to "accept for the sake of beautiful houses, . . . for the enjoyment of wives and concubines, . . . for the sake of the gratitude from needy acquaintances" (6A.10).

Mencius observed that the love for profit and pursuit of materialistic ends were almost always accompanied by a lack of scruples. *Mencius* 4B.33 tells the story of a man from Qi who obtained food and drink by begging for leftovers from people offering sacrifices to the dead. He was so despised that no one would speak to him when he went out, but he pretended to his wife and concubine that he wined and dined with "men of wealth and consequence" every day. When his wife and concubine found out, "they reviled their husband and wept in the courtyard." Mencius commented, "In the eyes of the gentleman, few of all those who seek wealth and position fail to give their wives and concubines cause to weep with shame." Although the willingness to do anything for profit or just to satisfy one's physical desires is shameful conduct rejected by exemplary persons, one should avoid being over-zealous in rejecting profit and wealth, lest the rejection itself leads us into unethical conduct. This is Mencius's apparent verdict on Chen Zhongzi, whose disapproval of his brother's income and wealth led him to "live apart from his brother and mother," something Mencius considered inappropriate.

> One day he came home for a visit and found that his brother had been given a present of a live goose, he knitted his brow and said, "What does one want this honking creature for?" Another day, his mother killed the goose and gave it to him to eat. His brother came home and said, "This is the meat of that honking creature." He went out and vomited it all out. He ate what his wife provided but not what his mother provided. He lived in Wu Ling but not in his brother's house. Did he think that he had succeeded in pushing his principle to the utmost limits? Pushed to the utmost limits his way of life would only be possible if he were an earthworm. (3B.10)

One might ask if Mencius is entirely consistent, especially given his view that there are some things more valuable than life, so much so that even a starving wayfarer would not accept food "given with abuse" and even a starving beggar would not accept food "given after being trampled upon" (6A.10)—sentiments that resonate much better with the earlier story of the man who shamed his wife and concubine. Mencius's verdict on Chen Zhongzi needs to be contextualized in his questioning of the latter's opinion that the income of his elder brother was unethical (*buyi* 不義). In the passage, Mencius pointed out that the elder brother had hereditary wealth generating a huge income.[20] Chen's scruples were judged as little more than a misguided sense of superiority in condemning wealth and eminence *per se*. It is also worth noting that Chen Zhongzi himself was not being required to commit any unethical acts in benefitting from his elder brother's wealth. On the contrary, Mencius seems to be hinting that Chen's behavior was ethically questionable as it undermined family harmony and propriety for the sake of unwarranted scruples in this case. Despite the strong criticism of materialistic desires in the *Mencius*, there is still a subtle balance to be struck that prevents a total rejection of all materialistic gains or pursuits.

To a certain extent, Mencius did not completely reject the strategy of harnessing materialistic desires that people already have to move people towards ethical life—he seemed to be following it in urging King Xuan of Qi, who loved money and women, to share his materialistic goods with his people who also had materialistic desires. However, Mencius did not actually concede that one could end up with an ethical life by following one's materialistic desires alone. Paying attention to others' materialistic desires, and not just one's own, activates emotions of sympathy that are the roots of ethical desires—this already transforms one's motivations from purely materialistic toward the ethical. It is a step toward recovering one's heart-mind that has "strayed" when one's attention is occupied by materialistic desires (6A.11). Unfortunately, Mencius's own failures in persuading people such as King Xuan show the chances of success for this strategy to be slim at best.

The discussions in *Analects* and *Mencius* about materialistic desires and their effect on one's pursuit of the ethical life leave us with the following possibilities: at one end, we have people so consumed with materialistic desires that they have lost their capacity to act ethically; at the other we have people so advanced in personal cultivation, whose characters are so strong, that they are able to eliminate most materialistic desires, and ignore those that remain, including even the desire for life, when these conflict with their ethical commitment. Most people fall between the two extremes where there is possibility of moving in either direction. The path in the materialistic direction is a slippery slope toward unscrupulous villainy, and gets more slippery the further one moves in that direction. Moving in the opposite ethical direction is difficult for most ordinary people, but becomes easier the closer one gets to the goal, or perhaps becomes easy once one passes a point where one recovers one's basic heart-mind. Even though Confucius emphasized that it is up to oneself to pursue an ethical life (12.1), and individual effort is certainly crucial, still one could criticize contemporary capitalist society for the extent to which it encourages the slide towards the materialistic or increases the difficulty of moving toward the ethical. I do not think that capitalism necessarily condemns us to a slide in one direction, despite more radical critiques that portray capitalism as rotten to the core, and incorrigible. Total condemnation of the status quo that we inevitably inhabit gives no guidance on viable change. Revolutions that had attempted to replace entire social realities with utopias have not given us much faith in such all-or-nothing approaches. Realistic reform requires efforts to separate positive and negative elements in experience. Learning from Confucius's and Mencius's experience, I do not think recommending that everyone follows Yan Hui's example will have much success. Setting such a high standard might even discourage many from even trying to improve. There is something to be said for an alternative model that seeks both ethical life and materialistic prosperity, even while we bear in mind Mencius's warning about the dangers of feeding materialistic desires. The next section will show that we can find such a "second best" option in the *Analects*.

"Most Precious and Sacred Kind of Vessel": Reconciling Materialistic Pursuits with Ethical Life

Contemporary capitalist societies could not by any stretch of imagination be considered a world "in which the Way prevails." If that is so, should it not follow that today "it is a disgrace to be wealthy and of noble rank"? The message of *Analects* 8.3 may need to be qualified when one considers the character and achievements of Zigong. In worldly terms, Zigong was the most successful of Confucius's students. According to Han historian Sima Qian, he had held high office in two states, as premier of both Lu and Wei, and was fabulously rich.[21]

> Zigong, after studying with Confucius, retired and held office in the state of Wey. By buying up, storing and selling various goods in the region of Cao and Lu, he managed to become the richest among Confucius' seventy disciples. While Yuan Xian, another of the Master's disciples, could not get even enough chaff and husks to satisfy his hunger, and lived hidden in a tiny lane, Zigong rode about with a team of four horses attended by a mounted retinue, bearing gifts of bundles of silk to be presented to the feudal lords, and whatever state he visited the ruler never failed to descend into the courtyard and greet him as an equal. It was due to Zigong's efforts that Confucius' fame was spread over the empire. Is this not what we mean when we say that a man who wields power may win greater and greater eminence?[22]

Confucius had thought that Yan Hui's early death spelled the end of his hopes that his teachings would make an impact on the world (11.9). (One wonders whether Yan Hui's delight in poverty also meant extreme neglect of materialistic well-being to the extent that it hastened his death.) Fortunately Confucius was wrong about his teachings dying with Yan Hui, and if we believe Sima Qian, we have Zigong to thank for the spread of Confucius's teachings, an accomplishment due in no small way to his worldly skills and success both as a merchant and a diplomat. Zigong had the longest biography in Sima Qian's biographies of Confucius's disciples. Most of the narrative was about Zigong's impressive diplomatic feats in saving the state of Lu from invasion: "[I]n one trip, Tzu-kung [Zigong] preserved Lu, troubled Ch'i, defeated

Wu, strengthened Chin and made Yüeh hegemon."[23] In *Analects* 6.8, Confucius commented that Zigong's understanding (*da* 達) equipped him well for taking office. Although the *Analects* singled out Zigong for his eloquence, his accomplishments as an official outshone even those singled out for statesmanship, Ran You and Zilu, who were only stewards of the powerful Ji family in Lu, whereas Zigong rose to be premier of two states.

Zigong appears frequently in the *Analects*, and he was one of the ten students whose accomplishments were singled out for comment (11.3). Although Confucius criticized Zigong on a few occasions—for overestimating his abilities (5.12) or having the wrong priorities cutting expenses in a ritual (3.17)—Confucius thought highly of this student.[24] Despite their occasional disagreements (14.17), Confucius valued his opinions (5.9; 17.24). Instead of simply accepting his teacher's words, Zigong often engaged Confucius more actively, and won praise for going beyond what he was taught.[25]

> The Master said: "Zigong, it is only with the likes of you then that I can discuss the *Songs!* On the basis of what has been said, you know what is yet to come."[26]

Often not satisfied with Confucius's initial reply to his questions, he would press for further clarification, question, or even disagree with his teacher, respectfully of course.[27] He was attentive and devoted to Confucius, explaining and defending him to others even after his death, and mourned him for six years, twice the length of time prescribed for ritual mourning for one's parents.[28] He even challenged Confucius's own self-assessment when the latter seemed to him overly modest (14.28). When Confucius, perhaps out of frustration at the little impact his views were having on the world, wanted to give up speech, Zigong objected: "If you do not speak, how will we your followers find the proper way?" (17.19) It is clear from the *Analects* that, even if he was not the teacher's favorite, Zigong was valued highly by Confucius and has enjoyed a high standing in the Confucian tradition.[29]

While generally not as highly regarded as Yan Hui by Confucius and subsequent generations, Zigong provides a much more realistic model for most people when it comes to the question of materialistic desires and ethical life. He was modest enough to acknowledge that he was not as good as Yan Hui who, "learning one thing he will know ten" compared with himself who, "learning one thing will know two" (5.9).

Despite the occasions when Confucius disagreed with or criticized him, he could still serve as a model for later Confucians because he was not incorrigible, compared to Zaiwo, who was also praised for eloquence (11.3) but was condemned by Confucius as "a piece of rotten wood that cannot be carved."[30] Zigong's conversations with Confucius elucidate important aspects of the Master's teachings. Confucius's assessment of him confirms that, for all his worldly ambitions, Zigong was a student genuinely interested, and not without accomplishments, in learning and the ethical life.

> Zigong inquired, "And what do you think of me?" The Master replied, "You are a vessel." Zigong asked, "What kind of a vessel?" The Master replied, "You are a most precious and sacred kind of vessel." (5.4)

This may seem like an admonishment, perhaps for the vanity of seeking the teacher's assessment of himself, in view of Confucius's remark, "The exemplary person is not a vessel (*qi* 器)" (2.12). However, being a vessel need not be a bad thing, as "exemplary persons employ others according to abilities (*qizhi* 器之)" (13.25). To use someone according to abilities is to make that person "a vessel" or an instrument (another possible translation of *qi*, 15.10). Zigong certainly used his abilities most effectively to gain worldly success. That Zigong's usefulness or effectiveness went beyond the materialistic is evident in Confucius's elaboration of the assessment to "a most precious and sacred kind of vessel" (*hulian* 瑚璉). Comparing Zigong to this sacrificial vessel used in the ancestral hall of the Xia and Shang dynasties, Confucius recognized that his materialistic success was not at the expense of his ethical character or his pursuit of the ethical life. Wealth and power, albeit instruments for gratifying materialistic desires, could be employed to serve ethical ends.

Given his impressive success at combining pursuit of wealth and ethical life, it is not surprising that Zigong has been singled out, even idolized, by modern "*rushang* 儒商" (Confucian merchants). An International Association for *rushang* Study was established in 1994, followed by branches being set up and a series of all kinds of *rushang* events all over the world; and there is serious interest in *rushang* studies among some Chinese academics.[31] The term has been used to describe overseas Chinese businessmen in South East Asia well-versed in Chinese culture, sometimes more narrowly understood as having literary ambitions, talents, and accomplishments. The broader understanding of their "cultural accomplishments" often includes adherence to Confucian ethics. Others see the ethical element as more central to the concept than culture.[32] Cheng Chung-ying maintained that "*rushang*" should be used normatively to refer to those who at least do business according to Confucian ethical standards, and at a higher level, those who devote themselves and their wealth to realize Confucian ideals in the economy and society.[33]

While some contributors to the "*rushang*" discussions since the nineties have emphasized the employment of Confucian ethical framework to constrain economic activities and sometimes criticized the excesses of "market economy," more are uncritically in favor of the latter and focus on explicating how Confucian values facilitate economic production and business management. The latter group's views recall and elaborate the "Post-Confucian thesis" of the late seventies and eighties, when Confucianism was revived through an academic discourse initiated in the West suggesting that Confucian values had contributed to the economic "miracles" of Japan and the four "Asian tigers" or "dragons" (South Korea, Taiwan, Hong Kong, and Singapore). Reflecting on Mencius's objections to Confucius's strategy of harnessing materialistic desires, one should be wary of too blithely promoting Confucianism as capitalism-friendly. Confucian sensibilities should make us uncomfortable if not outraged and disgusted by some of the injustices, systemic malfunctions, and malpractices prevalent in capitalist societies. Rather than instrumentalizing Confucian values and practices to aid capitalism unquestioningly, a modern Confucian should ask, not how Confucian values can aid capitalism, but how Confucian ethics can constrain and reform capitalism, and how capitalism can serve Confucian ethical life.

The above exploration of the relationship between materialistic desires, pursuit of profit, and wealth on the one hand, and ethical life on the other, reveals interesting complexities in Confucian attitudes to the tension between them in the *Analects* and the *Mencius*. There is no doubt that the highest ideal for both Masters is that of a person who loves the ethical so much that she is willing to sacrifice all materialistic goods and even her life. They are, however, realistic enough to recognize that materialistic desires are common and dominate the motivations of the average human being, and the idea that ethical life precludes these desires is more likely to turn people away rather than lead them toward the Confucian way. Nor is it necessarily the case that what is profitable and what is ethical are always opposed. It is possible to satisfy materialistic desires, gain wealth and honor while living ethically, at least in some cases. Confucius even occasionally resorted to the strategy of harnessing people's materialistic desires to lead them toward the good by arguing that ethical actions, besides having the guaranteed good of personal cultivation, sometimes could bring materialistic gains as well, while pursuit of materialistic goals is not guaranteed success. This is not without pitfalls we see from closer scrutiny of Mencius's less tolerant attitude toward pursuit of profit.

Although not always representing mutually exclusive choices, materialistic gains and the ethical good do often compete for people's attention. If materialistic gains are the focus of one's attention and drive one's conduct, then they tend to obscure ethical concerns, so that instead of leading one toward the ethical, they instrumentalize apparently ethical actions and may even corrupt the agent. Besides the highest ideal of Yan Hui's delight with the way while living in poverty, Zigong in the *Analects* presents us with an easier to attain model of worldly success combined with a more moderate ethical achievement. It is also a model that fits better with the pressures of contemporary life in capitalist societies. Although this may be an expedient second best option to attract to the Confucian way those who find the ideal character of Yan Hui too daunting or even totally unrealistic, we must remember that second best options are by their very nature limited. Unless one could move beyond materialistic desires, and becomes motivated by ethical concerns, turning profit and wealth into means rather than ends, the potential for corruption always remains and continues to threaten the Confucian ethical aspiration.

Acknowledgments

I thank Henry Rosemont Jr. and Chenyang Li for their comments, which helped me rethink and revise some key points in the paper. Several members of the audience at the panel celebrating Joel Kupperman's 50 years of teaching at the Tenth East-West Philosophers Conference also raised questions that were thought provoking, although I have not been able to address all of them. Errors and omissions are my sole responsibility.

Notes

1. *Analects* 8.12. Unless otherwise stated, citations from the *Analects* use the translation by Roger T. Ames and Henry Rosemont Jr. In-text citations give book and passage numbers.

2. By "materialistic desires" in this paper, I refer to physical desires, desire for physical objects, economic and other forms of power that enables one to acquire objects that gratify the physical senses. I exclude desire for honor and worldly reputation, even though these are often associated with what I call "materialistic desires" in contrast to the desire for the ethical.

3. Zhou Dunyi 周敦頤, *Penetrating the Book of Changes* (*Tongshu* 通書), Chapter 23 "Master Yan (Yanzi 顏子)" and Chapter 33 "On Wealth and Honor (*fugui* 富貴)" (Chan 1963, 475, 478; see also Chen 1991, 42–47).

4. Kupperman 1991, Chapter 6.

5. *Analects* 5.28; 6.3; 11.7.

6. Lau 1979; cf. Ames and Rosemont 1998: "If you get distracted by small opportunities, you won't succeed in the more important matters of government."

7. This is the topic of a famous lecture by Song dynasty Confucian Lu Jiuyuan, delivered at Zhu Xi's invitation in the White Deer Grotto Academy in 1181.

8. Yu 2004, 179–82.

9. Unless otherwise stated, translations from Lau 1970. In-text citations give book and chapter numbers.

10. The opposition between *li* and *yi* later came to be understood in terms of the opposition between private interests and public good.

11. *Mencius* 7A.8, translation modified from Lau 1970. Being in an "exalted position" (*shi* 勢) gives one power to gratify one's materialistic desires.

12. This claim is open to debate. However, this paper will not take up that issue but accepts the common reading that this is most likely the assumption in this passage.

13. Modified from Ames and Rosemont 1998.

14. *Analects* 7.30; see also *Analects* 4.6 and 6.12.

15. In a similar statement in 6A.6, what is sought is the human heart-mind with the beginnings of *ren*, *yi*, *li*, and *zhi*.

16. To "Seek it within oneself" (*qiu zhu ji* 求諸己) is often associated with personal cultivation, which is about making demands on oneself (*Analects* 15.21). See also *Mencius* 2A.7: the archer who misses his target should seek the cause within himself; *Mencius* 4A.4: "If others do not respond to your benevolence, look into your own benevolence . . . look into yourself whenever you fail to achieve your purpose"; *Mencius* 7A.4: "All the ten thousand things are there in me. . . ."

17. *Analects* 2.18, translation modified from Ames and Rosemont 1998.

18. This is also emphasized by Mencius in 5A.7.

19. Mencius repeatedly stressed the importance of accepting appointment to office only in accordance to proper ceremony and when the ruler's attitudes and motivations are appropriate (3B.3; 7A.8).

20. In a similar vein, the *Xunzi* refers to Chen Zhongzi as one who "would deceptively steal a reputation for humaneness," by "treating the rich and eminent as a group with arrogance or to be intent on demeaning oneself before

the poor and humble" (Knoblock 1988, 1:181–82). According to Yang Bojun 楊伯峻, Chen Zhongzi in *Mencius* 3B.10 is the same individual as Tian Zhong 田仲 and Chen Zhong 陳仲 in the *Xunzi* (Yang 1984, 160).

21. "Confucius' Disciples (仲尼弟子列傳)" (Nienhauser 1994, 74; Sima 1997, 558b).

22. "The biographies of the Money-makers (貨殖列傳)" (Watson 1971, 438; Sima 1997, 824a).

23. "Confucius' Disciples" (Nienhauser 1994, 74; Sima 1997, 558b).

24. According to Sima Qian, Zigong went on the diplomatic mission mentioned above in response to Confucius's encouragement to his student to save their home state of Lu from Tian Chang's threat, and Confucius refused permission to three other students—Zilu, Zizhang, and Zishi—who volunteered to undertake the task, but gave permission to Zigong (Nienhauser 1994, 71; Sima 1997, 557b). Cf. Amy Olberding's much more negative assessment of Zigong as a partial exemplar of moral failure (Olberding 2012, Chapter 7).

25. Examples of Zigong not satisfied with Confucius's initial replies and pressing for more are found in 11.16; 12.7; 13.20; 13.24; 14.35.

26. Cf. *Analects* 3.8 the only other person who won similar praise from Confucius is Zixia, who was noted for his accomplishments in the study of culture (11.3).

27. *Analects* 1.15; 5.4; 11.16; 12.7; 13.20; 13.24; 14.35; 17.19.

28. "The hereditary house of Confucius (孔子世家)" (Sima 1997, 494a). On Zigong's explaining Confucius to others, see *Analects* 1.10; 7.15; 19.22; he defended Confucius in *Analects* 9.6; 19.23; 19.24; 19.25.

29. In the *Analects*, we find people claiming that Zigong was superior to Confucius, something which Zigong himself denied (19.23; 19.25)

30. *Analects* 5.10, translation modified from Ames and Rosemont 1998. Confucius's disapproval of this student is implicit in 3.21; and 6.26; in 17.21, Confucius explicitly called him "unfeeling," perhaps even "inhumane" (*buren* 不仁).

31. Pan et al. 1996.

32. The definition of "*rushang*" as someone who earns his or her living doing business who have literary aspirations, talents or accomplishments is adopted by the collection of essays edited by the International Association for *Rushang* Studies Secretariat (1995). For a discussion of different meanings of "*rushang*" in popular and academic discourses, see Ji 2001, 3–7.

33. Cheng 2004.

References

Ames, Roger T., and Henry Rosemont Jr. (1998). *The Analects of Confucius*. New York: Ballentine.

Chan Wing-tsit (1963). *A Source Book in Chinese Philosophy*. Princeton, NJ: University of Princeton Press.

Chen Lai 陳來. *Song and Ming Confucianism* (宋明理學). Shenyang: Liaoning Education Press.

Cheng Chung-ying 成中英 (2004). "Creating the Human Destiny of the Twenty-first Century: Globalized Economic Development and Defining Confucianism and Confucian Merchant (創造二十一世紀的人類命運：全球化經濟發展與儒學及儒商的定位)." In Chen Qizhi 陳啟智 and Zhang Shuhua 張樹驊 (eds.), *Confucian Merchants and the Twenty-first Century* (儒商與二十一世紀), 1–11. Jinan: Qilu Shushe.

International Association for *Rushang* Studies Secretariat (1995). *Major Trend* of *Rushang* (儒商大趨勢). Guangzhou: Jinan University Press.

Ji Douyong 戢斗勇 (2001). *Rushang Spirit* (儒商精神). Beijing: Economic Daily Press.

Knoblock, John (trans.) (1988, 1990, 1994). *Xunzi: A Translation and Study of the Complete Works*, 3 volumes. Stanford, CA: Stanford University Press.

Kupperman, Joel J. (1991). *Character*. Oxford: Oxford University Press.

Lau, D. C. (trans.) (1970). *Mencius*. London: Penguin.

———. (trans.) (1979). *Confucius, the Analects*. Middlesex: Penguin.

Lennington, Robert L. (1996). *Managing Higher Education as a Business*. Phoenix: The American Council on Education and Oryx Press.

William H. Nienhauser, Jr. (ed.) (1994). *The Grand Scribe's Records*. Trans. Tsai-fa Cheng, Zongli Lu, William H. Nienhauser, Jr., and Robert Reynolds. Bloomington: Indiana University Press.

Olberding, Amy (2012). *Moral Exemplars in the* Analects. New York: Routledge.

Pan Yatun 潘亞暾 et al. (1996). *Rushang Studies* (儒商學). Guangzhou: Jinan University Press.

Seidman, Dov (2010, January 12). "Philosophy is back in business." *Business Week*. <http://www.businessweek.com/managing/content/jan2010/ca20100110_896657.htm> (accessed 26 December 2011).

Sima Qian 司馬遷 (ca.145–ca.86) (1997). *Record of the Grand Historian* (史記). Beijing: Zhonghua Shuju.

Stewart, Matthew (June 2006). "The Management Myth." *The Atlantic Online*. <http://www.theatlantic.com/magazine/archive/2006/06/the-management-myth/4883/> (accessed 26 December 2011).

Watson, Burton (trans.) (1971). *Records of the Grand Historian*. New York: Columbia University Press.

Yang Bojun 楊伯峻 (1984). *Translation and Annotation of the Mencius* (孟子譯注). Hong Kong: Zhonghua Shuju.

Yu Ying-Shih 余英時 (2004). "Interaction between Scholar-Officials and Merchants, and Confucianism's change in direction (士商互動與儒學轉向)." In Shen Guijia (Ed.), *Confucian Ethics and Merchant Spirit* (儒家倫理與商人精神), 162–212. Guilin: Guangxi Normal University Press.

9

Character and Ethics for Social Entities

Peimin Ni

The Discrepancy Between Ethics for Individuals and Ethics for Social Entities

People are so used to using economic measures for the development of nations that, when the concept of "happiness index" was brought up, it caused a wave of enthusiasm around the world.[1] For the first time many people suddenly realized that a tiny, almost primitive kingdom located at the foot of Himalayan mountains called Bhutan, could be considered more "advanced" than many industrially and financially well-developed nations in the world.

The fact that this came as a surprise is itself surprising. If the goodness of an individual person's life is not to be measured by his or her material possessions and consumption, why would the development of a society or a nation be measured mainly or even merely by economic indicators such as GDP? As Robert Kennedy once remarked, GDP "measures everything . . . except that which makes life worthwhile" (Kennedy 1968), yet we still see everywhere that social entities revolve around economic success at the cost of other vital values.

Governments, news agencies, publishers, medical and educational institutions, are heavily manipulated by the invisible hands of market economy. Media depends on advertisement. Publishers look at the market for what to publish. "Cultural industry" turns culture into commodity. It is taken for granted now that government election campaigns have to depend on fundraising. Symbolized by a scale, justice is supposed to be fair, but money is a heavy weight on the scale before any case is placed on the system. Not only are lawyers money-makers, lobbying, prison, and bail bond have all become multi-billion dollar industries in the United States. In international relations, leaders of nations feel no hesitation in speaking about "the interest of our nation" against the interest of the rest of the world, and by "interest," they clearly mean, mainly and above all, economic interest. Educational institutions ought to be the most sacred places for cultivating the young generation, and yet they are also heavily infested by market values. In an article titled "The Market-Model University, Humanities in the Age of Money," James Engell and Anthony Dangerfield used a large amount of statistical data to demonstrate that today's higher education is measured by three criteria of success: whether the field offers *a promise for money* (that it leads to a higher earning), whether the field offers *knowledge about money* (such as business, finance, and investment), and whether the field is itself *a source of money* (meaning that it can receive significant external funding from research contracts, federal grants, or corporate underwritings).[2] Whereas Socrates was known for being a gadfly who would force people to step out of their comfort zone, and his "teaching award" was a cup of hemlock, our teaching evaluations are now heavily based on student "satisfaction." As John McMurty observes, "More than ever before, policies, curricula, and salaries no longer follow what an institution thinks students and citizens need to prepare for life, . . . rather, they increasingly follow the voting feet of students from class to class" (McMurtry, 214), just like businesses follow the whim of the market.

These are all things that should look strange, but are strangely taken for granted. What would we say if an individual measured and managed everything in a money-based fashion? There is obviously a huge discrepancy between the ethics for individuals and the ethics for social entities. While we teach our children to be morally decent and caring, we have been paying little attention to cultivating the character of our social entities, groups, and social systems. We leave them largely to the hands of market economy, and restrict their behaviors only through laws and other forms of rules of conduct. Even the focus of professional ethics is on how individual professionals should behave, and very little attention is paid to nurturing the culture of our social entities. Given the strong influence of society upon individual persons, it is no less than hypocrisy to tell our children to stay away from material fetishism, and yet let our social entities be filled with it. Using Confucius's remark,

"Exemplary persons are persuaded by what is right; petty persons are persuaded by what is profitable" (*Analects* 4.16), how many of our social entities are exemplary in this sense?

One apparent cause for such a discrepancy seems to be that people tend to think that ethics is not really applicable to social entities. We often talk about social entities as if they were moral agents, but when it comes to attributing moral responsibilities, we always look for the individual persons whose decisions and actions play key roles in the operation of the relevant social entities. In other words, people tend to think that ethics for social entities is reducible to ethics for individuals. But is it so? In this paper, I want to extend Joel Kupperman's study of character and his insights about the value of Confucianism to the ethics of social entities. I find such an extension, though may be not intended by Kupperman himself, can be quite stimulating and fruitful.

Group Self

As I understand, Kupperman is reluctant to assign the concept of self to groups, and as a result, he rarely speaks about character of social entities.[3] It is well-known among philosophers that the issue of self is difficult. Kupperman is too familiar with all the philosophical challenges against our intuitive notion of an enduring self, whether they are from Western philosophers such as Hume, or from Eastern philosophical traditions, such as Buddhism. When we look for such enduring selves, "either we find nothing at all but psychic flux or what we find is rather far from what we would have termed individual selves" (Kupperman 1991, 33–4). Naturally and quite reasonably, Kupperman turns to a notion of self that does not contain anything like a soul or a mysterious substance, but a constructed "metaphysical term of art" (Ibid., 45, note 2) that allows us to account for the fact that:

> We somehow do manage to have a workable conception of individual persons that tracks people through their lives. Thus, X will have a self at least in the (minimal) sense that X has developed a consistent and meaningful usage of words such as *I* and *me* and also in that we, viewing X from the outside, can identify X as the same person at various points in her or his life. (Ibid., 35)

Notice that here the issue is "intertwined with the problem of personal identity, of determining the conditions under which X is or is not the same person as Y" (Ibid., 45–6), but it is certainly not simply reducible to the issue about identity. We can identify a ship as the same ship at various points of its life, but we do not say that the ship has a self. So there must be an additional requirement for having a self, which, in Kupperman's view, is a minimal degree of integration of consciousness.

> Someone who forgets everything and notices very little of what we think of as happening to himself or herself could not attain a concept of self. Because of such minimum standards, there is no realistic prospect of the formation of a human group-self. We are not sensitive enough to, knowledgeable enough about, or sufficiently coordinated with, one another. (Ibid., 37)

In other words, in the case of group-self, we not only need to have a consistent and meaningful usage of words such as *we* and *us* so that viewing social entities like "The United States" or "Wal-Mart" from the outside, we can identify them as the same entity at various points of their history, but also be able to say that the groups "have the possibility of self-knowledge and that self-knowledge will be of something more robust than the collection of characteristics and tendencies that someone [in this case, group] may have inherited" (Ibid., 44).

Certainly groups do not have integrated consciousness in the same way that an individual person normally does. Even in a most well-coordinated social group (imagine, for example, a well-disciplined army), people still do not literally feel each other's feelings, read each other's minds, and coordinate with each other in the same way that an individual's limbs coordinate. Yet if all that is required for having a self is "the possibility of self-knowledge" that is "more robust than the collection of characteristics and tendencies," then groups may very well qualify. Kupperman acknowledges that if a colony of intelligent termites were able to remember what happened to other members of the group, then one can consider this as a group-self. The reason for speaking about termites is of course because they seem to be well coordinated. But humans certainly also show good coordination, though not always as good as termites. As Kupperman also acknowledges, just as an individual human being does not retain every item of his own experience (Ibid., 37), the integration in a group does not have to be perfect. Using this less than "perfect" criterion, a social group may be said to have a "collective consciousness" and "collective conscience." In many cases a group can, as Burns and Egdahl put it, "be considered to possess agential capabilities: to think, judge, decide, act, reform; to conceptualize self and others as well as self's actions and interactions; and to reflect" (Burns & Egdahl, 72).

One might object this by saying that the so-called "collective consciousness" and "collective conscience" are actually *collections* of individual consciousness and conscience, *shared* by members of a group rather than *integrated* within the group. While a minimal degree of integration of *consciousness* is required for making sense of *self*, groups are often formed by *different kinds of integrations*, say the integration of a continuous history (e.g., a family line), or mutual relation (e.g., marriage), or a common space (e.g., a city or a neighborhood), or mission (e.g., a social organization). In these other kinds of integrations, patterns of thoughts and conducts of the relevant groups can be reduced to similar patterns of thoughts and actions of their individual members, especially those who are in leading positions.

Indeed, in the case of total absence of any integration of consciousness, we would not want to call these groups social entities, much less ones that have "selves." Following Kupperman's use of the relevant terms, we may take social group as a concept broader than social entity. A race, for instance, is a social group, but if there is not enough integration between its members, we would not call it an entity. A social entity, on the other hand, does not necessarily have a self. According to Kupperman, even individual humans do not necessarily have a self. "The psychological field which is present in a newborn infant and which continues throughout that infant's life would more accurately be termed a protoself" (Kupperman 1991, 43), because he or she is still incapable of the concept of I and a self-image. A new neighborhood may have mutual encounters between its residents, but without a neighborhood organization or other means of coordination that pulls thoughts and activities of the residents together consciously, it cannot claim to have a self, though it may perhaps qualify as a social entity.

Now looking at these other forms of integration, we find that, whether we call them merely groups, or groups that qualify as entities, or entities that can be said to have selves, is all a matter of degree of integration between their respective members. Furthermore, we find that the so-called "other forms of integration" are nothing but specific ways through which people's consciousness integrate with one another.

Exactly through their integration of consciousness, the history of a social group can continue, relationship within a group can sustain, and common mission of a social group can be formed.

It is important to keep in mind though that interpersonal integration of consciousness does not have to rely on having an organization (e.g., think of how people in the "occupy" moment coordinate their actions). There is certain truth in saying that, e.g., the French are more romantic than the British, and the Germans are more metaphysical than the French, even though members of the French, the British, and the Germans are not integrated by their respective governments, but by the culture or tradition of these places. The culture or tradition has a life of its own that lives within but goes beyond each individual, and it in turn exerts strong influences on individuals.[4]

In fact, when we find a group of people who share certain common pattern of thoughts and actions, we always believe that there is a culture or tradition behind, which influences these people and serves as the linkage that is "more robust than the collection of characteristic and tendencies." The saying that "the whole is more than the sum of its individual parts" applies here also. While a person is more than the sum of her body and mental constituents, a social group is also more than the sum of its individual members. A person's identity is typically drawn from the groups to which he or she belongs. That means, not only is a group different from a mere collection of individuals, but also a source of the individuals' selves. Confucius's relational notion of self can serve as a good example. Under such a notion, an individual is understood through one's particular position within a web of relations. Using Ames's words, Confucian selves are "foci of fields." Though this notion is also a "metaphysical term of art," which, as Rosemont puts it, is neither provable conclusively through experience nor demonstrable through a priori reasoning (see Rosemont 2001, 91), it is strongly supported by our own sense of being. It is no coincidence that everywhere in the world, bringing a person's parents, especially the mother, into a name calling, is commonly used as a vicious way to insult a person (e.g., "the son of a bitch" in English and "*gou niang yang de* 狗娘養的," the son of a mother dog, in Chinese). This shows that people universally take their parents as an important part of their identity. Going beyond the family, we find that gender, race, institutional affiliation, nationality, etc. are all sources of a person's pride or dignity. Social entities are different from groups of objects such as boxes of matches. An essential feature of social entities is that they consist of human beings as their constituents, and as extension of individual human beings, they entail more complex manifestation of human subjectivity. One's identity derived from being a member of a social group is a *sense* of belonging or an *awareness* of one's role in a web of social relations, and this sense or awareness is not reducible to the integration of memories etc., within individual persons' minds; quite the contrary, it requires these individuals to go beyond their own psychological fields in order to find themselves.

Of course, to analyze and articulate this group subjectivity will be more difficult than doing the same with individual subjectivity, which is by itself already notoriously difficult. But remember that here we are talking about a metaphysical term of art that will allow us to account for meaningful ways to talk about social groups through uses of words like "*we*" and "*us*," and in practice, able to address the fact that cultures and traditions have existences beyond individual persons. For such a purpose, we do not necessarily have to be able to spell out all the details about how it works before we are justified in using it, just like we do not depend on any satisfactorily articulated metaphysical account of personal self in order to meaningfully use terms like "*I*" and "*me*." Here we can again follow Kupperman's advice to be content with "a minimal sense of integration" of consciousness and apply this to social groups. By going beyond the limit of individual persons' psychological fields, the notion of group-self offers us a better and more realistic account to deal with group responsibilities, as it allows us to address how an individual is affected by, and in turn affects, the groups to which he or she belongs. By accepting the notion of group-self, we are better positioned to deal with what our experience teaches us, that is, no one is entirely responsible for a social group, and yet every member of a group is partly responsible for it. Group ethics requires one to take responsibility for groups, in proportion to one's role in a group and the degree of integration in the group.

What Does It Mean for a Social Entity to Have Character?

Kupperman defines character as: "X's character is X's normal pattern of thought and action, especially with respect to concerns and commitments in matters affecting the happiness of others or of X, and most especially in relation to moral choices" (Kupperman 1991, 17). From this definition, we can roughly understand the character of a social group as its culture,[5] which consists of a set of shared attitudes (habits and tendencies), values, goals, and pattern of practices that characterizes an institution, organization, or group. Like character of an individual person, the culture of a social group involves habits and tendencies of thought and action, which makes the tendencies and actions of the social group somewhat predictable (Ibid., 4).

The concept of group character was quite popular in Europe and America during the eighteenth and nineteenth centuries and the earlier part of the twentieth century. For instance Voltaire talked about *esprit des nations* (spirit of nations), and J. G. Herder also used the concept of *Volksgeist* (spirit of the people). In the early 1900s, many books and articles were written, both by Western authors and Chinese intellectuals, on characteristics of the Chinese people. The fact that the concept is no longer popular is in part due to the difficulties involved in making such generalizations; but I think it has more to do with people's concern with stereotypes or prejudices against certain groups of people based on their race, nationality, or even appearance. While these are all extremely important considerations, these are not reasons for evading the topic of group character altogether. Instead, they require us to take the topic seriously with more care and caution. After all, even in the case of individual persons, we also need to take caution not to base our judgment of people's actions solely on the basis of their character. That does not mean, however, that they do not have normal patterns of thoughts and actions which make their actions somewhat predictable.

With regard to social entities (that are more than merely groups), their character is often more clear than what we normally see in individual persons. One might even say that, unlike individual persons, social entities have their own purpose or unique function built into their existence. A business, for instance, is a profit-making entity, whereas an army is a military unit, and a church is organized for religious activities. Individuals, however, apparently have no such predetermined nature, at least not so clearly. The difference seems to have implications about whether ethics for individuals is applicable to ethics for social groups. Take economic entities, such as banks and manufacturers, for example. Isn't their aim naturally and necessarily about making profits and being selfish? We can set up rules to limit what they are allowed to do and what they cannot do (such as laws about fair competition, fair employment, etc.), but can we require them not to put profit making as their primary aim without abolishing them altogether?

This argument is actually not as strong as it appears. An individual can also be a business man/woman, a politician, or a church priest. Can we therefore say that it is unreasonable to ask a business person to go beyond profit making, a politician not to be preoccupied by winning or losing an election, a priest be more than a spokesperson for the divine? Metaphysically, it is an abstraction to take social entities as nothing but what they primarily aim to do. This is similar to the logic of seeing my flipping the switch, my turning on the light, my illuminating the room, and my unintentional alerting of a burglar as four entirely different actions, whereas in reality they are one and the same action described in four different ways.[6] The Chinese and Japanese term used for translating "economy," *jingji* 經濟, can serve as an illustration. *Jingji* originally meant "managing and providing," which came as an abbreviation for *jingshi jimin* 經世濟民—managing the world for the purpose of providing for the people. Though we do not know exactly who used it for "economy" first and what was in the person's mind,[7] the association of *jingji* with economy shows a Confucian understanding of what economic activities should be. Nowadays, most of our economic entities turned the internal good of *jingji* as their means for the external good of profit making. Instead of creating a product to serve the needs of the people and, in doing so, also to make a profit, now the standard format is, in order to make a profit, we make a product to create a need or want. As a social being, an economic entity can affect the society's politics, culture, security, and much more, and it is more than reasonable to expect them to be socially responsible in the broader sense.

But one might argue further that the purpose or function of a social entity is built into the structure designed for the purpose or function. Features of their structure play an important role in shaping their character. Thus, for instance, a totalitarian regime's normal pattern of behavior is very different from that of a democratic one. Indeed, some people might even take social entities as nothing but systems or the way their constituents are related, and argue from there that the culture or character of a social entity is fundamentally little more than the characteristics of the relevant systems. What this implies is that unless you change the structure of the system, there is no way one can change their character. The do-goods cannot survive in Capitalism because Capitalism is competitive by nature. Compared to an individual person who can use free will to make ethical decisions, social entities usually lack a centralized decision-making faculty (in whatever sense one may define it). Most people feel that they live within a social group, and are powerless in affecting its system or culture. This feeling is even found in most people who are heads of their respective social groups, including the emperors of China who supposedly had all the power to do whatever they liked. They are still constrained by the tradition passed down from history, by the officials in their court, and by the will of the people.[8]

While I do not think the character of social entities can be simply reduced to their structural features, as it involves much more, such as attitudes and styles of thoughts and actions, I do agree that structural features play important roles in shaping and defining the character of a social entity. Yet, again, we can draw insights from what is the case in individual persons. Often an individual's autonomy is exaggerated. As individuals, we are also constrained by our body which has its own "likes and dislikes," by our sentiments which are not always in agreement with our reason, and by our social surroundings and the traditions passed on to us through our family and community. A person becomes less malleable as one gets older when one's "structure" of thought and bodily dispositions is firmly established. Confucius even said, "When a person at forty still provokes dislikes, the person is hopeless" (*Analects* 17.26). Yet this does not mean a person has absolutely no control over these factors. One of the major contributions of Kupperman's analysis of character and his study of Eastern philosophy is that he shows us that ethics should not simply be a matter of decision making in the sense of a person "explicitly weights alternatives and then decides to do one thing or another" (Kupperman 1991, 69). It should include continuity of commitments, in which choices are "made without reflection or even the agent's explicit awareness that a choice is being made. These choices, nevertheless, can be made very well or badly. Bloggs does very well when, without thinking, he swerves to avoid driving over someone. Schmitt does very badly when, without reflection or any explicit awareness that he is making choices, he does his job as a concentration-camp guard" (Ibid., 71). Similarly, a social entity's system or structure may be seen as a larger scale "continuity of commitment." It is less perceivable as a choice (or a series of choices, from one moment to another) than in the case of an individual person, and is certainly more difficult to change, because social entities are often less well-coordinated than individual persons, but this does not mean that there is no way a social entity can make changes to it except by launching a revolution.

The difficulty can be illustrated by what I call, for the lack of any other exact term, the "Red Lantern Effect." The name is derived from a Chinese movie titled "Raise the Red Lantern," in which a girl who lived in 1920s China was forced to marry an old landlord, who already had three wives. Each night a red lantern would be lit in front of a wife's quarter to indicate the master's choice of the wife to spend the night with. As the master's attention carried power, status, and privilege, there was a competition among the wives over which red lantern would be lit. The newly arrived girl found herself in such a dilemma: Either she refuses to join this absurd competition, and as a consequence, she would be a victim of the game, or she joins the game, but then she becomes an enforcer of the absurdity.

Though the movie is a fiction, the Red Lantern Effect is actually everywhere in real life. In today's education system in China, little children are forced to do a ridiculous amount of homework every day, and yet parents and school teachers who know well that this is bad for children feel that they have no choice but to become the very ones who enforce this cruel practice, because otherwise their students will lose competitiveness in the society. In today's capitalist society, although saving financial institutions from their crisis with government bailout would only temporarily ease the problems while causing the problems to go deeper in the long run, it is still perceived as the only option. Even the Stockholm Syndrome, a paradoxical psychological phenomenon wherein hostages develop empathy and positive feelings toward their captors, might be considered a special case of the Red Lantern Effect, because hostages tend to feel that their chance of survival is dependent on the leniency of the captors.

All these actually point to the importance of paying more attention to character of social entities and the potential fruitfulness of extending achievements in moral psychology into the study of social entities. If a successful moral education and cultivation makes one a good person so that, as Kupperman puts it, one's real options of choice narrows down, and some immoral things (such as kicking a child for fun) would become unthinkable (Kupperman 1999, 77, 104–6, 136), and a bad moral upbringing or cultivation narrows down one's range of choices also, such as in the case of persistent habit of gambling, then, we are led to the view "in which one may have genuine choices in the long run that one does not have in the short run" (Ibid., 111). One has no choice in the short run because one apparently has no choice but to follow the already formed character; but one has choice in the long run, because one can still try to gradually lead to a change of character. The same can be applied to social entities: Instead of focusing on individual actions of social entities, which are more or less the result of their culture (often reflected in their structure), more attention must be paid to the change of their cultures.

Transforming Power of Role Models

We do expect our social entities to be morally responsible agents in our society. Indeed, the most horrible tragic things in the world are done by social entities rather than by individuals, and they are always done in the name of enforcing certain ideas of good. Karl Marx's idea of eliminating alienation in order for workers to live as "species-being" (to express the features that are characteristic of human being) is beautiful in many ways, yet the implementation of his idea through Communist revolution turned out to be one of the gravest disasters in human history. Religious fundamentalism is another reaction to the problems of our era, which has obviously caused more harm than good and has become one of the main sources of instability and violence in the world. The unprecedented level of cruelty displayed by some of the most "advanced" nations in the world during the two World Wars in the last century shocked the entire human race. After the two wars, the world continues to be an unsecure place to live, despite the amazing achievements in other areas. What happened in Kosovo, Rwanda, Khmer Rouge Cambodia, 9/11 in America, the Stalin era of the Soviet Russia, and the Cultural Revolution in China, is still happening in the world constantly, though in less devastating scales on a daily basis. One consequence of these is the intensified fear of imposition of value and any form of social programming.

To maintain peace and order and yet still retain human freedom, most people focus on trying to reach overlapping consensus on some most basic (and hence minimum) universal principles and appeal to value-free rules of conduct (laws and regulations). This "lowest-common-denominator" approach has commendable merits of allowing for freedom and bringing efficiency and regularity to the operation of society and its subentities. However, appealing to universal principles and value-free rules of conduct is by nature inadequate and problematic. In order to be universal, principles have to be formulated in very abstract terms. Even the so-called "golden rule" would have to admit exceptions in various circumstances. The logic of "doing to others what you would like" would not work in all cases because what I like or dislike may be moral or immoral.[9] It is the very inadequacies of the Kantian and the Utilitarian ethics of conduct that have led to the revival of virtue ethics—an ethics that focuses more on the goodness of the agent than on formulating principles and rules of conduct. The nature of rules is that they are imposed from without. Even when they are self-imposed, rules still *restrict* what we do, and hence entail a conflict between the rules and the self that is ruled. Rules are never fully consistent with freedom and autonomy, unless they become fully internalized and, in that case, they are no longer serving as rules.[10] Confucius says, "If the common people are led by administrative regulations and kept in order by punishments, they will try to avoid the punishment, but have no sense of shame" (*Analects* 2.3). Rules do not foster willingness. For this reason, they can only be minimalistic. They cannot demand us to reach beyond basic expectations to build long-term, harmonious relationships, or to actualize our full potential. Rules also fail because we cannot possibly come up with rules that cover every possible scenario, and consequently there will always be loopholes. When we write more and more rules to cover loopholes, soon the overwhelming amount of rules becomes part of the problem. Rules entail distrust, and no society can sustain without trust! The increasing complains and sarcasm about TSA (Transportation Security Administration) is a typical example.[11] As meticulous as the current TSA is (e.g., from taking passengers' nail clippers to scanning people's bodies), it still has to rely on a certain level of trust.

How do we retain freedom for social entities and yet, at the same time, demand more than what rules of conduct can achieve? Here is actually again an area where we can draw inspirations from ethics for individuals. Confucian scholars discovered very early on that the best way for character development, and hence for bringing a harmonious and prosperous society, is through model emulation—or what the modern psychology calls "observational learning."

> When Ji Kangzi asked Confucius about government, saying, "What do you say to kill those who have abandoned the Way and get closer to those who are with the Way?" Confucius replied, "Sir, in governing, why do you need to resort to killing? If you aspire what is good, the people will be good." (*Analects* 12.19)

> To govern (*zheng* 政) means to be correct (*zheng* 正). If you lead the people with correctness, who will dare not to be correct? (*Analects* 12.17)

Confucius not only set up ancient sages as his role models, he took the early Zhou society as a role model for later societies to emulate.

The Master said, "The Zhou looked downward (*jian* 監) at the two past dynasties. How rich and well developed is its culture! I follow the Zhou." (*Analects* 3.14).

Though a model social entity cannot be separated from having model individual human beings in them, it cannot be reduced to having such individuals. Among the ancient sages, Confucius spoke most highly of those who devoted themselves to the establishment of a great culture for the society, such as King Shun, King Yao, King Wen, and Duke of Zhou. They are not only morally exemplary individuals with great sense of mission to benefit the world; they also had prominent social positions to implement their ideals. Confucius himself spent a considerable amount of his life traveling from one state to another, seeking employment. "If anyone employs me, may I not make an Eastern Zhou?" (17.5) Unfortunately, he was unable to make the rulers listen to him. On the other hand, for Confucius, politics is not limited to official government affairs. Someone said of Confucius, "Why is the Master not engaged in government?" The Master said, "The *Book of Documents* says: 'Filial, simply in being filial, and befriend your brothers, the influence will extend to government.' This is also an engagement in governing. Why must there be any extra 'engagement in government'?" (*Analects* 2.21) In other words, one can start affecting the world even through family affairs. By making a family a model family, one sets an example for other families. By making whatever social groups to which one belongs a little better, one is affecting the world. No matter how insignificant one's position is in a group, one can still make contributions to bettering it. This is what we came up to before: While no one is entirely responsible for the character of a group, everyone is partially responsible for it, though the proportion is dependent on one's role within the group.

Perhaps one example will serve better than many words. Despite the fact that General Electric (GE), the largest corporation in the United States, does not have a reputation of being morally exemplary,[12] one subdivision of the corporation, GE Aircraft Engine Assembly plant in Durham, North Carolina, is quite an extraordinary role model for social entities. According to a report published in *Fast Company* magazine (Fishman 1999), at GE/Durham, there is no clock for punching in or out. Every worker is free to show up and leave as they like. There is only one boss, the plant manager, who everybody reports to, or rather, does not report to. The only command the workers receive from her is the date that their engine is scheduled to ship. There is no special monetary incentive for the workers' high performance. Besides the regular three pay grades at GE/Durham, tech-1, tech-2, and tech-3, which are all based on skill level and training, the only monetary incentive is to become better educated in "multiskilling" so that there is a better technical continuity between the teams. The manager, Paula Sims, says simply, "They [financial incentives] are not part of the culture at GE Aircraft Engines." Yet in five years in the 1990s, the plant reduced the cost of airplane engine assembly by over 50 percent, and reduced quality defects by 75 percent. They release a much lower rate of toxic chemicals into the air than other plants of the same kind. In short, they truly reached a state-of-the-art level of efficiency, quality, and low cost to the environment.

The secret is the culture. The most challenging part of her job, says the plant's manager, is that it "requires a different level of listening skills," because most decisions are made by the working teams collectively. Her job is coordinating the process to make sure it goes smoothly. While in one sense no one there has a boss, the opposite is also true: Keith McKee, a technician in the plant, says, "I have 15 bosses. All of my teammates are my bosses." To get a job at GE/Durham, you need to be good in 11 areas. "Only one of those involves technical competence or experience," says Keith McKee. The other areas include "helping skills, team skills, communication skills, diversity, flexibility, coaching ability, work ethic, and so forth." Sim's boss Bob McEwan, who is also the general manager of GE assembly operations at Evendale, just outside of Cincinnati, says "I think what they've discovered in Durham is the value of the human being." He points to the ceiling—the plant he directs—"Upstairs, you've got wrench turners. In Durham, you've got people who think."

The author of the report says: "At a place where the morale is high and the performance is extraordinary, something is going on that is often overlooked in an economy obsessed with fringe benefits, gratuitous flattery, and today's closing stock price. At GE/Durham, the work itself is the thing." Why do they do that? "It matters," says Bill Lane, a 35-year-old tech-2. "I've got a 3-year-old daughter, and I figure that every plane we build engines for has someone with a 3-year-old daughter riding on it." The reporter writes, "There is something so extraordinary about this place that you wish you could walk through it with Karl Marx and Max Weber—just to hear them explain how its revolutionary culture squares with their theories about the dehumanization of work in modern society."

What the model shows is very rich. One asset is the commitment to values higher than economic gain. "At GE/Durham, people strive for perfection, expecting no reward other than their own satisfaction." The system they have is indeed more minimalistic, more liberal, and more democratic than any minimal liberalist has envisioned, because there are so few rules and almost no bosses. But this is possible only because there is a thick culture in which higher values are in perfect harmony with personal freedom and creativity. It illustrates that by embracing higher values, the people at GE/Durham achieved the freedom and creativity that are unthinkable in a society governed by rules. When they disconnected work from financial incentive, they replaced it with the satisfaction of the good activity itself—a remarkable success in turning work into what MacIntyre calls "practice," and an illustration of the ideal of the Chinese concept *jingji*. And yet in this way, they dramatically increased their financial success! It illustrates that economic prosperity not only does not have to be in conflict with commitment to values; it is the very result of commitment to values. It reminds us of Mencius's saying that seeking for profit and yet going contrary to human-heartedness and appropriateness is like looking for fish by climbing a tree (see *Mencius* 1A.7 and 4A.7). Drawing from this example, Dov Seidman, the CEO of LRN business consulting company, says, "The success of GE/Durham lies in the unique way people there have chosen to relate to each other, to organize their endeavors, and to govern themselves—in short, their culture. . . . Culture is a company's unique character, its lifeblood. . . . Much as some people say that character is one's destiny, culture can be thought of as the destiny of an organization" (Seidman, 218).

One will naturally question whether such a model is applicable or universalizable for all varieties of social entities. Of course different social groups have unique features. The culture at GE/Durham will have to manifest in different ways in different groups and places. One most challenging difficulty in model learning is to mimic a model without mechanically copying the model in every detail.[13] This brings us to another, and the final issue I want to touch on before I end this paper: Would mimesis lead to the "end of history," since when people all mimic the same model, there will be carbon copies of the same character everywhere? If so, it would certainly be the enemy of multiplicity and individuality, and would lead to the annihilation of itself, because logically, in the end everything will be the same and there will be nothing to imitate.

Putting aside the fact that modern liberal democracy and market economy, aided by the fast development of digital technology, has made the world "flat" by standardizing everything, from language to the style of shopping malls, mimesis is, properly understood and practiced, far from mere duplication. The key is to differentiate mimesis from repetition and mere similarity in form. It should be understood as a process of acquisition of abilities, art, or *gongfu* (kung fu). Heidegger insists that representation is not what mimesis is about; to the contrary it is "doing-after: production that comes afterwards. The mimesis is in its essence situated and defined through distance" (Heidegger, 215). Derrida also finds that "true mimesis [is] between two producing subjects and not between two produced things" (Derrida, 67ff). Actually, mimesis is the very process through which one gains the ability to be creative—creative not in the sense of making something new out of blue, but in the sense of being able to base one's own creativity on the ground of the greatness of the model. In Chinese martial arts and calligraphy, for instance, mimicking the master is always stressed as fundamental, because more often than not, simple creation of one's own is worthless, or even worse, a hindrance to one's opportunity to develop real creativity.

The issue about whether modeling after exemplary persons is limiting one's creativity and freedom is closely tied to Kupperman's point about freedom as narrowing down options (see Kupperman 1999, 97–114) and about the "mixed blessing" of having strong and good character in general, for it can make one predictable (Kupperman 1991, 140–1). In Confucius's famous statement about himself reaching the stage of being able to "follow his heart's will without overstepping the line" (*Analects* 2.4), he shows this paradoxical nature of true freedom—facing with wrong or bad options, he would not need to make a choice because he is no longer tempted. This is a point even Descartes recognizes. In his Meditations IV, Descartes says that the freedom of indifference is the lowest kind of freedom (Descartes, 81). True freedom is gained exactly through internalization of knowledge, instructions, and "rules" so deep that they become one's second nature, or character (see Ni 2002).

Of course the danger of misunderstanding mimics as mechanical duplications is real. Just as any instruction can be taken mechanically or properly, mimicking a model is itself an art. Caution must be taken to follow models with reflection and sensitivity to the cultural, historical, and other specific conditions and limitations of particular models (Munro 2011, 14). But this danger is no greater than the danger of lacking proper guidance and, after having internalized bad influences, people lose their freedom to develop into decent humans and live good lives. The same can be said about social entities.

The reporter of GE/Durham used a pun in the title of his article "Engines of Democracy." Not only is GE/Durham an aircraft engine assembly plant, it also exemplifies what will drive democracy and lift it off the minimalist ground. Its culture or character makes it an "exemplary person" among social entities. The special significance of this "exemplary person" is that it offers us a model richer than any individual exemplary person is able to offer. The plant is a community. Its real strength is not in any of its particular member's exceptional moral cultivation, much less in the size of its muscles (budget, monetary incentive), but in the way its members connect and cooperate with each other. This character allows each of its members to truly actualize their human potentials, including compassion and trust, and work—or more accurately *live*—together harmoniously, without having to rely on conceptual formulations of overlapping consensus, or rules of conduct. The only thing it needs for exerting its strong influence all over is a ritual position—to be set on a seat, "facing due south."[14]

Will others follow? A study done by LRN shows that "an overwhelming majority of employees—94 percent—say it is critical that the company they work for have a strong commitment to values. In fact, 82 percent said they would prefer to be paid less and work for that value-driven company than receive higher pay at a company with questionable commitment" (Seidman, 136). This seems to be the very basis for Confucius's optimistic assessment: "The virtuosity of exemplary persons is like the wind, and the virtuosity of the small men is like the grass. The grass will for sure bend when the wind blows across it" (*Analects* 12.19).

Acknowledgment

While the formation of the ideas in this paper is benefited from more people than I can acknowledge here, I want to thank particularly Chenyang Li, Henry Rosemont Jr., and Stephen Rowe for their helpful comments and suggestions.

Notes

1. Coined in 1972 by Bhutan's former King Jigme Singye Wangchuck, the notion developed into an instrument to measure the population's general level of well-being, including sustainable development, cultural integrity, ecosystem conservation, and good governance. It was further specified through eight general

contributors to happiness—physical, mental, and spiritual health; time-balance; social and community vitality; cultural vitality; education; living standards; good governance; and ecological vitality. The concept quickly caught wide attention all over the globe. Since then five global-scale conferences have been held on the topic, some of them were attended by around 800 participants.

2. Of course the humanities satisfy none of these three criteria in any direct way. Here are some alarming data that the authors of the article provide: Between 1970 and 1994, in 25 years, the number of BAs conferred in the United States rose 39 percent. Among them three majors increased five- to tenfold: computer and information sciences, protective services, and transportation and material moving. Two majors tripled: health professions and public administration. Already popular, business management doubled. In contrast, English, foreign languages, philosophy, history, and religion all declined. In 1960, one of every six faculty members professed the liberal arts. Twenty-eight years later, the ratio had shrunk to one of thirteen. In 1960, for every 100 students in college, 16 enrolled in foreign languages. In 1970 it was 12, and by 1995, with a global economy in full swing, fewer than 8. Not only did the ratio of faculty and students in the humanities drop about 50 percent in the span of about 30 years, humanists received the lowest faculty salaries by thousands or tens of thousands of dollars. Nationally in the United States, in 1976, a newly hired assistant professor teaching literature earned $3,000 less than a new assistant professor in business. By 1996 the gap exceeded $25,000!

3. When he does, e.g., in 1991, p. 97, where he used expression "the character of their society," he seems to treat it more as a collective for the characters of the majority of individuals within the group, which warrants attention mainly in its effects on the character of each individual.

4. Recently, Daniel Bell and Avner de-Shalit co-authored a book titled "The Spirit of Cities," which examines various characteristics of great cities in the world (Bell and de-Shalit 2011).

5. "Roughly" because culture is a complicated concept that does not have a clear-cut definition.

6. The logic of abstraction is displayed in Jaegwon Kim (1980) and Alvin Goldman (1970)'s view about events as "exemplifications of a property," which opposes the more commonsensical view about events held by G. E. M. Anscombe (1957) and Donald Davidson (1963).

7. Although we know that the term was first used by the Japanese for economy and this use of the term was introduced into China by Sun Yat-sen.

8. One illustration of this is the famous story about Emperor Xuanzong of the Tang Dynasty. Facing the pressure from his own subjects and the army, he had to let his most favorite concubine die.

9. See Ni 2006 for more analysis. One relevant point I made in the article is this: The Confucian statement "do not do to others what you don't like others do to you" should be taken as a *gongfu* 功夫 instruction rather than a moral imperative. Taken as a moral imperative, the "golden rule" becomes

absolute, allowing no exceptions, and will hence subject to the rejection of the counterexamples, but taken as a *gongfu* instruction, it becomes an effective way (*gongfa* 功法) of reaching a stage where one can "give one's heart-mind free rein without overstepping the boundaries" (*Analects* 2.4). The counterexamples will not apply, because an instruction is instrumental for getting a skill or ability, not a universal rule.

10. I realize that my view here is in conflict with Kant's. For a more detailed analysis and defense of my view, see Ni 2002.

11. One only needs to do a quick online search to find an overwhelming amount of sarcasm about TSA, such as calling the TSA "Thousands Standing Around," or "Thousands Sexually Assaulted."

12. Particularly due to its very controversial practice in avoiding taxes. See Kocieniewski 2011.

13. Donald Munro calls this mechanical copying "problem solving models," in contrast to the proper way of model learning, which he calls "character models." He uses Daqing oil fields in Heilongjiang Province China as an extreme case of mechanical copying. During the Cultural Revolution, the Chinese government set up Daqing as the role model for all industries, both in terms of its production process as well as a "spirit" to conquer extraordinary difficulties. In 1979, the officials in the Ministry of Petroleum took the Daqing process model and applied it to an offshore drilling platform called Bohai No. 2. In doing this they ignored the difference between Daqing, a land oil field, and the ocean oil platform, and failed to provide the information about water and weather conditions. Consequently Bohai No. 2 capsized under the impact of a force-ten wind, drowning 72 of the team members abroad. See Munro 2005, 35–7.

14. Confucius said, "May not Shun be instanced as having governed efficiently without exertion? What did he do? He did nothing but seating himself reverently, facing due south" (*Analects* 15.5). Facing due south is a ritual position of being an authority. Here it is used to imply that the larger society needs to set up models like GE/Durham for others to follow.

References

The Analects of Confucius, a Philosophical Translation (1998). Translated by Roger Ames and Henry Rosemont. New York: Ballentine Books. (Quotes from the book contain the author's occasional modification of the translation.)

Anscombe, G. E. M. (1957). *Intention*. Oxford: Blackwell.

Bell, Daniel A., and Avner de-Shalit (2011). *The Spirit of Cities: Why the Identity of a City Matters in a Global Age*. Princeton, NJ: Princeton University Press.

Burns, T. R., and E. Engdahl (1998). "The Social Construction of Consciousness. Part 1: Collective Consciousness and its Socio-Cultural Foundations," in *Journal of Consciousness Studies*, 5.1.

Davidson, Donald (1963). "Actions, Reasons and Causes," in *The Journal of Philosophy*, 60.23.

Derrida, Jacques (1975). "Economimesis," in *Mimesis—des articulations*. Paris: Flammarion.

Descartes, René (1980). *Discourse on Method and Meditations on First Philosophy*. Trans. by Donald A. Cress. Indianapolis, IN: Hackett Publishing Company.

Engell, James, and Anthony Dangerfield (1998). "The Market-Model University, Humanities in the Age of Money," *Harvard Magazine*, 1998, 05.

Fishman, Charles (1999). "Engines of Democracy," *Fast Company*, 28 (September, 1999): 174.

Goldman, Alvin I. (1970). *A Theory of Human Action*, Princeton, NJ: Princeton University Press.

Heidegger, Martin (1961). *Nietzsche*, Vol. 1. Pfullingen: Neste.

Hume, David (1985). *Essays, Moral, Political, and Literary*, New York: Liberty Fund, Inc.

Kennedy, Robert (1968). "On the Gross National Product and What It Does not Measure," Speech at the University of Kansas, March 18.

Kim, Jaegwon (1980). "Events as Property Exemplifications," in M. Brand and D. Waiton, ed. *Action Theory*. Dordrecht, Holland: Reidel, 159–77.

Kocieniewski, David (2011). "G.E.'s Strategies Let It Avoid Taxes Altogether," in the *New York Times*, March 24, 2011.

Kupperman, Joel (1999). *Learning from Asian Philosophy*, New York & Oxford: Oxford University Press.

———. (1991). *Character*, Oxford: Oxford University Press.

MacIntyre, Alasdair (1981). *After Virtue: A Study in Moral Theory*. London: Duckworth.

McMurtry, John (1991). "Education and the Market Model" in *Journal of Philosophy of Education*, 25.2: 209–217.

Munro, Donald J. (2005). *A Chinese Ethics for the New Century*. Hong Kong: The Chinese University Press.

———. (2011). "Unequal Human Worth," forthcoming in Brian Bruya, ed. *The Philosophical Challenge from China*, MIT Press.

Ni, Peimin (2002). "The Confucian Account of Freedom," in Xinyan Jiang, ed. *The Examined Life—Chinese Perspectives: Essays on Chinese Ethical Traditions*, 119–140. Binghamton, NY: Global Publications.

———. (2006). "Rules with Exceptions, A Discussion on Confucian Ethics," in *International Journal of Decision Ethics*, Fall 2006, 2.1: 151–164.

Rosemont, Jr., Henry (2001). *Rationality and Religious Experience—The Continuing Relevance of the World's Spiritual Traditions*. Chicago and La Salle, IL: Open Court.

Seidman, Dov (2007). *How—Why How We Do Anything Means Everything . . . in Business (and in Life)*. Hoboken, NJ: John Wiley & Sons, Inc.

10

When Good Relationships Are Not Enough for Business

Understanding Character in Confucian Ethics

Karyn Lai

Introduction

Many proposals for a Confucian approach to business identify good relationships as a key feature of Confucian ethics. Accordingly, notions such as reciprocity, loyalty, leadership, virtue, harmony, trustworthiness, superior-subordinate relationships, and business partnerships are explained in Confucian terms. I concur that it is not inappropriate to identify good relationships and the cluster of its associated implications as a key feature of Confucian ethics. However, I suggest in this paper that Confucian philosophy can make a more significant contribution if we draw on one of its more fundamental themes, that of the cultivation of character. An analysis of character highlights: (a) the nature of development as an ongoing process, (b) the nurturing of meaningful relationships not for self-gain but as a manifestation of the exemplary person's[1] character and (c) the ethical stature of the exemplary person that seeks to maintain harmonious relationships but does not seek simply to satisfy others at the cost of virtue. I draw some implications for an ethical understanding of character and how this can inform our understanding of the *image* of the business organization.

Confucian Philosophy and Business Ethics

In the last ten years, some scholarly journals in Business Ethics—such as the *Journal of Business Ethics* and *Business Ethics Quarterly*—have focused their attention on the possible contributions of Confucian philosophy to discussions in business ethics.[2] The majority of these publications deal with how Confucian philosophy might be plumbed to shed relevant and valuable insights on contemporary discussions on business ethics. The majority of these papers focus on relationships in Confucianism, expressed in pre-Han Confucian texts as *renlun* (人倫; human relationships) and in pre-modern texts and contemporary discourse as *guanxi* (關係; have a bearing on, a relation to).[3] The general thrust of these papers suggests that the Confucian focus on relationships is grounded in Confucian notions such as ethical responsibility, trustworthiness, exemplary conduct, and harmony. These ethical aspects of relationships are important in informing our understanding of business ethics at a range of levels: business relationships,[4] organization structures[5] and the role of the organization in society.[6]

Some of these papers are more cautious in approach as they are wary of the optimism in some accounts of Confucianism's value to Business Ethics.[7] One scholar remarks, for example, on how keenness to emphasize the relevance of Confucian ethics can overshadow the question of its real-world applications in business contexts:

> . . . the bulk of discussion in the literature seems to focus on the positive sides of Confucianism (Chan 2008; Koehn 2001; Lam 2003; Romar 2002, 2004). These studies are largely based on fairly sympathetic readings of a few often quoted textual extracts from the Confucian corpus. Argued in loose language and using analyses often couched in generic and vague terms, they are particularly weak in making the connections between the concepts with the real world of business. They have little to say in concrete terms on how Confucianism can combat corporate malfeasance. More importantly, they contain very little critical work, especially on the darker side of Confucianism. (Chan 2008, 473)

The argument in this paper takes the side of caution. The focus here, however, is not so much on the inadequacies of Confucian philosophy in this field but the way it is characterized in argument. In particular, some of the proposals seem to engage with issues in business ethics by positing (Confucian) relationships as a starting point, and then by propping up the notion with other Confucian values or virtues. I suggest that this is a wrong-headed approach: although relationships are a *key* aspect of Confucianism—especially in its conception of selfhood—what is *fundamental* in Confucian ethics is the cultivation of character. From this cornerstone, good relationships ensue. In other words, good relationships are an important *manifestation* of a person's successes in character cultivation; the two phenomena must occur concurrently. However, it is clear which has priority: the cultivated person *necessarily* has good relationships but the person who has good relationships may not necessarily have an ethically developed character. In brief, good relationships are necessary but not sufficient for an ethical life.

In some of the discussions that draw on Confucian insights for business ethics, there seems to be an assumption that the cultivation of good or harmonious relationships is the fundamental distinguishing feature of Confucian philosophy. For example, Tai K. Oh, in "Inherent Limitations of the Confucian Tradition in Contemporary East Asian Business Enterprises," writes that:

> It is important to note that the major focus of Confucian thought is on family relationships. (Oh 1992, 156. See also Romar 2004)

However, problems arise when relationships are the primary focus, as this can require compromises from the individual:

> . . . social relationships and their harmony are of utmost importance in human society. The family is seen as the most revered and an almost sacred form of human relationships and institution . . . Hierarchy in loving family relationships may be benign. However, in less than loving situations, it can be a source of coercion and domination. When hierarchy is aligned with prescribed authority, domination and subjugation may be its natural consequences, as has been the case in many Chinese families throughout history from feudal eras to modern times. (Ip 2009, 464, 466)[8]

There are other problems, too. These relate to nepotism, as Gary Chan articulates:

> In the *Analects*, Confucius seemed to suggest that favoritism should be shown towards family members [citation of *Analects* 13.19]. . . . the *specific* illustration about the father concealing the misconduct of the son and vice versa is problematic as it appears to not merely condone, but to praise the act of concealment of a wrongdoing. (Chan 2008, 353–4)

To prevent such misconduct, Chan suggests that *li*, Confucian rules of propriety, be implemented as restraints:

> The Confucian moral actor cleaves towards ethical standards to be found in a set of societal rituals and propriety (*li*) though the self is not completely surrendered or submerged, as it were, in the sea of ritualised standards. (Chan 2008, 355)

It is questionable whether *li*, as Chan suggests, might be sufficient to rescue Confucianism from this difficulty. This is because, typically, *li* may further entrench the greater moral weight of significant relationships (e.g., *Analects* 2.5; cf. Lai 1995). More importantly, however, to take relationships or *guanxi*[9] as the starting point might be a factor that contributes to these difficulties. This is because to do so eclipses the Confucian ethical self which is rightly at the center of the relationships. In this way, some of the proposals could sell Confucianism short in terms of what it has to offer to contemporary discussions in business ethics. I suggest that the Confucian theme of cultivated personhood might shed some light on the ethical character of business. In the following section, I examine the notion of the Confucian cultivated person at the center of relationships.

The Confucian Self at the Center of Relationships

From its origins during the Spring and Autumn period (*Chunqiu*; 771–476 BCE), the Confucian tradition has prioritized learning and reflective self-examination precisely because these are processes central to the cultivation of the self. The *preparation for an official career*—for a life engaged in ethico-political reform—is indeed the distinguishing feature of the Confucian tradition. Even if we were to dwell on debates such as those between Mengzi (Mencius, ca. 390–305 BCE) and Xunzi (ca.

310–219 BCE), or those in Song-Ming Confucianism (Song, 960–1279 CE; Ming, 1368–1644 CE) and beyond, we see that, notwithstanding important differences in themes, key concepts, emphases, borrowings, frameworks, and methodological approaches, the discussions cenetr on the ethical development of self for such engagement. At the core of Confucian self-cultivation is the ethically-developing person.

In contemporary discussions of Confucian ethics there is an influential characterization of self-cultivation provided by Tu Weiming, of the self as being "at the center of relationships":

> . . . the person in ordinary daily existence is the basis for the full realization of humanity. The Confucian insistence that learning is for the sake of the self, an end in itself rather than a means to an end, speaks directly to this. . . . The self as the center of relationships has always been the focus of Confucian learning. (Tu 1985, 52, 55)

Tu proceeds to explain the nature of relationships grounded in this distinctively-Confucian notion of self:

> Self-cultivation can very well be understood as the broadening of the self to embody an ever-expanding circle of human rel atedness. . . . Nevertheless, the self is not reducible to its social roles. The dramatic image of the modern person who assumes a variety of social roles is definitely un-Confucian. (Tu 1985, 57)

Tu's logical framework is different from those we have seen in the previous section. In the former proposals, relationships are problematic *because* they carry moral weight in and of themselves, thereby demanding that individuals dispense special favors or requiring other compromises. In Tu's account, relationships are a natural and *correlative* aspect of the ethically developing self. Relationships are not a metaphysically distinct stream of a person's life that occasionally impinge on other aspects of personhood; such a notion is alien to Confucian thought.[10]

Some of the conversations in the *Analects* seem deeply aware of how the *junzi* (君子), an exemplary person, upholds standards that set him apart from conventional expectations (*Analects* 2.21; 9.13). *Analects* 13.24 notes:

> Zigong enquired, saying, "What do you think about someone who is loved by everyone in his village?
>
> "It is not enough," said the Master.
>
> "What if everyone in the village despises a person?"
>
> "It is not enough. It would be better that the best villagers love, and the worst despise, this person." (Trans. Ames and Rosemont, Jr. 1998, 169)

There is an element of tension arising from the mismatch of the *junzi*'s commitment and values with those of the status quo.[11] This is quite different from the image of a person mindlessly yielding to the demands of relationships, or who seeks to uphold harmony at the expense of other morally weighty considerations. Indeed, in some conversations in the *Analects*, it is stated explicitly that an exemplary person does not seek simply to maintain harmony across all of his relationships (*Analects* 4.3; 12.22). In order to understand the notion of harmony more fully, we need to explore its corresponding terms in the *Analects*. The key term here is *he* (和), often translated as "harmony." This notion *he* is specifically addressed in *Analects* 13.23:

> The Master said, "Exemplary persons seek harmony not sameness; petty persons, then, are the opposite." (Trans. Ames and Rosemont, Jr. 1998, 168–9).

According to this passage, the *junzi* is harmonious *but he does not seek to be like others* (*he er butong* 和而不同). Here, the term *he*, typically translated "harmony," is given more depth by contrasting it with *tong* (likeness, similarity). By contrast, the small person (*xiaoren* 小人) strives to be is similar but is not harmonious (同而不和). This explicitly captures the mood of the previous conversation, *Analects* 13.24, that an exemplary person is not necessarily liked by everyone. Hence, it seems simplistic to present harmonious relationships as the overriding concern of Confucianism, as Po-Keung Ip does:

> Harmony, a cardinal value of Confucianism, is seen as the primary goal of personal and social life. People should strive to achieve harmony with their own selves, and with lives of others. Harmony is the basic and overlapping goal of familial, organizational, communal, and political lives. (Ip 2009, 466)

There are other important reasons for a more nuanced understanding of relationships in Confucianism. Those who focus primarily on the maintenance of harmony in relationships might also fail to notice the different shades of relationships. For example, in *Analects* 4.18 where Confucius addresses the topic of remonstration with one's parents, we get a fuller picture of the dynamics of close relationships, where one is not simply charged with pressing their point but with careful consideration of others. Indeed, many of the passages in the *Analects* address carefulness across a range of relationships (*Analects* 1.2; 2.6–8; 5.16; 9.16; 11.22; 19.10). Just as importantly, relationships enrich the individual; some conversations emphasize the joys of friendship (*Analects* 1.1; 1.4). In his relationships, Confucius had reasons to *enjoy* Yan Hui's (顏回) company. Confucius praised Yan Hui for his love of learning and looked forward to being challenged by him (*Analects* 2.9; see also 5.9; 6.3, 7, 11; 9.20; 11.4, 7, 11, 19). Just as revealing is Confucius's disdain for many of Zaiwo's (宰我) decisions and actions, including especially his laziness (*Analects* 5.10; 11.21).

In Confucian philosophy, the way a person relates to others must be understood over time and across different relationships. Indeed, this is true for all of a person's behaviors and actions; how a person conducts himself or herself and responds to others are expressions of the self. Yet, at the same time, they are constitutive of personhood (Lai 2003). The Confucian notion of personhood and moral cultivation is foundational in Joel Kupperman's characterization of virtue in Confucianism (Kupperman 2009). Kupperman compares Confucian with Aristotelian virtue ethics, although he is careful to draw a fundamental distinction between the two. According to Kupperman, in Chinese philosophy, the focus is on "a general state of being a virtuous person" that "involves mostly (although not always) 'narrow' character traits, which involve a strong tendency to function well in certain kinds of choices in certain kinds of situations" (2009, 252, 253). This conception of virtue contrasts with that typically articulated in Aristotelian ethics, where particular virtues take center-stage and are assumed to be consistent across different situations.

By contrast, the Confucian notion of virtue is a "longitudinal" one which emphasizes "how people can come to be virtuous and on the rewards of a life that centers on being virtuous" (2009, 250). Kupperman's account of virtue is centered on the development of *character* over time. In his work on character (esp. 1991; 2001, 2009), Kupperman emphasizes the distinctiveness of how it is conceived in the Confucian tradition.

Importantly, he draws on particular features of the tradition to address gaps in modern and contemporary moral theories including Kantian morality, Utilitarianism and, more recently, findings in psychological research that impact on how we think about morality. Focus on character contrasts with "big-moment" ethics (Kupperman 1971, 194), trolley-case ethics (Kupperman 2009, 250–1) or snapshot views of moral behavior at a fixed time (Kupperman 2001, 245). This is a view of ethics that expects to see some mistakes and failures rather than perfect instantiations of a particular virtue in every context. What is important is to examine the person's character as manifest in situations (Kupperman 2001; 2009); over time these will allow us to understand the person's character in terms of their reliability (or lack thereof) in realizing specific virtues in particular situations.

These discussions on the Confucian notion of self serve to convey a picture of a person engaged in ongoing reflection about his or her actions, behavior, and relationships with others. In the following section, I suggest how this notion of self might inform debates on ethical business, focusing in particular on the character of businesses.

Ethical Character in Business

In this final section, I discuss some features of character-based ethics that are helpful in business ethics. I begin with an outline of an exemplary person in Confucian ethics before proceeding to suggest some of its implications for business. The key aspects of Confucian character cultivation include:

(a) *Engagement in activities and projects that bring benefits not only for oneself.* The idea of cultivating character traits through engagement in projects that only benefit the self is alien to Confucian philosophy. The *Mengzi* (《孟子》; *Works of Mencius*, e.g., 1A.1) in particular speaks out against the accrual of *li* (利), normally translated "profit," at the expense of *ren* (仁). In the *Analects*, there are statements such as "Exemplary persons (*junzi* 君子) understand what is appropriate (*yi* 義); petty persons understand what is of personal advantage (*li* 利)" (4.16. Trans. Ames and Rosemont Jr. 1998, 92). The term *li* 利 in the Confucian texts is sometimes taken literally as if Confucius disapproved of profit and, by extension, of profit-making in business.[12] We need to be careful about how we *apply* the translation of *li* 利, however, as it seems that the *Analects* is not simplistically rejecting the pursuit of profit but rather the *focus on personal gain* that sets the self against others. Hence, although the person who seeks personal gain will incite much dislike (*Analects* 4.12), benefiting the people (*min* 民) is encouraged (*Analects* 20.2). In contrast to the person who seeks self-gain, a person who seeks to enhance the lives of others is highlighted in *Analects* 6.30: the person is "broadly generous with the people and is able to help the multitude. . . . Authoritative persons establish others in seeking to establish themselves and promote others in seeking to get there themselves" (Trans. Ames and Rosemont Jr. 1998, 110).

(b) *A picture of ethical attainment over time.* A person's decisions and actions are understood not as single, disconnected events. This prevents unrealistic expectations being placed on how an individual is to perform in *every situation* (as measured against particular virtues or moral principles). The longitudinal understanding of ethics suggested by Kupperman allows for a more substantial and meaningful picture of a person's *moral development* over time. As Kupperman has argued, this is integral to our conception of self.

(c) *Constant reflection on oneself and attunement with others.* The exemplary person is, on a daily basis, engaged in practice and self-reflection. He puts into practice what he has learnt and reflects on his actions (*Analects* 1.1; 1.4; 2.15; 15.16). In light of the points previously articulated, these are essential processes in the cultivation of character. The cultivation of character *includes*: familiarity with a wide range of scenarios and possibilities for the realization of one's value commitments, awareness of individual needs where possible and relevant (cf. *Analects* 1.16; 12.22), and an understanding of consequences. This process of self-reflection is not an inward-looking exercise but rather one that is grounded in legitimate and familiar ways of acknowledging humanity. After all, Confucian *li*, behavioral propriety, is a language of respect shared with others in the community (*Analects* 12.1). This is where Confucian harmony, *he*, bears its distinctive mark: an exemplary person is part of the community but he does not simply and unthinkingly do as others do. Hence, *Analects* 17.13 points out that "[t]he 'village worthy' is excellence (*de* 德) under false pretenses" (Trans. Ames and Rosemont Jr. 1998, 207; see also the discussion in Hall and Ames 1987, 49–50). How does an exemplary person maintain his ethical stature (*he er bu tong*)? An important resource in attunement and reflection is to be found in friends with similar value commitments (*Analects* 4.1; 9.30). *Analects* 16.5 presents an eloquent expression of the enjoyment of one's improvement:

> Confucius said, "Finding enjoyment in three kinds of activities will be a source of personal improvement . . . One stands to be improved by the enjoyment found in attuning oneself to the rhythms of ritual propriety (*li* 禮) and music (*yue* 樂), by the enjoyment found in talking about what others do well (*shan* 善), and by the enjoyment found in having a circle of many friends of superior character (*xian* 賢). . . ." (Trans. Ames and Rosemont Jr. 1998, 197–8)[13]

How can some of these features of cultivated character inform our understanding of business ethics? I suggest that some of the elements of character outlined here are relevant especially in terms of how we might conceive of the *ethical character* of a business.[14] Naturally, the relevant parameters for understanding personhood and a business organization are significantly different in many ways. Fundamentally, businesses are run by people and/or teams to maximize profits: this is a primary goal, though it is not necessarily an exclusive one. The fundamental aim to maximize profits contrasts sharply with aims in human lives, which are not constrained by or reducible to any one measure of significance. Yet, I suggest it is not out of place to think about a business as having a character, especially in terms of how this image develops over time, in the way a business treats its employees, its customers, its competitors, its stakeholders, and its products.

The idea of businesses as participants in and contributors to society is not new. It has been articulated recently, and extensively, in the literature in terms of *corporate social responsibility* (CSR), that is, in general, to think of how businesses fulfil their economic, ethical, social, and charitable responsibilities. The definition of CSR and its evaluation has developed over the years and it is not the place here to revisit its many formulations.[15] Drawing on the point made in (a) above, I suggest that, instead of prohibiting profit, Confucianism upholds that profit should be understood in context. Clearly, while relationships between business, government, industry and the public are different from those between individuals, it is at least as important for a business to think of its embeddedness within society, not merely as a profit-making enterprise but also as a contributor to human well-being.

This image of a business stands in contrast to one that is focused primarily on strategies to trump competitors without heed for the costs that might be borne by the public or other stakeholders as a result of such competition.[16] For example, attempts by businesses to maximize profits at all costs can result in unethical and unsustainable practices, including price collusion, squeezing of suppliers and lowering of employees' real wages. While, in the short term, the negative consequences are borne by affected individuals, in the longer term, entire communities will feel their far-reaching impacts.

The view of human character being developed over time (point (b)) and manifest in contexts has important parallels in businesses seeking profits in context: what are the foreseeable impacts of intended measures and schemes on the wider community? This question should be located within a more meaningful one, that is, what *kind of character* of the business is portrayed and manifest in its proposals and projects, *across a period of time*? As with the case of character in human personhood, it is not the occasional ethical deed that counts. An ethically-engaged business does not aim merely to fund the occasional charitable project but rather understands that part of its core business is to contribute to society. It is also imperative that it does not see its contribution simply in narrowly-conceived economic terms. In other words, businesses need actively to seek out opportunities for contributing to society, in the same way they seek to increase profits. This is a fundamental step in its engagement with society in order to understand where it can make meaningful contributions.

As it is with character, frequent and rigorous evaluation of initiatives is a necessary aspect of development (point (c)). This is perhaps even more crucial in the case of businesses as personnel, employees and organizational structures will change over time. Continual review must be integrated in the organizational schedule whereby there is genuine and honest evaluation that takes into account a wider (community or public) view of its image as an ethical business. This attunement is critical for businesses that understand their objectives in light of their situatedness within particular social, political, legal and ethical contexts. It is important for businesses not to respond only to legal and regulatory pressures but also to public perceptions of its undertakings and decisions. As in the case of the exemplary person in Confucianism, the business is regularly reflecting on what to do, taking its cues thoughtfully from its wider environment.

Finally, I note that these perspectives on the ethical character of businesses rely heavily on the ethical persuasion of key persons. In the case of character, the motivation ethically to cultivate the self must originate from the person himself or herself. While regulation might provide some constraining and some guiding principles, the person must be persuaded by a picture of ethical character attuned to his or her relationships within, and responsibilities to, others in society.[17] The same applies to businesses, or, more accurately, to its key decision makers. The question to stakeholders, executives and employees is whether they are concerned to foster a character—a reputation, perhaps—that is ethical. I will let Confucius have the last word here on the centrality of the reflective self to the cultivation of character. What he had to say about this in relation to a person is also applicable in ethical business: The Master said, "There is nothing that I can do for someone who is not constantly asking himself: 'What to do? What to do?'" (*Analects* 15.16. Trans. Ames and Rosemont, Jr. 1998, 188).

Notes

1. I use the phrase "exemplary person" in this discussion to capture two aspects of the term "exemplary." The first denotes a sense of *quality*, in which the case in point is noteworthy or extraordinary. This does not necessarily mean, however, that the exemplary person's actions or behaviors should be *imitated*. The second aspect of exemplary derives from its root "example," where the exemplary person provides an example of how life *might* be lived well. This

means there can be different *good* examples—not just one—of how to live life *well*. According to this account, to insist there is *only one* model of excellence is misdirected.

2. This is not to say that other scholarly journals do not publish in this area, or that these journals did not publish in this area prior to this period. Rather, a quick review of the publications of these two journals over this period reveals a high number of papers published in this area.

3. See, for example, Koehn 1999, Koehn 2001, Romar 2004, Chan 2008, Ip 2009, and Zhu 2009. Refer to Fan 2002 for an interesting classification of different types of *guanxi*.

4. E.g., Koehn 2001, Romar 2004, and Zhu 2009.

5. E.g,. Koehn 2001 and Ip 2009.

6. E.g., Chan 2008.

7. E.g,. Chan 2008 and Ip 2009.

8. Ip argues that the notion of the Confucian Firm (when understood in terms of these features) is "incompatible with the core value of equality presupposed by the human rights norm." (2009, 472).

9. Daryl Koehn notes the continuing impact of the Confucian focus on relationships, "*Guanxi* is typically seen as an outgrowth of the Confucian emphasis on personal relations. . . . To this day Chinese businesspeople will often treat classmates, friends, and family members preferentially when making hiring or other business decisions" (Koehn 2001, 421).

10. In contemporary discussions of Confucian ethics, it is important that Confucian personhood be understood on its own terms rather than as defective when held up against a Kantian account of autonomy. See, for example, Michael Martin's argument that contrasts Confucian personhood (in terms of a performer) unfavorably with Kantian personhood (in terms of a composer). Martin claims, "[T]he Kantian will want to know who creates the *tao*; even more, the Kantian will want to create it himself, autonomously, and with suitable justification" (1995, 18). See my response to this in *Learning from Chinese Philosophies* (2006, 139–56). Joseph Chan (2002) argues against the use of Kantian autonomy against which to measure the Confucian conception of self.

11. For a detailed discussion of the Confucian exemplary person's engagement in social reform, see Hourdequin 2010.

12. For example, Gary Chan notes, "One major task pertaining to Confucian Ethics in the business arena is to understand and explain the apparent negative attitude of Confucius against profit-making in business activities. . . . In the course of advocating the virtues, the concept of profit-making was employed as a foil. Hence, in contrast to the aim of developing human virtues, the profit-making activity represents man's efforts to attain material wealth at the expense of virtuous living" (2008, 349, 350).

13. The phrase in Chinese is likewise imbued with depth of meaning: "孔子曰：'益者三樂 . . . 樂節禮樂，樂道人之善，樂多賢友，益矣。'"

14. My reflections in this essay pertain to business organizations and not to individual persons. That is, I do not discuss the character of the *business person* or of particular *personnel* but rather of the business as a whole.

15. See the influential discussion by Carroll (1999) on the history of the phrase. For recent discussions of CSR and its connections with Confucian philosophy, refer, for example, to Lei and Heikki 2009 and Ip 2009.

16. An ancient Chinese text, Sunzi's *Bingfa* (孫子兵法), is (mis)appropriated to apply to discussions of business strategies. Steven Heine discusses the misappropriation: "This thriving subfield [of business strategies and management] is based largely on appropriations of the Art of War and applications of it to corporate battles, as Western businesses seek to learn the fine 'art' of conquering opponents, as practiced for centuries by ancient Chinese generals and now applied to the corporate realm. As in the case of warring opponents, business giants such as Sears and JC Penney or Coke and Pepsi learn that to be effective and master the competition in turbulent times it is necessary to create leverage and gain advantage through cunning and deception. This is done in order to hide one's real intentions in such a way that rivals are caught off guard and kept guessing so that they are left bewildered, unprotected, and vulnerable to attack" (2008, 130). Refer also to Wawrytko 2007 for an important argument against "distorted views of Chinese cultural values, past and present, fueled by intercultural misunderstanding and even cultural imperialism" (p. 561).

17. In *Analects* 17.21, Confucius seems to have "given up" on Zaiwo, who is keen to present arguments against the traditional three-year mourning period. It is clear that Confucius in this passage regards the mourning period as a manifestation of a child's respect and love for his or her parents, and their grief at a parent's passing-on. Interestingly, Confucius does not attempt to dissuade Zaiwo from excusing himself from this ritual. Confucius's primary question to Zaiwo was, "Would you be *comfortable* [ceasing the mourning ritual before the prescribed three years]?" To which Zaiwo replied, "Yes" (安, *an*: comfortable). Confucius then said, "If you are comfortable, then do it" (Sections trans. by Ames and Rosemont, Jr. 1998, 208–9).

References

Bernasek, A. (2003). "Banking on Social Change: Grameen Bank Lending to Women," *International Journal of Politics, Culture, and Society*, 16.3: 369–85.

Chan, Gary Kok Yew (2008). "The Relevance and Value of Confucianism in Contemporary Business Ethics." *Journal of Business Ethics*, 77: 347–60.

Chan, Joseph (2002). "Moral Autonomy, Civil Liberties, and Confucianism." *Philosophy East and West*, 52.3: 281–310.

Carroll, Archie B. (1999). "Corporate Social Responsibility: Evolution of a Definitional Construct." *Business and Society*, 38.3: 268–95.

Dowla, A. (2006). "In Credit We Trust: Building Social Capital by Grameen Bank in Bangladesh." *Journal of Socio-Economics*, 35.1: 102–22.

Hassan, M. Kabir (2002). "The Microfinance Revolution and the Grameen Bank Experience in Bangladesh." *Financial Markets, Institutions and Instruments*, 11.3: 205–65.

Heine, Steven (2008). "From Art of War to Attila the Hun: A Critical Survey of Recent Works on Philosophy/Spirituality and Business Leadership." *Philosophy East and West*, 58.1: 126–43.

Koehn, Daryl (1999). "What Can Eastern Philosophy Teach Us About Business Ethics?" *Journal of Business Ethics*, 19: 71–79.

———. (2001). "Confucian Trustworthiness and the Practice of Business in China." *Business Ethics Quarterly*, 11.3: 415–29.

Fan, Ying (2002). "Guanxi's Consequences: Personal Gains at Social Cost." *Journal of Business Ethics*, 38.4: 371–380.

Hourdequin, Marion (2010). "Engagement, Withdrawal, and Social Reform: Confucian and Contemporary Perspectives." *Philosophy East and West*, 60.3: 369–90.

Ip, Po-Keung (2009). "Is Confucianism Good for Business Ethics in China?" *Journal of Business Ethics*, 88: 463–76.

Kupperman, Joel J. (1971). "Confucius and the Nature of Religious Ethics." *Philosophy East and West*, 21.2: 189–94.

———. (1991). *Character*. New York: Oxford University Press.

———. (2001). "The Indispensability of Character." *Philosophy*, 76.2: 239–50.

———. (2009). "Virtue in Virtue Ethics." *Journal of Ethics*, 3: 243–55.

Lai, Karyn L. (1995). "Confucian Moral Thinking." *Philosophy East and West*, 45.2: 249–271.

———. (2003). "Confucian Moral Cultivation: Some Parallels with Musical Training." In Kim-Chong Chong, Sor-Hoon Tan, and CL Ten (eds.) *The Moral Circle and the Self: Chinese and Western Perspectives*. Chicago, USA: Open Court Publishing. 107–39.

———. (2006). *Learning from Chinese Philosophies: Ethics of Interdependent and Contextualised Self*. Aldershot, UK: Ashgate Publishing.

Lei, Wang, and Heikki, Juslin (2009). "The Impact of Chinese Culture on Corporate Social Responsibility: The Harmony Approach." *Journal of Business Ethics*, 88: 433–51.

Martin, Michael R. (1995). "Ritual action (*li*) in Confucius and Hsun Tzu." *Australasian Journal of Philosophy*, 73.1: 13–30.

Oh, Tai K. (1992). "Inherent Limitations of the Confucian Tradition in Contemporary East Asian Business Enterprises." *Journal of Chinese Philosophy*, 19: 155–69.

Romar, Edward J. (2004). "Globalization, Ethics, and Opportunism: A Confucian View of Business Relationships." *Business Ethics Quarterly*, 14.4: 663–78.

Tu Wei-ming (1985). "A Confucian Perspective on Learning to be Human." In *Confucian Thought: Selfhood as Creative Transformation*. Albany, NY: State University of New York Press: 51–66.

Wawrytko, Sandra A. (2007). "Winning Ways: The Viability (*Dao*) and Virtuosity (*De*) of Sunzi's Methods of Warefare (*Bingfa*)." *Journal of Chinese Philosophy*, 34.4: 561–79.

Zhu, Yunxia (2009). "Confucian Ethics Exhibited in the Discourse of Chinese Business and Marketing Communication." *Journal of Business Ethics*, 88: 517–28.

PART III

Responses and Comments

11

Responses and Comments

JOEL J. KUPPERMAN

This excellent set of papers highlights a real change in conceptions and practice of philosophy since my time as a beginning philosophy teacher and writer. In that era, which now seems in some respects to have been benighted, the central feature of philosophy was held to be argument. This in turn suggested that there was an agonistic element built in to philosophy, that it was normally a struggle between or among philosophers. It was widely regarded as helpful if, in starting to write on a topic, you could refer to someone who had got things wrong. This, over time, evolved in a baroque way into Reviews of the Literature, offering ways of approaching one's own views (and perhaps boring non-philosophers who were presuming to read some philosophy).

All of that seems to me to have been a bit peculiar. One feels lucky not to feel obligated to criticize the papers in this volume, because I did not encounter a single thing that I was inclined to criticize in any significant way—which in the old days would amount to my failure.

There are of course some differences between my views and those of some of the papers. But they are not major differences, and the appropriate image is not one of philosophical combat. Rather, one might use the metaphor of a number of blind people examining an elephant. As such a philosophically "blind" person, I can gain from having access to other people's reports.

What Rosemont and Ames say is very good, and connects nicely with Roger Ames's revelatory book on roles. (I have written a highly favorable review of this book.) They refer to my view of a "reified self."

Perhaps this view is a result of the influence of Indian philosophy—and also of David Hume—on me. In any case it is clear that many people have a sense of what they are like and what their lives are like. There is room in this for self-criticism. One might think "I should try to be less disposed to feel angry," or "It would be a good idea to focus on the interests of the people I talk with." My sense is that many thoughtful people at some point in their lives take stock, and work on modifying features of their nature that they are not entirely satisfied with. This self-modification can occur at any time in life. For many people, it takes place during college age.

Let me concede that the image of an individual agent functioning in an autonomous way is overworked in recent Western philosophy. That it is overworked though (and factors of context, culture, social roles, etc. not given sufficient regard) does not mean that it can be disposed of. In passing, let me say that this reminds me of something striking. Recent psychological studies (e.g., the Milgram Report, the Stanford Prison Experiment) have cast considerable light on human behavior and misbehavior. However in none of these trials has every single one of the subjects behaved in the same way. Individual selves are definitely part of this picture. We typically praise or blame individual agents for their behavior or attitudes.

If we look at our own lives, we are unlikely to encounter a smooth and even continuing surface. Much of life normally will involve carrying on, pursuing a pattern of behavior that already had been adopted. But there may well be moments when we step out of this, and consider behaving in a way that is not typical of us. Something may have happened that puts us in a not entirely familiar position, and we have to decide what to do. It is at such points that we especially appear (to ourselves, and to others) as individual agents functioning in an autonomous way. The individual emerges out of the person.

Let me emphasize that in most lives—especially ones that do not involve crises of various sorts—such moments are not very frequent. But they do occur, at least occasionally in most lives (and often in some lives), and it is then that the idea of the individual agent functioning in an autonomous way takes on personal meaning.

P. J. Ivanhoe"s paper is excellent in a number of ways, including the careful comparison between Confucius's and Aristotle's forms of virtue ethics. One might note that Aristotle's emphasis on the "intellectual" virtues has a residual influence on much in modern Western culture. There are inherent complications in this. Intellectual activities have their own problems, and there can be difficult questions as to whether some matters require close consideration, and as to how open to others one's lines of thought should be. Sometimes it might be suggested that data should be suppressed or downplayed, for various reasons, such as the possibility that many people would be demoralized or tempted to behave badly. In a world with highly developed systems of communication, many of the decisions connected with intellectual activities can be taken quite seriously.

As Ivanhoė points out, identifying with a strong cultural tradition (while valuable) requires work at "interpreting, understanding, and applying an inherited body of wisdom." "Practical and theoretical forms of reasoning" have an important role in this, even given a genuine desire to be virtuous.

Part of the appeal of Confucianism is that it crosses the boundary between, on one hand, high pressure choices in which a poor decision amounts to immorality, and our general dispositions in interacting with other people. The moral choices are important, but the general dispositions are important also in that they connect with the quality of our lives most of the time, when we are not making moral decisions. Most Western ethical philosophy in recent decades has concentrated on morality, and has paid rather little regard to the qualities of personal interactions.

To put this succinctly: Confucianism illuminates a much larger part of our lives than recent Western ethics has addressed.

Bryan Van Norden gives a very apt treatment of Confucius as a virtue ethicist, in some ways anticipating Hume's emphasis on care and benevolence. He also provides a thoughtful and convincing discussion of Xunzi as an anthropocentric realist about values, which strengthens one's sense of his importance. It can be added that the claim that our natures typically involve elements of (or tendencies toward) care and benevolence has great weight in assessing human lives. Of course, there are some people whose lives do not exhibit these features. Hume mentions the emperor Nero. But perhaps most people are not like that.

Some people allow benevolent elements and tendencies to come forward in their lives, and others are inclined to view them as impractical. There is a strong case for contending that the first group tends to have better (and more satisfying) lives than the second group. The great problem in this area is that of whether it is (in some sense) a fact that certain activities or forms of life have very much value—or not much value. Ordinary thought suggests a positive answer. But much recent philosophy is built around a distinction between facts and values. Very sophisticated philosophers have argued that any judgment of values will be based on sentiments or emotions, and in this respect will lack the support that judgments of fact normally have.

I have argued, in *Ethical Knowledge* (1970), and in much subsequent writing, against the view characterized above. Clearly sentiments and emotions influence someone's acceptance or rejection of judgments of value or about morality. All the same, we have ways of evaluating such judgments. Both in ethics and aesthetics there can be reasons (good or bad). There can be what amounts to evidence that some patterns of life, or personal decisions, are life-enhancing, leading to personal fulfilment, and that some others are the opposite. The issues usually are not easy to pin down, but that does not mean that they are never considered intelligently (or unintelligently).

David Wong's paper on love raises some interesting issues. He is surely right to suggest that accounts that work in some contexts might not work in others. Part of the fascination of all of this is that "love" is far from having a definite or precise meaning, and cases of what we might speak of as love can vary widely in their natures. It might make sense to regard "love" as one of those words that covers a range of cases, each of which has some similarities with some of the others. We might think immediately of romantic love, which typically has a strong element of desire to be with the beloved, etc. But we can love institutions, social customs, or ideas, and in all these cases very different factors will play a part. Perhaps the most salient thing that these examples of "love" have in common is that they involve a person, as it were, going outside of herself or himself. Perhaps most of us are, so to speak, too much inside ourselves. If so, love in its various forms can play a highly positive role in human life.

Kwong-loi Shun's paper comes very close indeed to areas of concern in my own work. Indeed, I have learned a great deal from him, and expect to reread his paper more than once. His discussion of two levels of thought seems to me to be very important. We need to remind ourselves that a life with some continuity and coherence is usually better and more gratifying than one that lacks these qualities. This is especially important in the twenty-first century, in which popular culture focuses especially on momentary, transient thrills or satisfactions. Generally speaking there is nothing wrong with having an occasional thrill, but our sense of our own lives will be determined far more by its ongoing qualities and connections.

Many of us, in some periods of time, deal mainly with what is happening at the moment. This leads to what might be termed a "presentist" outlook on life. It has often seemed to me that this represents a weakness not only in popular culture but also in educational systems. There is a lot to be said for introducing into the schools courses in playing chess. This could instill habits, in various situations, of thinking about "what comes next."

A number of the papers raise issues connected with "market values" or material well-being. Peimin Ni comments incisively on the growing emphasis on market values. He adeptly points out that groups do not have an integrated consciousness in the way that an individual person normally does, and yet groups may nevertheless play the role of being agents, and are thus are subject to moral evaluations and cultivation. Individual concern with market values does not of course conflict in any very simple way with a strong emphasis on virtue and the development of character, although in some cases it might be a distraction. As Chenyang Li points out, there are significant connections between material well-being and the cultivation of virtue. The insight here goes back to what Confucius said about enriching the people, and Li very nicely brings it up to date.

A book that connects with this is one on happiness, written by the Oxford psychologist Michael Argyle. "Happiness" of course is a slippery concept. People are sometimes happy—an immediate state, often short run—with something that has happened. But there is also a long-term version of happiness, which enables people to have sunny, gratifying lives. In *The Psychology of Happiness* Argyle cites data that indicate that by and large people who have a moderate amount of money (or even more) tend to be happier (in this long-term sense) than the poor. But the data also indicate that people who have a lot of money tend not to be significantly happier than people who have only a moderate amount.

One paper that centers on the problems here is Sor-hoon Tan's, which points out that in Confucianism there is "not a simple opposition but varied and more complex attitudes toward materialistic desires and the pursuit of wealth." This leaves room, of course, to deprecate materialistic concerns without flatly rejecting them. She effectively points out how Mencius thought that materialistic desires and an ethical life could reasonably be combined. This paper also provides an interesting discussion of Confucius's highly successful disciple, Zigong.

It could be argued that materialistic desires and the pursuit of wealth—to a degree—could play a reasonable part in most lives. It is not merely that most of us would like to have more money than we have. There may be innocent gratifications that more money would make possible. All the same, our concerns in this area ought to be a matter of degree. To have some materialistic interests looks harmless. For those to play a major part in our lives looks pathological.

That said, we have to be aware of the resonance of money in our culture. In social and political matters its weight has become so great that the United States might be termed a plutocracy rather than a democracy. In people's lives it is often taken as a measure of personal success. We repeatedly encounter accounts of people (successful business people and the like) who equate the amount of wealth with the degree of personal success. Often this is harmless. But cumulatively it leads to an excessively narrow view of what amounts to a good life. We need to bear in mind Michael Argyle's data on the relation (real, but not unlimited) between money and happiness.

One of the complications of the Confucian tradition is the way in which concerns about individual development are woven into an emphasis on the quality of social interactions. A number of the papers exhibit this. Karyn Lai, for example, admirably brings together cultivation of character and the role of good relations for someone with a well-developed character. A number of factors may affect whether someone gains the ability to have good relations with others. Many recent studies have taken a longitudinal view of this, in some cases looking at family relations in the pre-school years as setting the tone for much that follows.

Karyn Lai's paper especially connects with longstanding interests of mine. The cultivation of character is of great importance, both for the society and for the individual. The health of a society requires (as Hobbes and others have argued) that most of its members have characters that make them reliable and cooperative. A society that falls short of this is in real trouble.

A person who lacks a character that is reliable and cooperative also is in real trouble. Personal relations are very likely to suffer, as others notice or sense what is not there. Many activities benefit from the help and support of others, and someone whose character does not invite such help and support is likely to miss out on a great deal. More deeply, in the last analysis one of the factors that most determine the quality of a person's life will be how much that person likes herself or himself. Michael Argyle's data indicate that this has considerable weight in determining a person's level of happiness.

Pace Rosemont and Ames, individual character matters a great deal in life. Not everyone, of course, has what we would term "character." Many people act largely on impulse, and as a result their lives lack coherence and predictability. What is colloquially termed "character" is something that small children normally do not have: they are said to have temperaments, which may be reflected in their later character development. To have "character" or something like character, one must be to some degree predictable. There are some things that a person with character would never do. By and large, we count in various ways on people who we believe to have character. However, none of this means that a person with character is entirely predictable. For various reasons a person can act "out of character."

It is arguable that most of us construct our characters as we go along, through our teenage years and afterward. The construction may involve habits of mind that we develop. It also can be influenced by reflection. "Why did I do that?" can be a question that leads to self-conscious modification of character. Character need not be static.

Robert Neville makes it clear that development as an individual could not be simply reduced to a personal decision, but rather normally has roots in "important rituals of life." The important rituals of life can be individuated. Character development typically takes place in relation to others who develop their characters in the context of "the dense fabric of ritual roles." In the process of this examination, he highlights important elements in the philosophy of Xunzi. There is a connection here between individuated rituals and the "harmonious ease" in ritual referred to in *Analects* 1.12.

"Ritual" has a broad meaning, covering a wide range of activities. It could include such things as carefully discussing important decisions with a spouse. A good teacher may have rituals that communicate to students that there is some degree of approachability. Brushing one's teeth daily can be a ritual, as can voting in an election. Probably the most familiar rituals, for most of us, are those of saying "thank you" when someone has done us a favor, or holding a door open for someone who is walking behind you. A lot of this is in a way trivial. But it often contributes to social cohesion. Much current thought views the interactions with other people in a matter of fact way. Bloggs does the appropriate thing, or perhaps he does not. But how Bloggs does the appropriate thing (or not), and the attitude that he evinces, can matter a great deal. If Bloggs, with a silly smile on his face, shuts the door on the person behind him, this amounts to significant misbehavior. Perhaps not much harm is done, but our opinion of Bloggs will surely plummet.

The basic point here is that in reporting or assessing human behavior we normally will consider not only the broad nature of what is said or done, but also the spirit and attitude involved in this. In Western culture this would be taken seriously in part because the way in which Bloggs performs an action can be an important indication of what we can expect of Bloggs in the future. Helping a needy person with an expression of disdain is not a hopeful sign.

However, more broadly, we can consider what is indicated as, so to speak, the inner life of the agent. Someone who does the "proper" thing in a variety of cases, but with signs of feelings of contempt or boredom, is not likely to gain our respect or trust. Most basically, we would not want to be that kind of person—not merely because it looks bad, but also because it points toward what might be termed an impoverished soul.

Confucianism can be appealing not merely because of its emphasis on community and on the rewards of virtue, but also because of its attention to the style and attitude involved in various forms of behavior. What might be termed a bureaucratic view of Bloggs's behavior is that either he meets the standards or he does not. A more personal, existential view would go well beyond that. Bloggs's characteristic manner in interacting with others will count heavily in this, as will any sense of what Bloggs's emotions and interests are like.

We have to keep in mind that many of the issues addressed are not merely of concern to the discipline of philosophy, but also are of personal and social concern for each of us and for the societies in which we live. Our interactions with friends, students, colleagues, and the wider society are very much connected with the judgments at which we arrive.

Finally, the complexity of issues has to be acknowledged. Often, when there is a question of whether something is justified, the best answer may be "it depends." Chenyang Li in effect gives this answer in relation to the connection between material well-being and the moral life.

Li points out an apparent tension between a view that material well-being is (or can be) a precondition for moral refinement, and on the other hand the view that sometimes moral refinement does not require material well-being. Further, sometimes we may have a negative attitude toward material well-being, as when it is the material well-being of someone who is wicked. Li points out that there are "qualified goods."

Does material well-being add to a person's life? It depends. Also, if we ask whether someone could achieve moral refinement, personal factors do matter.

The distinction between being influenced by external conditions and having one's behavior be determined by them is important here, as is the distinction between strong external influence and quite mild influence. The word "conducive" is very apt in relation to all of this. Some factors may (or may not) be conducive to moral development, and some factors may be more conducive than others. All things considered, it is plausible to say that reliable material well-being can be conducive to successful moral cultivation.

Appendix

Publications by Joel J. Kupperman

Books

Human Nature: A Reader (Indianapolis, IN: Hackett, 2012)
Theories of Human Nature (Indianapolis, IN: Hackett, 2010)
Ethics and Qualities of Life (New York: Oxford University Press, 2007)
Six Myths About the Good Life: Thinking About What Has Value (Indianapolis, IN: Hackett, 2006) [Korean translation by Son Jeongsug, Hawangsojali Press, 2010]
Classic Asian Philosophy: A Guide to the Essential Texts (New York: Oxford University Press, 2001; second edition, 2006) [Korean translation 2005]
Learning From Asian Philosophy (New York: Oxford University Press, 1999) [Chinese translation, Renmin Press, Beijing, 2009]
Value . . . And What Follows (New York: Oxford University Press, 1999)
Character (New York: Oxford University Press, 1991, paperback 1995)
The Foundations of Morality (London and Boston: Geo. Allen & Unwin, 1983)
Philosophy: The Fundamental Problems (New York: St. Martin's Press, 1978)
Ethical Knowledge (London: Geo. Allen & Unwin, Muirhead Library of Philosophy, 1970; reprint by Routledge, 2002)
Fundamentals of Logic (with A. S. McGrade) (Garden City: Doubleday, 1966)

Articles

Ethics

"Why Ethics Needs Comparative Philosophy," *Philosophy*, 85 (2010): 185–200
"Virtue in Virtue Ethics," *Journal of Ethics*, 13 (2009), 243–255
"Classical and Sour Forms of Virtue," in *Morality and Self-Interest*, ed. Paul Bloomfield (New York: Oxford University Press, 2007)

"The Ethics of Style and Attitude," in *Moral Cultivation*, ed. Brad Wilburn. (Lanham, MD: Lexington Books, 2007)

"A New Look at the Logic of the 'Is'–'Ought' Relation," *Philosophy*, 80 (2005): 345–59

"The Epistemology of Non-Instrumental Value," *Philosophy and Phenomenological Research*, 70 (2005): 659–80

"Morality, Ethics, and Wisdom," in *Handbook of Wisdom: Psychological Perspectives*, eds. Robert Sternberg and Jennifer Jordan (Cambridge: Cambridge University Press, 2005), 245–71

"Comfort, Hedonic Treadmills, and Public Policy," *Public Affairs Quarterly*, 17 (2003): 17–28

"A Messy Derivation of the Categorical Imperative," *Philosophy*, 77 (2002): 485–502

"The Indispensability of Character," *Philosophy*, 76 (2001): 239–50

"Metaphysics as Prologomenon to Ethics," *Midwest Studies in Philosophy*, 24 (2000): 1–16

"How Values Congeal Into Facts," *Ratio*, 13 (2000): 37–53

"Virtues, Character, and Moral Dispositions," in *Virtue Ethics and Moral Education*, eds. David Carr and Jan Steutel (London: Routledge, 1999), 199–209

"Axiological Realism," *Philosophy*, 71 (1996): 185–203

"Suffering, Joy, and Social Choice," *Public Affairs Quarterly*, 8 (1994): 51–65

"Ethics for Extraterrestrials," *American Philosophical Quarterly*, 28 (1991): 311–20

"Ethical Fallibility," *Ratio*, n.s. 1 (1988): 33–46

"Character and Ethical Theory," *Midwest Studies in Philosophy*, 13 (1988): 115–25

"Moral Realism and Metaphysical Anti-Realism," *Metaphilosophy*, 18 (1987): 95–107

"Francis Hutcheson: Morality and Nature," *History of Philosophy Quarterly*, 2 (1985): 195–202

"Utilitarianism Today," *Revue Internationale de Philosophie*, 36 (1982): 318–30

"Value Judgments," *Philosophy and Phenomenological Research*, 42 (1982): 506–18

"A Case for Consequentialism," *American Philosophical Quarterly*, 18 (1981): 305–13

"Vulgar Consequentialism," *Mind*, 89 (1980): 321–37

"Do We Desire Only Pleasure?" *Philosophical Studies*, 34 (1978): 451–8

"Inhibition," *Oxford Review of Education*, 4 (1978): 277–87

"Nuance and Ethical Choice," *Ethics*, 79 (1969): 105–13

Metaphysics and Philosophy of Mind

"Half Truths," *Ratio*, 25, (2012): 148–63

"The Disunity of Emotion," in *Emotion in Postmodernism*, ed. Alfred Hornung (Heidelberg: C. Winter Universitätsverlag, 1997), 363–81

"An Anti-Essentialist View of the Emotions," *Philosophical Psychology*, 8 (1995): 341–51

"Character and Self-Knowledge," *Proceedings of the Aristotelian Society*, 85 (1984–5): 219–38

"Chisholm's View of Person and Object," *Metaphilosophy*, 10 (1979): 62–73

"Is the Nature of Physical Reality Unknowable?" *American Philosophical Quarterly*, 15 (1978): 99–105

"Precision in History," *Mind*, 84 (1975): 374–89

"Realism vs. Idealism," *American Philosophical Quarterly*, 12 (1975): 199–210

Asian and Comparative Philosophy

"Confucian Civility," *Dao*, 9 (2010): 11–23

"Fact and Value in the *Analects*: Education and Logic." in *Educations and Their Purposes*, eds. Roger T. Ames and Peter D. Hershock (Honolulu: University of Hawaii Press, 2008), 405–419

"Tradition and Community in the Formation of Character and Self," in *Confucian Ethics: A Comparative Study of Self, Autonomy and Community*, eds. David Wong and Kwong-loi Shun (New York: Cambridge University Press, 2004), 103–23

"Losing Place: The Risks of Cosmopolitanism," in *Technology and Cultural Values: On the Edge of the Third Millenium*, eds. Peter Hershock, Marietta Stepaniants, and Roger Ames (Honolulu: University of Hawaii Press and East-West Philosophers' Conference, 2003), 416–430

"Naturalness Revisited," in *New Essays on Confucius and the Analects*, ed. Bryan Van Norden (New York: Oxford University Press, 2002), 39–52

"Xunzi: Morality As Psychological Constraint," in *Virtue, Nature and Agency in the Xunzi*, eds. T. C. Kline III and P. J. Ivanhoe (Indianapolis, IN: Hackett, 2000), 89–102

"Feminism as Radical Confucianism: Self and Tradition," in *The Sage and the Second Sex: Confucianism, Ethics and Gender Issues*, ed. Chenyang Li (LaSalle: Open Court, 2000). 43–56

"Spontaneity and Education of the Emotions in the Zhuangzi," in *Scepticism, Relativism, and Ethics in the Zhuangzi*, eds. P. J. Ivanhoe and Paul Kjellberg (Albany: State University of New York, 1996), 183–95

"Falsity, Psychic Indefiniteness, and Self-Knowledge," in *Self and Deception: A Conversation in Comparative Philosophy*, eds. Roger T. Ames and Wimal Dissanayake (Albany: State University of New York, 1996), 161–76

"Atman and Self-Realization," in *Man, Meaning and Morality*, eds. R. Balasubramanian and R. Misra (New Delhi: Indian Council of Philosophical Research, 1995), 185–95

"The Emotions of Altruism, East and West," in *Emotions in Asian Thought*, eds. Joel Marks and Roger Ames (Albany: State Universiity of New York, 1995), 123–38

"Tradition and Moral Progress," in *Culture and Modernity*, ed. E. Deutsch (Honolulu: University of Hawaii Press, 1991), 313–28

"Confucius, Mencius, Hume, and Kant on Reason and Choice," in *Rationality in Question*, eds. S. Biderman and B. A. Scharfstein (Leiden: E.J. Brill, 1989), 119–39

"Not in So Many Words: Chuang-tzu's Techniques of Communication," *Philosophy East and West*, 41 (1989): 311–7

"Wong's Relativism and Comparative Philosophy," *Philosophy East and West*, 38 (1986): 169–172

"Investigations of the Self," *Philosophy East and West*, 36 (1984): 37–51

"Confucian Ethics and Weakness of Will," *Journal of Chinese Philosoph*, 8 (1981): 1–8

"The Supra-Moral in Chinese Ethics," *Journal of Chinese Philosophy*, 1 (1974): 153–60

"The Supra-Moral in Religious Ethics: The Case of Buddhism," *Journal of Religious Ethics*, 1 (1973: 65–71

"Confucius and the Nature of Religious Ethics," *Philosophy East and West*, 21 (1971): 89–94

"Confucius and the Problem of Naturalness," *Philosophy East and West*, 18 (1968): 175–85

Applied Philosophy

"How Not to Educate Character," in *Character Psychology and Character Education*, eds. Dan Lapsley and F. Clark Power (Notre Dame: University of Notre Dame Press, 2005), 201–17

"Autonomy and the Very Limited Role of Advocacy in the Classroom," *Monist*, 80 (1996), 488–98

"Pluralism and the Tradition of Democracy," in *Can Democracy Be Taught?*, ed. Andrew Oldenquist (Bloomington, IN: Phi Delta Kappa Educ. Fdn., 1996), 45–60

"Affirmative Action: Relevant Knowledge and Relevant Ignorance," in *Affirmative Action and the University*, ed. Steven M. Cahn (Philadelphia: Temple University Press, 1993), 181–8

"Relations Between the Sexes: Timely vs. Timeless Principles," *San Diego Law Review* (1989): 1027–41

"Educating Character as the Integration of Choice," in *Content, Character and Choice* (Washington: National Council on Educational Research, 1986), 63–71

"Perfectionism and Educational Policy," *Public Affairs Quarterly*, 1 (1987): 111–9

"Why Some Topics Are Controversial," *Educational Leadership*, 42 (1984–85): 73–6

"The Teaching of Values," in *Challenges to the Humanities*, eds. C. Finn, D. Ravitch, and H. Roberts (New York: Holmes and Meier, 1985), 128–44

Aesthetics

"Art and Aesthetic Experience," *British Journal of Aesthetics*, 15 (1975): 29–39
"Aesthetic Value," *American Philosophical Quarterly*, 9 (1972): 259–64
"Reasons in Support of Evaluations of Works of Art," *Monist*, 50 (1966): 222–36

Contributors

Roger T. Ames is Professor of Philosophy and editor of *Philosophy East & West*. His publications include translations of Chinese classics: *Sun-tzu: The Art of Warfare* (1993); *Sun Pin: The Art of Warfare* (1996) and *Tracing Dao to its Source* (1997) (both with D. C. Lau); the *Confucian Analects* (1998) and the *Classic of Family Reverence: A Philosophical Translation of the* Xiaojing (2008) (both with H. Rosemont), *Focusing the Familiar: A Translation and Philosophical Interpretation of the* Zhongyong (2001), and *A Philosophical Translation of the* Daodejing: *Making This Life Significant* (2003) (both with D. L. Hall). He has also authored many interpretative studies of Chinese philosophy and culture: *Thinking Through Confucius* (1987), *Anticipating China: Thinking Through the Narratives of Chinese and Western Culture* (1995), and *Thinking From the Han: Self, Truth, and Transcendence in Chinese and Western Culture* (1998) (all with D. L. Hall). He has most recently been engaged in projects promoting a conversation between American pragmatism and Confucianism.

Fred Dallmayr is Packey J. Dee Professor Emeritus in the departments of philosophy and political science at the University of Notre Dame (USA). He holds a Doctor of Law degree from the University of Munich and a PhD degree from Duke University. He has been a visiting professor at Hamburg University in Germany and at the New School in New York, and a Fellow at Nuffield College in Oxford. During 1991–92 he was in India on a Fulbright research grant. He is past President of the Society for Asian and Comparative Philosophy (SACP) and Executive Co-Chair of the World Public Forum—Dialogue of Civilizations. Among his recent books are: *Dialogue among Civilizations* (2002); *In Search of the Good Life* (2007); *Integral Pluralism* (2010); *The Promise of Democracy* (2010); and *Being in the World: Dialogue and Cosmopolis* (2013).

Philip J. Ivanhoe, who earned his PhD from Stanford University, is Chair Professor of East Asian and Comparative Philosophy and Religion at City University of Hong Kong. He has written, edited, or co-edited more than twenty books and published more than fifty articles and numerous dictionary and encyclopedia entries on Chinese and Western religious and ethical thought and its contemporary implications. Among his more recent publications are *The Essays and Letters of Zhang Xuecheng* (Stanford University Press), the co-edited anthology *Taking Confucian Ethics Seriously: Contemporary Theories and Applications* (with Yu Kam-por and Julia Tao, SUNY Press), *Readings in the Lu-Wang School of Neo-Confucianism* (Hackett Publishing Company) and the co-edited anthology *Working Virtue: Virtue Ethics and Contemporary Moral Problems* (with Rebecca Walker, Oxford University Press).

Joel J. Kupperman is Board of Trustees Distinguished Professor of Philosophy Emeritus at the University of Connecticut. He is author of 12 books and numerous articles. Known as a strong advocate for character ethics, Kupperman's work covers Western, Chinese, and Indian philosophies. He has been a fellow of the National Endowment for the Humanities (1981, 2004), Earhart Foundation (1995–1996), Rockefeller Foundation (1988), and Cambridge University (1988) and the University of Oxford (1985).

Karyn Lai is Associate Professor of Philosophy at the School of Humanities and Languages, University of New South Wales in Sydney, Australia. Her primary research area is in pre-Qin Chinese philosophy (i.e., between 600–200 BCE). Her work is often of a comparative nature, drawing insights from Chinese philosophies to address issues in a number of philosophical areas including moral philosophy, environmental ethics, reasoning and argumentation, and epistemology. She is the section editor of the Chinese Comparative Philosophy section of the journal, *Philosophy Compass* and Associate editor of the *Australasian Journal of Philosophy*. Her publications include *Introduction to Chinese Philosophy* (2008, Cambridge, UK: Cambridge University Press) and *Learning from Chinese Philosophies* (2006, Aldershot, UK: Ashgate Publishing). Her current research projects include ethics and character in the Confucian tradition and epistemology in pre-Qin Chinese philosophy.

Chenyang Li is Associate Professor of Philosophy at Nanyang Technological University, Singapore. Prior to joining Nanyang, he was Professor and Chair of the Philosophy Department at Central Washington University (1999–2010), where he received the Distinguished Research

Professor Award, Outstanding Department Chair Award, and Keys to Success Award (Student Service). His publications include *The Confucian Philosophy of Harmony* (2013), *The Tao Encounters the West: Explorations in Comparative Philosophy* (1999), *The Sage and the Second Sex: Confucianism, Ethics, and Gender* (ed., 2000), *The East Asian Challenge for Democracy: Political Meritocracy in Comparative Perspective* (co-edited with Daniel A. Bell, 2013), and about 100 journal articles and book chapters. He is the vice president of the International Society for Chinese Philosophy and a former president of the Association of Chinese Philosophers in North America. He currently serves on the editorial/academic/advisory boards of 22 publications and organizations.

Robert Cummings Neville is Professor of Philosophy, Religion, and Theology at Boston University. He is past president of the American Academy of Religion and the International Society for Chinese Philosophy, and the author of *Boston Confucianism* and *Ritual and Deference*, among other writings. His most recent publications are *Ultimates: Philosophical Theology, Volume One*, and *Existence: Philosophical Theology, Volume Two*, treating religion from the perspective of world religions.

Peimin Ni is Professor of Philosophy at Grand Valley State University in Michigan. In addition to being the author of several books, including *On Confucius* (2002), *On Reid* (2002), *Confucius—Making the Way Great* (2010), he published numerous journal articles, book chapters, and some articles in the *New York Times*. As a Chinese calligraphy artist, he co-authored a book (with S. Rowe) titled *Wandering—Brush and Pen in Philosophical Reflection*. He is a former president of the Association of Chinese Philosophers in America, former president of the Society of Asian and Comparative Philosophy, and is serving as the editor-in-chief of the ACPA book series on Chinese and Comparative Philosophy. He served as a visiting professor at the University of Hawaii and the University of Hong Kong, and was invited to be a plenary speaker at the World Public Forum "Dialogue of Civilizations" numerous times.

Henry Rosemont, Jr. is the author of *A Chinese Mirror* (1991), *Rationality and Religious Experience* (2001), and with Huston Smith, *Is There a Universal Grammar of Religion?* and most recently, *A Reader's Companion to the Confucian* Analects. He has edited and/or translated ten other books, including *Leibniz: Writings on China* (with D. J. Cook, 1994), and with Roger T. Ames, *The Analects of Confucius: A Philosophical Translation*

(1998) and *The Chinese Classic of Family Reverence: A Philosophical Translation of the* Xiaojing (2008). He has spent three years as Fulbright Senior Professor of Philosophy and Linguistics at Fudan University in Shanghai. An anthology of essays dedicated to his work was published in 2008, edited by Marthe Chandler and Ronnie Littlejohn, *Polishing the Chinese Mirror: Essays in Honor of Henry Rosemont, Jr.*

Kwong-loi Shun has been Professor of Philosophy and an academic administrator at UC Berkeley, the University of Toronto, and the Chinese University of Hong Kong. He has now returned to teaching at UC Berkeley and is currently working on a multivolume work in Confucian ethics. The first volume, *Mencius and Early Chinese Thought*, was published by Stanford University Press in 1997. A manuscript of the second volume, *Zhu Xi and Later Confucian Thought*, is under revision, and the third volume, *From Philology to Philosophy*, is close to completion. The fourth volume, *On Self and Self Transformation*, will discuss a central theme in Confucian moral psychology, while the fifth volume, *A Study in Confucian Ethics*, will provide a primarily philosophical discussion of Confucian ethics.

Sor-hoon Tan is Associate Professor of Philosophy at the National University of Singapore. Her research interests include Comparative Moral and Political Philosophy, and she has published on Confucianism and American Pragmatism. Her articles have appeared in *Philosophy East and West*, *Journal of Chinese Philosophy*, *Dao: A Journal of Comparative Philosophy*, *Asian Philosophy*, *Contemporary Pragmatism*, and the *Transactions of the Charles S. Peirce Society*. She has contributed to edited volumes such as *Routledge History of Chinese Philosophy*, *Cambridge Companion to Modern Chinese Culture; Confucianism in Context; Rorty, Pragmatism, and Confucianism, Educations and their Purposes*. She is author of *Confucian Democracy: A Deweyan Reconstruction*; editor of *Challenging Citizenship: Group Membership and Cultural Identity in a Global Age*; and co-editor of *Filial Piety in Chinese Thought and History*, *The Moral Circle and the Self: Chinese and Western Perspectives*, and *Democracy as Culture: Deweyan Pragmatism in a Globalizing World*.

Bryan W. Van Norden is Professor in the Philosophy Department and in the Department of Chinese & Japanese at Vassar College (USA). He has a BA from the University of Pennsylvania and a PhD from Stanford University. Among his recent publications are *Introduction* *to Classical Chinese Philosophy* (Hackett, 2011), *Mengzi: With Selections from Traditional Commentaries* (Hackett, 2008), and *Virtue Ethics & Consequentialism in Early Chinese Philosophy* (Cambridge, 2007).

David B. Wong is the Susan Fox Beischer and George D. Beischer Professor of Philosophy at Duke University. He is the author of *Moral Relativity* and *Natural Moralities: A Defense of Pluralistic Relativism*. He is the co-editor with Kwong-loi Shun of *Confucian Ethics: A Comparative Study of Self, Autonomy and Community*. He has written articles and chapters in ethical theory, Chinese and comparative philosophy, and moral psychology.

Index